THE
FINAL
QUEST
TRILOGY

RICK JOYNER

MorningStar Publications

The Final Quest Trilogy
by Rick Joyner
Copyright ©2016
Third Printing 2018

The Final Quest
Copyright ©1996

The Call
Copyright ©1999

The Torch and the Sword
Copyright ©2003

Distributed by MorningStar Publications, Inc.,
a division of MorningStar Fellowship Church
375 Star Light Drive, Fort Mill, SC 29715

www.MorningStarMinistries.org
1-800-542-0278

Cover: Esther Jun
Layout Design: Michael R. Carter

ISBN— 978-1-60708-665-9; 1-60708-665-4

TABLE OF CONTENTS

THE CALL

[4]

The Torch and the Sword

Introduction to
the New Edition

I've been blessed to have a number of bestselling books, but *The Final Quest* has been my top seller by a huge margin. After twenty years it still remains popular around the world. Why? I've spent twenty years trying to understand this, and why the two sequels, *The Call* and *The Torch and the Sword*, struck such a chord. I think such things need to be understood because they can reveal where people are presently.

THE DEVIL KILLS BABIES

We see in Revelation 13 that the devil sought to destroy the Messiah when He was an infant. He tried to kill Moses the same way. I think for just about every major thing God seeks to do, the devil tries to kill it at the earliest stage of life—in the womb if possible, but at least while still an infant. It encourages me that this was also the case with this trilogy.

When I finished the manuscript for *The Final Quest* and shared it with a number of close friends who were Christian leaders, it provoked a response unlike anything I had ever said or written. The group was united in asking me not to publish this book. When I asked why, they said that if I did it would destroy my ministry. I asked if they thought there was any doctrinal error in the message, and they agreed that there was not. They were convinced that the body of Christ was not ready for the message in this book.

I appreciated their concern for my ministry. I also thought this group was probably right, and publishing this book could be the end of my ministry. At the time our ministry was growing fast. I took their warning seriously, but concluded that I knew the word was true and it had been given to me by the Lord. I decided that it was better to lose my ministry and go back to flying airplanes for a living than bury something the Lord had entrusted me with. The whole experience had changed my life, and many who read the sections I published in our newsletter said the same. So I published the book and waited for the firestorm.

The storm came, but not as I expected—it came in the form of a massive flood of orders. I hoped to distribute ten or twenty thousand copies over a lifetime, but we received orders for that many in a week. Our staff was overwhelmed; our printers were overwhelmed.

THE GREAT DISCONNECT

The first message I took from this was that I had grossly underestimated the body of Christ—so had my friends. To this day I am concerned about how out of touch much of the leadership in the body of Christ is with their people. When a Presidential candidate asked if we could help mobilize pastors my response was, "Why would you want to do that? The people do not follow them." Granted, we may have some of the greatest pastors living today, but they are rare. Most are out of touch with where their congregations are spiritually, but they think that they are very much in touch with them. There is a major disconnect here.

This was highlighted to me when the leader of a large state church publicly condemned a conference we were having in his country. About nine hundred pastors and thousands of members came from that denomination—it was the best free advertising. This has been repeated a number of times so that now when I hear that a leader has attacked us in some way, I tell our people to get ready for a big growth spurt.

I am not gloating about this, but I'm lamenting it. The body of Christ, in general, needs a new breed of leader. It is coming, but as the Lord is prone to do, He often lets them die off naturally, as He treated the first generation of Israelites in the wilderness. This waiting period is also one of the Lord's greatest opportunities to fashion the new generation of leaders. So let's not waste our waiting!

Another surprise was that the biggest group buying this book was not Pentecostals or Charismatics, but Southern Baptists and conservative Evangelicals. One of the most influential conservative Evangelicals of this time told me that he thought the book was "a *Pilgrim's Progress* for our times." This was the last group I expected to be receptive to this message, but they were immediately the most enthusiastic. Why?

The most obvious answer is that this group, one with a rich tradition of being strong in the Scriptures, is possibly the hungriest for the Spirit. Many in this part of the body of Christ have come to understand that true faith in the Bible is more than just believing the things in it happened—it is believing to see them happen in your own life.

The second biggest group drawn to this book was the "high churches"—the Anglicans, Catholics, and traditional Protestants. I think that many in these groups are also starving for an experience with God and for the reality of life in the Spirit.

The Main Reason—The Quest

The above being the case, probably the main reason so many were drawn to the message of these books is because of the adventure they contained. What is missing from the typical Christian's life is adventure. The true Christian life is the greatest adventure that can be lived on this earth. Yet why are our churches led by those who are almost always afraid of anything that might offend anyone in the church?

The most popular books and movies of our times are about adventure. They include epic battles of good against evil. They also include stories of a group bonding as a band of brothers and sisters to confront evil. We are drawn to these stories because we yearn for the same experience. We yearn for this because we were created for it. There is no life more exciting, compelling, or difficult as the true Christian life. The greatest adventure is serving the King as we are called to. The fellowship we are called to have in the body of Christ is the ultimate band of brothers.

Since *The Final Quest's* publication, I don't think a week went by that I did not hear from someone how this book impacted their life. My question to them is did it really impact their life or just encourage or entertain them? Did it help them to actually get in the fight? Did it compel them to find other believers in the fight that they could join with?

For many the book was an encouragement but it did not really change them. Others could no longer be satisfied with a life not engaged in the greatest adventure, the greatest cause, and the greatest quest. I'm thankful if it helped anyone in any way, but what I wrote about in this book is not a story—it is a calling to live in the ultimate reality.

Where are the Detractors?

Of course, not everyone liked *The Final Quest*, or me, and that is to be expected. What I did not expect was that even though some attacks were vicious, there were so few of them. I take attacks as encouragement that I am doing enough to threaten the powers of darkness. Try to find one thing in the Scriptures that Jesus said or did publicly that He was not attacked for. That is how the darkness reacts to the light.

The Call and *The Torch and the Sword* have likewise received a large and diverse reception in the body of Christ. Because each of these pressed further into the supernatural realm of revelation, I wondered if they were more than most could handle. Again I was wrong. In many ways, the body of Christ was much more mature and spiritually experienced than I thought, and I was happy to be wrong about this.

Finding Our Home in the Spirit

One widely respected evangelical theologian told me that the message in these books was beyond human creativity. This is true. For this reason, I rejected publishing these as fictional allegories, as was proposed to me—I did not think that was honest. This is not creative fiction. If I had released it as fiction it may have reached more people, but that was never my goal. I write to convey truth that impacts lives to live for the truth. I want the favor of the Spirit of Truth more than I want book sales.

The messages in these books all came in dreams or prophetic experiences so real that I felt I was living another life in that realm. Then I did live them in this realm. Many others have too.

As I have studied psychology and psychiatry for years, I understand why some would think this is disconnected from reality. However, this is an ultimate reality. The spiritual realm is far more real than what we tend to think of as "reality." We live in far greater deception if we do not see the spiritual reality.

According to Scripture, the physical universe is but "a shadow" of the spiritual—meaning that spiritual substance is as great as you are compared to your shadow. That is a reality the sanest people on earth know well. In the not too distant future, this will become clear to all. Again, my greatest hope for this trilogy is that it will not just convince people of the unseen world's power and influence over the natural realm, but that people would be compelled to experience it for themselves.

As one of the ancients said, "We are not called to be natural beings that have occasional supernatural experiences, but supernatural beings that have occasional natural experiences." According to the New Testament, our main warfare **"is not against flesh and blood"** **(see Ephesians 6:12).** It is not in the natural realm, but in the spiritual realm. The Apostle Paul indicated that we should be more at home in the spiritual realm than in the natural. We are called to be a "new creation"— more spiritual than natural, but also learning to live and function in both realms.

Before being born again I did not believe in the supernatural, though I admit to being of an inclination that never thought much about it. I came to know Christ through a powerful supernatural experience that was so real I have never had the luxury of doubting the supernatural, or Christ, again. I consider this a great advantage—grace from God for me. He may have done this because He knows I am so weak that I could not have made it without such a conversion. For whatever reason, I have been thrust into knowledge of the supernatural—the spiritual realm—that I must live with and cannot escape.

That being said, I never want to escape it! I love it and am thankful for it. I cannot imagine a more interesting, fulfilling life, even though it can be scary at times. It was not easy, but it was worth it. I saw the depths of some evils behind the madness of human events. This was hard to see, but I learned that the Lord always counterbalances it by letting me see His glory. The power of all evil cannot in any way be compared to the power of His truth and glory. Evil will certainly be vanquished. Even so, He has let it run its course on the earth for our sake.

How could this be for our sake? To face and overcome it is the ultimate test of the human heart. He is looking for hearts that will be joined to Him forever as members of His own family—joint heirs with Christ. This high calling can only be for those who love His truth, and Him, more than they love their own lives. Our ultimate quest is to love Him that much.

THE ULTIMATE ANSWER

I Corinthians 13:8 is often translated **"love never fails,"** but it could have been translated "love never quits." There is a limit to what people will endure, except for those in love. Those in love never quit. It is not those with the truth who are not deceived, but those who love the truth. So it is not those with the truth who will not quit, but those who love the truth will not quit.

There was a time when I was afraid to go to sleep because of what I might see in my dreams. I was told this would end if I wanted it to. I decided to persevere, and it was not long before I could not wait to sleep because my dreams were so wonderful. It was almost like living another life in my dreams, and it was an exciting and wonderful life.

I do wonder if those who do not have such dreams, visions, and experiences were asked the same question and decided that they did not want them. I can understand this because it was a hard choice to keep going. We see in Revelation 3:21 that Jesus would not even enter His own church without the church opening the door for Him. He will not force Himself on His bride. We have to want Him and I want all that He is, especially the Holy Spirit.

Experiencing the spiritual realm has almost been like getting the bonus of an additional life. I have had the experience of making friends in the spiritual realm that impacted me as much as any I've had in the natural. We would experience the glory of God together, and there is a bonding in this unlike any other bond. However, in these experiences I would also go through trials and seeming dangers. I would experience everything in them that I did in natural experiences. This may sound weird and crazy, but it is a wonderful weird!

I love when I am having such experiences, whether awake or asleep. However, I have gone through two periods of about seven years each when I had almost no supernatural experiences. I learned to love the spiritually dry times too. Not only did I learn that they usually preceded a higher level of coming spiritual experiences, but I used those times to sink my roots deeper into the Scriptures, studying history and other fields of knowledge that I needed for my assignment. I love knowledge, so this was a great time too.

It seems that just as I start to really love one state that I am in, it ends and I go to another. I'm okay with this because it is always a better place, but also more challenging. The trials are the tests we take so we can be promoted, but one basic trial is learning to love the place we are at. We have a well of living water inside of us, so we can be in the driest desert, or the driest meetings, and still be having wonderful fellowship with the Lord and His truth.

CLIMBING THE LADDER

There is a theological principle of first mention. This principle says that the first mention of a subject in Scripture is often a revelation of its basic purpose. The first place in Scripture mentioning that God had a house is when Jacob dreamed of a ladder reaching into heaven. The messengers of God ascended into heaven, and then descended, on that ladder. This is a revelation of a basic purpose of the house of God, now the church—it is supposed to be a place of access to heaven. The messengers of God are to continually ascend into the heavenly realm and bring back to earth what they received as evidence of heaven's reality and its authority over the natural realm.

Almost as often as people tell me these books helped them, I have people tell me they had the same revelations but never shared them. They seem to think it would impress me to hear they had the same revelations. I don't doubt this, but it does not impress me that they did not share them. What we receive from heaven is not just for our own encouragement or entertainment. There is a real connection between what goes on in the spiritual realm and in the natural, as we see in the Scriptures. What we see must be conveyed so that God's people can take the proper actions. When Daniel saw in the

[16]

prophecies of Jeremiah that it was time for Israel to return to the land from captivity, he did not just rejoice—he prayed and fasted for God's word to come true. Why was this necessary?

In Psalm 115:16 we are told, **"The heavens are the heavens of the Lord, but the earth has been given into the hands of the sons of men."** The Lord has delegated authority in the earth to men, which is why He will not act on the earth unless we pray. This is why He said through Isaiah that He needed an intercessor, a mediator.

The Lord certainly has the power to do whatever He wants, but He does not do things on the earth without going through the chain of authority He established. I learned as a young businessman that not going through my managers and department heads to give instruction or correction—but instead bypassing them to go directly to employees—usually led to discord and morale problems. Maybe this is why the Lord said that the Centurion had a greater faith than anyone He had found in Israel—the Centurion knew the chain of command and how it operated.

My point is that having spectacular revelations doesn't mean much if not converted into what will help people. The greatest impact we can have is to draw men to God. You cannot see the Lord without loving Him, because He is love. Loving God is the main thing we were created for. There is nothing that will elevate us or others like loving God. Only by loving Him as we should can we love others as we should.

I realize that prophetic revelation has many strategic and tactical purposes in giving directions and assignments. Even so, as Peter Lord used to say often, "The main thing is to keep the main thing the main thing." There is nothing higher or greater that we can do than to keep growing in our love for our King. He is worthy of it.

So my first hope for these books is to see them impart a desire for a closer relationship with God. Next I pray that they convey the majesty of God that I experienced and the majestic nature of His cause. After that, it is to convey to His people the resolve to fight the good fight that we have been called to.

There is a saying in the military that there are many soldiers but not many warriors. Every Christian is called to be a warrior. We are told that the whole world lies in the power of the evil one; to live on earth now as a Christian is to have been dropped behind enemy lines. However, we have been given divinely powerful weapons for destroying the enemy's strongholds. It is time to use them.

It was said of Jesus that He came to destroy the works of the devil. He then stated in His great prayer the night before He was crucified that just as He was sent into the world, He has sent us. Therefore, every Christian should have a resolve to destroy the works of the enemy and bring down his strongholds by which he has kept mankind in bondage. Christians are called to be the ultimate freedom fighters.

The greatest prophets rose up in times of great darkness. As the world slips into the deepest darkness, the greatest lights will emerge. They will be a fellowship of true knights of the cross, warriors who have not come to kill and destroy, but to heal and set the captives free. Will you be one of them? If so, when you read the message in these books, resolve that you will live the greatest adventure that they call you to. Make your own story, don't just enjoy this one.

Rick Joyner
2016

THE FINAL QUEST

INTRODUCTION

This book stems from an extraordinary dream I had in early 1995. I published a condensed version of the first dream in *The MorningStar Prophetic Bulletin* and *The Morning Star Journal* under the title "The Hordes of Hell Are Marching." As I continued to seek the Lord about this great spiritual battle that I had seen, I received a series of related visions and prophetic experiences. Condensed versions of these were published in *The Morning Star Journal* as "The Hordes of Hell Are Marching, Parts II and III."

The articles in this series became the most popular writings I have ever published. We were deluged with requests to have all of the parts published together in a book. I determined to do this and set out to fill in all that had been left out of the condensed versions. However, just when I was ready to give this to our editing department, I had another prophetic experience that was obviously related to this vision, containing what I felt were the most important parts of all. These are included in Parts IV and V of this book.

HOW I RECEIVED THE VISION

This is the most common question I receive about this vision, so I will attempt to briefly answer it here. First, I must explain what I mean by visions and "prophetic experiences."

Prophetic experiences are numerous and diverse and include all of the primary ways that God spoke to His people in the Scriptures. Because the Lord is the same today as He was yesterday, He has never ceased to speak to His people in the same ways, which we see continued in the New Testament just as in the Old. The same supernatural experiences found in the Scriptures can be seen throughout church history and are becoming increasingly common today. In the sermon of the Apostle Peter recorded in Acts 2:14-21, he explains that dreams, visions, and prophecy are primary signs of the outpouring of the Holy Spirit in the last days. As we are obviously getting closer to the end of this age, these signs are therefore becoming increasingly common with Christians.

One reason why experiences such as dreams, visions, and prophecy are becoming so much more common now is because we will need them for accomplishing our purposes in these times. It is also true that Satan, who unfortunately knows the Scriptures better than many Christians, understands the importance of prophetic revelation in God's relationship with His people. Satan is therefore pouring out his own counterfeit gifts in great measure to those who serve him. However, there would be no counterfeit if there was not a genuine reality, just as there are no counterfeit three-dollar bills because there are no real ones.

Soon after I became a Christian in 1972, I read Peter's sermon in Acts chapter two and realized that if we were in the end times, it was important to understand the ways that the Lord speaks to us. I do not remember praying at first to have the experiences myself, but I did begin having them, which gave me an even greater impetus for understanding them, which I continue to pursue.

Since that time, I have gone through periods when prophetic experiences were very frequent. I have also gone through long periods of time when I did not have any such experiences. Yet, after each period of not having them, they returned, and were either much more powerful or much more frequent. Through all of this I have learned a great deal about prophetic gifts and prophetic people, and I have addressed the full scope of the prophetic ministry in my book, *The Prophetic Ministry.*

DIFFERENT LEVELS OF REVELATION

There are many levels of prophetic revelation. The initial level is prophetic "impressions." These are genuine revelations or guidance from the Holy Spirit, and a primary way that He speaks to believers. They can be extraordinarily specific and accurate when interpreted by those who are experienced and sensitive to them. However, on this level our "revelations" can be affected by our own feelings, prejudices, and doctrines. I have therefore resolved not to use expressions such as "thus says the Lord" with any revelations that come on this level.

Visions can also come on the impression level. They are gentle and must be seen with "the eyes of our hearts." These, too, can be very specific and accurate, especially when received and/or interpreted by those who are experienced. The more the eyes of our hearts are opened, as Paul prayed in Ephesians 1:18, the more powerful and useful these can be.

The next level of revelation is a conscious sense of the presence of the Lord, or the anointing of the Holy Spirit, which gives special illumination to our minds. This often comes when I am writing or speaking, and it gives me much greater confidence in the importance or accuracy of what I am saying. However, while we may be emboldened by this sense of God's presence, we need to realize that this is still a level where we can be influenced by our pre-existing viewpoints and attitudes. I believe this is why, in certain matters, Paul would say he was giving his *opinion*, but that he *thought* he had the agreement of the Spirit of the Lord (see I

Corinthians 7:40). In general, we need humility rather than dogmatism when we deal with the prophetic.

"Open visions" occur on a higher level than impressions, and they tend to give us even more clarity than we feel with the presence of the Lord or the anointing. Open visions are external and are like watching a movie screen. Since they cannot be controlled by us, there is far less possibility of mixture in revelations that come this way.

Another higher-level prophetic experience is a trance, which is like dreaming when you are awake. Instead of just seeing a "screen" like in an open vision, you feel as if you are in the movie—actually *there* in some strange way. Peter fell into a trance in Acts 10:10, when he was instructed to go to the house of Cornelius and preach the gospel to the Gentiles for the first time. Paul, likewise, refers in Acts 22:17 to a trance he experienced while praying in the temple.

Trances were common experiences among the biblical prophets. The depth of trances can range from being rather mild—so that you are still conscious of your physical surroundings and can even still interact with them—to feeling as if you are literally in the place of your vision. This seems to be what Ezekiel experienced rather frequently, and what John probably experienced when he had the visions recorded in the Book of Revelation.

The visions contained in this book all began with dreams. Dreams can also be a powerful level of revelation as it is hard for us to control our dreams. However, this is not to imply that our dreams cannot be influenced by what we are occupied with, or even what we ate before we went to sleep. However, prophetic dreams are unmistakably different. If you have to ask what that difference is you probably have not had one. It is unmistakable, but it is also hard to explain, just as it is hard for me to explain my wife's voice, but I know it instantly when I hear it.

Dreams from God also have that same unmistakable quality so that you know they are from Him.

Some of these visions also came under a very intense sense of the presence of the Lord, but the majority were received in some level of a trance. Usually the visions came on a level where I was still conscious of my surroundings and could even interact with them, such as answering the phone. When the visions were interrupted, or when things got so intense I had to get up and walk around, they would immediately continue once I sat down again. One time the experience became so intense that I actually got up and left the mountain cabin where I had gone to seek the Lord and drove home. Over a week later, I returned and almost immediately was right back where I left off in the experience.

I have never known how to "turn on" such experiences, but I have almost always had the liberty to turn them off at will. Twice, large portions of this vision came at what I considered to be very inconvenient times, when I had gone to my cabin to get some important work done while facing deadlines. Two issues of *The Morning Star Journal* were a little late being published because of this, and one of my books was delayed a few months from when I had hoped to finish it. However, the Lord does not seem to be very concerned about our deadlines!

In the dreams and the trances, I had what I consider to be greatly magnified gifts of discernment and words of knowledge. Sometimes when I look at a person or pray for a church or ministry, I start to know things about them of which I have no natural knowledge. During the prophetic experiences recorded in this book, these gifts were operating on a level that I have never personally experienced in "real life." For example, in this vision I could look at a division of the evil horde and immediately know all of its strategies and capabilities.

I do not know how this enhanced knowledge came to me, but I just knew it, and in great detail. At times I would look at things or people and know their past, present, and future all at once. To save time and space in this book, I have included this knowledge as a matter of fact, without going into an explanation of how I received it.

USING PROPHETIC REVELATIONS

I must state emphatically that I do not believe that any kind of prophetic revelation is for the purpose of establishing doctrine. We have the Scriptures for that. There are two basic uses for the prophetic. The first is for revealing the present or future strategic will of the Lord in certain matters. We have examples of this in Paul's dream to go to Macedonia (see Acts 16:6-10) and in the trance where he was told to quickly leave Jerusalem (see Acts 22:17-18). We also have examples of this in the ministry of Agabus. One of these concerned a famine that was coming upon the whole world (see Acts 11:27-30), and the other had to do with Paul's visit to Jerusalem (see Acts 21:10-12).

Such revelations are also given for illuminating doctrine that is taught in the Scripture, but may not have been clearly understood yet. For example, Peter's trance in Acts 10 not only illuminated God's will for Peter, it also provided timely insight on a matter in which Scriptures were very clear (the Gentiles being able to receive the gospel), but which had not yet been understood by the church.

While the visions in this book do contain some strategic revelations, they also shed light on some biblical doctrines that I honestly had not seen before, but now see quite clearly. However, for years I had known and taught most of the truths illuminated to me in these experiences, even though I cannot say that I had lived them all very well. Many times I thought about the warning Paul gave Timothy—to pay attention to his own teachings (see I Timothy 4:16). Confronted by my failure to live up to some of my own teachings, I therefore accepted many of these messages as a personal rebuke. Even so, I also felt they were general messages to the body of Christ, and so I included them here.

Some of my friends encouraged me to write this as an allegory, in the third person, like *The Pilgrim's Progress*. I decided against that for several reasons. First, I feel that some would have taken this to be the result of my own creativity, which would have been wrong. I would like to be this creative, but I am not.

I also felt I could be much more accurate if I related these experiences just as I received them, and I endeavored to do so. However, I consider my memory of details to be one of my greatest weaknesses. At times I have questioned my memory about certain details in this vision, and you should therefore have the liberty to question some of them too. I think such scrutiny is wise with any such messages. Only the Scriptures deserve to be considered infallible. As you consider these experiences, I pray that the Holy Spirit will lead you to the truth and separate any chaff that may be present from the wheat.

Rick Joyner
1996

CHAPTER I

The Hordes of Hell
Are Marching

The demonic army was so large that it stretched as far as I could see. It was separated into divisions, with each carrying a different banner. The foremost divisions marched under the banners of Pride, Self-Righteousness, Respectability, Selfish Ambition, Unrighteous Judgment, and Jealousy. There were many more of these evil divisions beyond my scope of vision, but those in the vanguard of this terrible horde from hell seemed to be the most powerful. The leader of this army was the Accuser of the Brethren himself.

The weapons carried by this horde were also named. The swords were named Intimidation; the spears were named Treachery; and the arrows were named Accusation, Gossip, Slander, and Faultfinding. Scouts and smaller companies of demons with such names as Rejection, Bitterness, Impatience, Unforgiveness, and Lust were sent in advance of this army to prepare for the main attack.

These smaller companies and scouts were much fewer in number, but they were no less powerful than some of the larger divisions that followed. They were smaller only for strategic reasons. Just as John the Baptist was given an extraordinary anointing for baptizing the masses to prepare them for the Lord, these smaller demonic companies were given extraordinary evil powers for "baptizing the masses."

A single demon of Bitterness could sow his poison into multitudes of people, even entire races or cultures. A demon of Lust would attach himself to a single performer, movie, or advertisement and send what appeared to be bolts of electric slime that would hit and "desensitize" great masses of people. All of this was to prepare for the great horde of evil which followed.

Although this army was marching specifically against the church, it also was attacking anyone else that it could. I knew it was seeking to preempt a coming move of God, which was destined to sweep great numbers of people into the church.

The primary strategy of this army was to cause division on every possible level of relationship—churches with each other, congregations with their pastors, husbands and wives, children and parents, and even children with each other. The scouts were sent to locate the openings in churches, families, or individuals that such spirits as Rejection, Bitterness, and Lust could exploit and enlarge. Through these openings would pour demonic influences that completely overwhelmed their victims.

ON THE BACKS OF CHRISTIANS

The most shocking part of this vision was that this horde was not riding on horses, but primarily on Christians! Most of them were well-dressed, respectable, and had the appearance of being refined and educated, but there also seemed to be representatives from almost every walk of life. While these people professed Christian truths in order to appease their consciences, they lived their lives in agreement with the powers of darkness. As they agreed with those powers, their assigned demons grew and more easily directed their actions.

Many of these believers were host to more than one demon, but one of the demons would clearly be in charge. The nature of the one in charge dictated which division it was marching in. Even though the divisions were all marching together, it also seemed that the entire army was on the verge of chaos. For example, the demons of Hate hated the other demons as much as they did the Christians. The demons of Jealousy were all jealous of one another.

The only way the leaders of this horde kept the demons from fighting each other was to keep their hatred focused on the people they were riding. However, these people would often break out in fights with each other. I knew that some of the armies which came against Israel in the Scriptures had ended up destroying themselves in this same way. When their purpose against Israel was thwarted, their rage was uncontrollable, and they began fighting each other.

I noted that the demons were riding on these Christians, but they were not in them as was the case with non-Christians. It was obvious that these believers had only to stop agreeing with their demons in order to get free of them. For example, if the Christian on whom a demon of Jealousy was riding just started to question the jealousy, that demon would weaken very fast. When this happened, the weakened demon would cry out and the leader of the division would direct all the demons around that Christian to attack him until the jealousy would build up on him again. If this did not work, the demons would begin quoting Scriptures, perverting them in a way that would justify the bitterness, accusations, or other satanic influences they were spreading.

[31]

The power of the demons was clearly rooted almost entirely in the power of deception, but they had deceived these Christians to the point where they could use them and the Christians would think they were being used by God. This was because banners of Self-Righteousness were being carried by almost everyone, so that those marching could not even see the banners that marked the true nature of these divisions.

As I looked far to the rear of this army, I saw the entourage of the Accuser himself. I began to understand his strategy, and I was amazed that it was so simple. He knew that a house divided could not stand, and his army represented an attempt to bring such division to the church that she would be powerless and ineffective.

It was apparent that the only way the Accuser could do this was to use Christians to war against their own brethren, and that is why almost everyone in the forward divisions was a Christian, or at least a professing Christian. Every step these deceived believers took in obedience to the Accuser strengthened his power over them. This made his confidence and the confidence of all his commanders grow with the progress of the army as it marched forward. It was apparent that the power of this army depended on the agreement of these Christians with the ways of evil.

THE PRISONERS

Trailing behind these first divisions was a multitude of other Christians who were prisoners of this army. All of these captive Christians were wounded, and they were guarded by smaller demons of Fear. There seemed to be more prisoners than there were demons in the army.

Surprisingly, these prisoners still had their swords and shields, but they did not use them. It was a shock to see that so many could be kept captive by so few of the little demons of Fear. If the Christians had just used their weapons, they could easily have freed themselves and probably done great damage to the entire evil horde. Instead, they marched submissively along.

Above the prisoners, the sky was black with vultures named Depression. Occasionally these vultures would land on the shoulders of a prisoner and vomit on him. The vomit was Condemnation. When the vomit hit a prisoner he would stand up and march a little straighter for a while, and then slump over, even weaker than before. Again, I wondered why the prisoners did not simply kill these vultures with their swords, which they could have easily done.

Sometimes the weaker prisoners would stumble and fall. As soon as they hit the ground, the other prisoners would begin stabbing them with their swords, scorning them for their weakness. The vultures would then come and begin devouring the fallen ones even before they were dead. The other Christian prisoners stood by and watched this approvingly, occasionally stabbing the fallen ones again with their swords.

As I watched, I realized that these prisoners thought the vomit of Condemnation was truth from God. Then I understood that these prisoners actually thought they were marching in the army of God! This is why they did not kill the little demons of Fear or the vultures—they thought these were God's messengers! The darkness from the cloud of vultures made it so hard for these prisoners to see that they naively accepted everything which happened to them as being from the Lord. They felt that those who stumbled were under God's judgment, which is why they attacked them the way they did—they thought they were helping God!

[33]

The only food provided for these prisoners was the vomit from the vultures. Those who refused to eat it simply weakened until they fell. Those who did eat it were strengthened for a time, but with the strength of the evil one. Then they would weaken unless they drank the waters of bitterness that were constantly being offered to them. After drinking the bitter waters, they would begin to vomit on the others. When one of the prisoners began to do this, a demon that was waiting for a ride would climb up on him and ride him up to one of the front divisions.

SATANIC SLIME

Even worse than the vomit from the vultures was a repulsive slime that these demons were urinating and defecating upon the Christians they rode. This slime was the pride, selfish ambition, etc. that was the nature of their division. However, this slime made the Christians feel so much better than the condemnation had that they easily believed the demons were messengers of God. They actually thought this slime was the anointing of the Holy Spirit.

I had been so repulsed by the evil army that I wanted to die. Then the voice of the Lord came to me saying, *"This is the beginning of the enemy's last-day army. This is Satan's ultimate deception. His greatest power of destruction is released when he uses Christians to attack one another. Throughout the ages he has used this army, but never has he been able to use so many for his evil purposes as he is now. Do not fear. I have an army, too. You must now stand and fight because there is no longer any place to hide from this war. You must fight for My kingdom, for truth, and for those who have been deceived."*

This word from the Lord was so encouraging that I immediately began yelling to the Christian prisoners that they were deceived, thinking they would listen to me. When I did this, it seemed that the whole army turned to look at me. The cloud of fear and depression that was over them started to come toward me.

I still kept yelling because I thought the Christians would wake up and realize what was happening to them. Instead, many of them started reaching for their arrows to shoot at me. The others just hesitated, as if they did not know what to make of me. I knew I had spoken out prematurely and that it had been a very foolish mistake.

THE BATTLE BEGINS

Then I turned and saw the army of the Lord standing behind me. There were thousands of soldiers, but they were still greatly outnumbered. I was shocked and disheartened, for it seemed there were actually many more Christians being used by the evil one than there were in the army of the Lord. I knew that the battle about to begin was going to be viewed as the Great Christian Civil War because very few would understand the dark powers that were behind the impending conflict.

As I looked more closely at the army of the Lord, the situation seemed even more discouraging. Only a small number were fully dressed in their armor. Many only had one or two pieces of their armor on; some did not have any at all. A large number were already wounded. Most of those who had all their armor still had very small shields, which I knew would not protect them from the onslaught that was coming. Very few of those who were fully armed were adequately trained to use their weapons. To my further surprise, the great majority of these soldiers were women and children.

Behind this army was a trailing mob, which seemed very different in nature from the prisoners who followed the evil horde. Those in the mob seemed overly happy, as if intoxicated. They were playing games and singing songs, feasting and roaming about from one little camp to the next. This reminded me of Woodstock.

I ran toward the army of the Lord to escape the onslaught I knew would be coming at me from the evil horde. In every way, it seemed we were in for a mostly one-sided slaughter. I was especially concerned for the mob that was trailing the Lord's army, so I tried to raise my voice above the clamor to warn them that a battle was about to begin. Only a few could even hear me. Those who heard gave me the "peace sign" and said they did not believe in war.

When those in the mob assured me that the Lord would not let anything bad happen to them, I tried to explain that He had given us armor because we needed it for what was about to take place. To this they retorted that they had come to a place of peace and joy where nothing like that could happen to them. I began praying earnestly for the Lord to increase the shields of those with the armor, and to help protect those who were not ready for the battle.

Then a messenger came up to me, gave me a trumpet, and told me to blow it quickly. When I did, those who had at least some of their armor on immediately responded, snapping to attention. More armor was brought to them, which they quickly put on. I noticed that those who were wounded did not put armor over their wounds, but before I could say anything about this, enemy arrows began raining down on us. Everyone who did not have all of his armor on was wounded. Those who had not covered their wounds were struck again in the same wound.

Those who were hit by arrows of Slander immediately began to slander those who were not wounded. Those who were hit with Gossip began to gossip, and soon a major division had been created within our own camp. I felt that we were on the verge of destroying ourselves, just as some of the heathen armies in Scripture had done by rising up to kill each other. The feeling of helplessness was terrible.

THE VULTURES APPEAR

Then vultures swooped down to pick up the wounded and deliver them into the camp of prisoners. The wounded still had swords and could have easily struck down the vultures, but they did not. They were actually carried off willingly because they were so angry at those who were not wounded like they were.

I quickly thought about the mob behind the army and ran to see what had happened to them. It seemed impossible, but the scene among them was even worse. Thousands lay on the ground, wounded and groaning. The sky over them was darkened by the vultures that were carrying them off to become prisoners of the enemy.

Many of those who were not wounded just sat in a stupor of unbelief. They, too, were easily carried away by the vultures. Even though a few had begun trying to fight off the vultures, since they did not have the proper weapons, the vultures did not even pay them any attention. The wounded were so angry they would threaten and drive away anyone who tried to help them, but they became docile and submissive to the vultures.

Those from this mob who had not been wounded and had tried to fight off the vultures began running from the scene of battle. This first encounter with the enemy was so devastating that I was tempted to join them in their flight. Then, incredibly fast, some of those who had fled began reappearing with full suits of armor on, holding large shields. This was the first bit of encouragement that I remember seeing.

These warriors who were returning no longer had the mirth of the party, but an awesome resolve had now replaced it. I knew that although these had been deceived once, they would not be easily deceived again. They began to take the places of those who had fallen, and even began forming new ranks to protect the rear and flanks. This caused such great courage to spread through the army that the determination of everyone to stand and fight again began to rise. Three great angels named Faith, Hope, and Love immediately came and stood behind the army. As we looked at them, all of our shields began to grow. It was amazing how quickly despair had turned to faith. It was a solid faith too, tempered by experience.

THE HIGH WAY

Now everyone had swords named The Word of God and arrows named for different biblical truths. We wanted to shoot back, but we did not know how to avoid hitting the Christians that the demons were riding on. Then it occurred to us that if these Christians were hit with Truth, they would wake up and fight off their oppressors. I fired off a few arrows, as did some of the others. Almost all the arrows hit Christians. However, when the arrows of Truth went into them, they did not wake up or fall down wounded—they became enraged and the demons riding on them grew much larger.

This shocked everyone, and we began to feel that this was an impossible battle to win. Even so, with Faith, Hope, and Love we were confident that we could at least hold our own ground. Another great angel named Wisdom then appeared and directed us to fight from the mountain behind us.

On the mountain, there were ledges at different levels for as high as we could see. At each higher level the ledges became narrower and more difficult to stand on. Each level was named for a biblical truth. The lower levels were named after foundational truths such as "Salvation," "Sanctification," "Prayer," and "Faith," and the higher levels were named after deeper biblical truths. The higher we climbed, the larger both our shields and our swords grew, and fewer of the enemy arrows could reach our positions.

A Tragic Mistake

Some who had stayed on the lower levels began picking up the enemy arrows and shooting them back. This was a very grave mistake. The demons easily dodged the arrows and let them hit the Christians. When a Christian was hit by one of the arrows of accusation or slander, a demon of bitterness or rage would fly in and perch on that arrow. He would then begin to urinate and defecate his poison upon that Christian. When a Christian had two or three of these demons added to the pride or self-righteousness he already had, he was transformed into the contorted image of the demons themselves.

We could see this happening from the higher levels, but those on the lower levels who were using the enemy's arrows could not see it. About half of us decided to keep climbing, while the other half descended back to the lower levels to explain to those below what was happening. Everyone was then warned to keep climbing and not stop, except for a few who stationed themselves on each level to keep the other soldiers moving higher.

SAFETY AT LAST

When we reached the level called "The Unity of the Brethren," none of the enemy's arrows could reach us. Many in our camp decided that this was as far as they needed to climb. I understood this because with each new level the footing was more precarious. However, I also felt much stronger and more skillful with my weapons as I went higher, so I continued climbing.

Soon my skills were good enough to shoot and hit the demons without hitting the Christians. I felt that if I kept going higher I could shoot far enough to hit the main leaders of the evil horde, who stayed behind their army. I regretted that so many had stopped on the lower levels where they were safe but could not hit the enemy. Meanwhile, the strength and character that grew in those who kept climbing made them great champions, each one able to destroy many of the enemy.

At each level there were arrows of Truth scattered about, which I knew were left from those who had fallen from that position (many had fallen from each position). All of the arrows were named after the Truth of that level. Some were reluctant to pick up these arrows, but I knew we needed all we could get to destroy the great horde below.

I picked up one of the arrows, shot it, and so easily hit a demon that the others also started picking up arrows and shooting them. We began to decimate several of the enemy divisions. Because of this, the entire evil army focused its attention on us. For a time it seemed that the more we achieved, the more the enemy attacked us. Though our task seemed endless, it had become exhilarating.

Since the enemy forces could not hit us with their arrows on the higher levels, swarms of vultures would fly above us to vomit down on us. Other vultures carried demons that would urinate or defecate upon the ledges, making them very slippery.

THE ANCHOR

Our swords grew after we reached each new level, but I almost left mine behind because I did not seem to need it at the higher levels. I almost casually decided to keep it, thinking that it must have been given to me for a reason. Then, because the ledge I was standing on was so narrow and slippery, I drove the sword into the ground and tied myself to it while I shot at the enemy.

The voice of the Lord then came to me, saying: *"You have used the wisdom that will enable you to keep climbing. Many have fallen because they did not use their swords properly to anchor themselves."* No one else seemed to hear this voice, but many saw what I had done and did the same.

I wondered why the Lord had not spoken to me to do this sooner. I then knew that He had already spoken this to me somehow. As I pondered this, I began to understand that my whole life had been training for this hour. I knew that I was prepared to the degree that I had listened to the Lord and obeyed His voice throughout my life. I also knew that for some reason the wisdom and understanding I now had could not be increased or taken away while in this battle. I was very thankful for every trial I had experienced in my life, and I was sorry for not appreciating them more at the time.

Soon we were hitting the demons with almost perfect accuracy. Rage ascended from the enemy army like fire and brimstone. I knew that the Christians trapped in that army were now feeling the brunt of that rage. Some of the demons became so angry that they were now shooting at each other. Normally this would have been very encouraging, but those who suffered the most were the deceived Christians in the camp of the enemy. I knew that to the world this was appearing to be an incomprehensible meltdown of Christianity itself.

Some of those who had not used their swords as anchors were able to strike down many of the vultures, but they were also more easily knocked from the ledges where they were standing. Some of these landed on a lower level, but some fell all the way to the bottom and were picked up and carried off by the vultures. I spent every free moment trying to drive my sword deeper into the ledge, or trying to tie myself more securely to it. Every time I did this, Wisdom would stand beside me, so I knew that it was very important.

A NEW WEAPON

The arrows of Truth would seldom penetrate the vultures, but they hurt them enough to at least drive them back. Every time they were driven back far enough, some of us would climb to the next level. When we reached the level called "Galatians Two Twenty," we were above the altitude that the vultures could withstand. At this level the sky above almost blinded us with its brightness and beauty. I felt peace like I had never felt before.

Until I reached this level, my fighting spirit had been motivated almost as much by fear, hatred, or disgust for the enemy as it had been for the sake of the kingdom, truth, or love for the prisoners. But it was on this level I caught up to Faith, Hope, and Love, which before I had only been able to see from a distance. Here, I was almost overpowered by their glory. Even so, I felt that I could get close to them.

When I got next to Faith, Hope, and Love, they turned to me and began repairing and shining my armor. Soon it was transformed enough to brilliantly reflect the glory that was coming from them. When they touched my sword, great bolts of brilliant lightning began flashing from it.

Love then said, "Those who reach this level are entrusted with the powers of the age to come." Then, turning to me with a seriousness that was very sobering, he said, "I still must teach you how to use them."

The "Galatians Two Twenty" level was so wide that there did not seem to be any danger of falling. An unlimited supply of arrows was available, with the name Hope written on them. We shot some of them down at the vultures and killed them easily. About half of those who had reached this level kept shooting, while the others began carrying the arrows down to Christians still on the lower levels.

The vultures kept coming in waves upon the levels below, but with each wave there would be fewer than before. From "Galatians Two Twenty" we could hit any enemy in the army except the leaders themselves, who remained just out of our range. We decided not to use the arrows of Truth until we had destroyed all the vultures because the cloud of depression they created made the truth less effective. This took a very long time, but we did not get tired. Finally, it seemed as if the sky over the mountain was almost completely rid of the vultures.

Faith, Hope, and Love, who had grown like our weapons with each level, were now so large that I knew people far beyond the battle area could see them. Their glory even radiated into the camp of prisoners who were still under a great cloud of vultures. I was very encouraged that they could be seen this way. Maybe now the prisoners and the Christians who had been used by the enemy would understand that we were not the enemy, but they in fact had been used by him.

But this was not to be the case, at least not yet. Those in the camp of the enemy who began to see the light of Faith, Hope, and Love started calling them "angels of light" who were sent to deceive the weak or undiscerning. I knew then that their bondage was much greater than I had realized.

The non-Christians, who were not a part of either of these armies, saw the glory of Faith, Hope, and Love and started to come closer to the mountain to get a better view. Those who came closer to see them also started to understand what the battle had really been about. This was a great encouragement.

THE TRAP

The exhilaration of victory continued to grow in each of us. I felt that being in this army and in this battle had to be one of the greatest adventures of all time. After destroying most of the vultures that had been attacking our mountain, we began picking off the vultures that still covered the prisoners. As the cloud of darkness dissipated, the prisoners were bathed in sunlight and began to wake up as if they had been in a deep sleep. They were immediately repulsed by their condition, especially by the vomit that still covered them, and started cleaning themselves up. As they beheld Faith, Hope, and Love, they also saw the mountain and ran toward it.

Though the evil horde sent arrows of Accusation and Slander at their backs, the former prisoners did not stop. By the time they got to the mountain many had a dozen or more arrows stuck in them, yet they seemed to not even notice. As soon as they began to scale the mountain, their wounds began to heal. With the cloud of depression largely dispelled, it seemed as if everything was now getting much easier.

The former prisoners had great joy in their salvation. They seemed so overwhelmed with appreciation for each new level of the mountain that it gave us a greater appreciation for those truths too.

Soon a fierce resolve to fight the enemy arose in the former prisoners. They put on the armor provided and begged to be allowed to go back and attack the enemy who had held them captive and abused them for so long. We thought about it, but then decided we should all stay on the mountain to fight. Again, the voice of the Lord spoke, saying, *"A second time you have chosen wisdom. You cannot win if you try to fight the enemy on his own ground. You must remain on My holy mountain."*

I was stunned that we had made another decision of such importance just by thinking and briefly discussing it. I then resolved to do my best to not make another decision of any consequence without prayer. Wisdom then stepped up to me quickly, took both of my shoulders firmly, and looked me straight in the eyes, saying, *"You must do this!"*

As Wisdom said this to me, he pulled me forward as if he were saving me from something. I looked back and saw that, even though I had once been on the broad plateau of "Galatians Two Twenty," I had drifted to the very edge without even knowing it. I had come very close to falling off the mountain. I looked again into the eyes of Wisdom, and he said with the utmost seriousness, *"Take heed when you think you stand, lest you fall. In this life you can fall from any level."*

I thought about Wisdom's words for quite a while. In the exuberance of the victory we were starting to achieve and the unity we were beginning to experience, I had become careless. It was more noble to fall because of the onslaught of the enemy than to fall because of carelessness.

THE SERPENTS

For a long time, we continued killing the vultures and picking off the demons that were riding the Christians. We found that the arrows of different truths would have greater impact on different demons. We knew it was going to be a long battle, but we were not suffering any more casualties now, and we had continued to climb past the level of "Patience."

It was troubling that after these Christians had the demons shot off of them, few would come to the mountain. Many had taken on the nature of the demons and continued in their delusion without them. As the darkness of the demons dissipated, we could see the ground moving around the feet of these Christians. Then I saw that their legs were bound by serpents. As I kept looking at the serpents, I saw that they were all the same kind and had the name Shame written on them.

We shot arrows of Truth at the serpents, but the arrows had little effect. We then tried the arrows of Hope, but without results. From "Galatians Two Twenty" it had been very easy to go higher because we all helped each other. Since there now seemed to be little that we could do against the enemy, we decided to just try to climb as far as we could until we found something that would work against the serpents.

We passed levels of truth very fast. On most of them we did not even bother to look around if there was not a weapon in sight that might work on the serpents. Faith, Hope, and Love stayed right with us, but I had not noticed that we had left Wisdom far behind. It would be a long time before I understood what a mistake this was. He would catch up to us on the top, but leaving him behind cost us a much quicker and easier victory over the evil horde.

THE BEAUTIFUL GARDEN

Almost without warning, we came to a level that opened up into a Garden. It was the most beautiful place I had ever seen. Over the entrance to this Garden was written, "The Father's Unconditional Love." This entrance was so glorious and inviting that we could not resist entering. As soon as I entered, I saw a tree that I knew was the Tree of Life. It was in the middle of this Garden, and it was still guarded by angels of awesome power and authority. When I looked at them, they looked back. They seemed friendly, as if they had been expecting us. I looked back and there was now a host of other warriors in the Garden. This gave us all courage, and because of the angels' demeanor, we decided to pass them to get to the tree. One of the angels called out: "Those who make it to this level know the Father's love and can eat of the tree."

I did not realize how hungry I was. When I tasted the fruit, it was better than anything I had ever tasted. Yet, it was also somehow familiar. It brought pleasant memories of such things as sunshine, rain, beautiful fields, and the sun setting over the ocean, but even more, it reminded me of the people I loved. With every bite, I loved everything and everyone more. Then my enemies started coming to mind, and I loved them too. The feeling was soon greater than anything I had ever experienced, even the peace we felt when we first reached the level of "Galatians Two Twenty." Then I heard the voice of the Lord saying, *"This is now your daily bread. It will never be withheld from you. You may eat as much and as often as you like. There is no end to My love."*

I looked up into the tree to see where the voice had come from, and I saw that the tree was filled with pure white eagles. They had the most beautiful, penetrating eyes I have ever seen. They were looking at me as if waiting for instructions.

[47]

"They will do your bidding," one of the angels said. "These eagles eat snakes."

"Go!" I told the eagles. "Devour the shame that has bound our brothers."

They opened their wings, and a great wind came and lifted them into the air. The eagles filled the sky with a blinding glory. Even as high as we were, I could hear the sounds of terror from the enemy camp at the sight of the eagles descending.

THE KING APPEARS

The Lord Jesus Himself then appeared right in our midst. He took the time to greet each one personally, congratulating us for reaching the top of the mountain. Then He said to us, *"I must now share with you what I shared with your brothers after My resurrection—the message of My kingdom. The enemy's most powerful army has now been put to flight, but not destroyed. Now it is time for us to march forth with the gospel of My kingdom. The eagles have been released and will go with us. We will take arrows from every level, but remember that I am your Sword and your Captain. It is now time for the Sword of the Lord to be unsheathed."*

I then turned and saw that the entire army of the Lord was standing in the Garden. There were men, women, and children from all races and nations, each carrying their banners, which moved in the wind with perfect unity. I knew that nothing like this had been seen on the earth before. Although the enemy had many more armies and fortresses throughout the earth, I knew that none could stand before this great army of God.

Almost under my breath, I said, "This must be the day of the Lord." To my amazement, the whole host then answered in an awesome thunder: "The day of the Lord of hosts has come!"

REFLECTING ON THE DREAM

Months later, I sat pondering this dream. Alarmingly, certain events and conditions in the church had already seemed to parallel what I had seen when the hordes from hell began to march. I was then reminded of Abraham Lincoln. The only way he could become a great emancipator and the preserver of the Union was to be willing to fight a Civil War. Not only did he have to fight it, but he had to be determined not to compromise until the victory was complete.

Lincoln also had to have the grace to fight the bloodiest war in our history without "demonizing" the enemy with propaganda. If he had done that, he might have been able to galvanize the resolve of the North much faster, facilitating a quicker military victory. However, it would have made the reunion after the war much more difficult. Because he was truly fighting to preserve the Union, Lincoln never made the men and women of the South the enemy, but rather the evil that held them in bondage.

A great spiritual civil war now looms before the church. Many will do everything they can to avoid it. This is understandable and even noble. However, compromise will never maintain a lasting peace. It will only make the ultimate conflict that much more difficult when it comes, and it will come.

The Lord is now preparing courageous leaders who will be willing to fight a spiritual civil war in order to set men free. The main issue, as in the American Civil War, will be slavery versus freedom. The secondary issue, which will be the primary issue for some, will be money.

[49]

Just as the American Civil War at times looked like it would destroy the entire nation, that which is coming upon the church will sometimes appear as if it will bring the end of the church. However, just as the United States not only survived, but went on to become the most powerful nation on earth, the same is going to happen to the church. The church will not be destroyed, but the institutions and doctrines that have kept men in spiritual slavery will be.

Even after this, perfect justice in the church will not be attained overnight. There will still be struggles for women's rights and to set the church free from racism and exploitation. These are all causes that must be confronted. Yet, in the midst of the coming spiritual civil war, Faith, Hope, and Love, and the kingdom of God they stand upon, will be seen as they never have before. This will begin drawing people to the kingdom. God's government is about to be demonstrated as greater than any human government.

Let us always remember that with the Lord "a thousand years is as a day" (see II Peter 3:8). He can do in us in one day what we think will take a thousand years. The work of liberating and raising up the church will be accomplished much quicker than we may think is humanly possible. However, we are not talking about human possibilities.

CHAPTER II

The Holy Mountain

We stood in the Garden of God under the Tree of Life. It seemed that the entire army was there, many of them kneeling before the Lord Jesus. He had just given us the charge to return to the battle for the sake of our brothers who were still bound and for the world that He loved. It was both a wonderful and a terrible command. It was wonderful because it came from Him. It was terrible because it meant that we would have to leave His manifest presence and the Garden that was more beautiful than any place we had ever been before. To leave all of this to go into battle again seemed incomprehensible.

The Lord continued His exhortation: *"I have given you spiritual gifts and power, and an increasing understanding of My Word and My kingdom, but the greatest weapon you have been given is the Father's love. As long as you walk in My Father's love, you will never fail. The fruit of this tree is the Father's love, which is manifested in Me. This love, which is in Me, must be your daily bread."*

In this setting of such beauty and glory, it did not seem that the Lord was appearing in His glory. In fact, His appearance was rather ordinary. Even so, the grace with which He moved and spoke made Him the most attractive person I had ever seen. He was beyond human definition in dignity and nobility. It was easy to understand why He is everything that the Father loves and esteems. Seeing Him this way, so full of grace and truth, made it seem that nothing but grace and truth should ever matter.

As I ate the fruit from the Tree of Life, the thought of every good thing I had ever known filled my soul. When Jesus spoke, it was the same, only magnified. All I wanted to do was stay in this place and listen to Him. I remembered how I had once thought it must be boring for those angels who do nothing but worship Him continually before the throne. Now I knew that there was nothing more wonderful or exhilarating that we would ever do than to simply worship Him.

Such worship was what we were created for, and it would surely be the best part of heaven. I could not imagine how wonderful it would be if all of the heavenly choirs were added. It was hard to believe that I had struggled so much with boredom during worship services. I knew that it was only because I had been almost completely out of touch with this heavenly reality.

I was almost overwhelmed with the desire to go back and make up for those times during worship services when I had allowed my mind to wander or had occupied myself with other things. The desire to express my adoration for Him became almost insatiable. I had to praise Him! As I opened my mouth, I was shocked by the spontaneous worship that erupted from the entire army at the same time. I had almost forgotten that anyone else was there, yet we were all in perfect unity. The glorious worship that followed could not be described in human language.

As we worshiped, a golden glow began to emanate from the Lord. Then silver appeared around the gold. We were all then enveloped in colors, the richness of which I have never seen with my natural eyes. With this glory, I entered a realm of emotion that I had never experienced before. Somehow I understood that this glory had been there all along, but when we focused on Him in worship, we began to see more of His glory. The more intensely we worshiped, the more glory we beheld. If this was heaven, it was much, much better than I had ever dreamed.

His Dwelling Place

I have no idea how long this worship lasted. It could have been minutes or it could have been months. There was just no way to measure time in that kind of glory. I closed my eyes because the glory I was seeing with my heart was as great as what I was seeing with my physical eyes.

When I opened them, I was surprised to see that the Lord was not there any longer, but a troop of angels was standing where He had been. One of them approached me and said, "Close your eyes again." When I did, I beheld the glory of the Lord. This was no small relief. Now that I had experienced the glory, I knew I simply could not live without it.

Then the angel explained, "What you see with the eyes of your heart is more real than what you see with your physical eyes."

I had made this statement myself many times, but how little I had walked in it! The angel continued, "It was for this reason that the Lord told His first disciples it was better

[53]

for Him to go away so the Holy Spirit could come. The Lord dwells within you. You have taught this many times, but now you must live it for you have eaten from the Tree of Life."

The angel then began to lead me back to the gate. I protested that I did not want to leave. Seeming surprised, the angel took me by the shoulders and looked me in the eyes. This was when I recognized him—it was Wisdom.

"You never have to leave this Garden," he assured me. *"This Garden is in your heart because the Creator Himself is within you. You have desired the best part, to worship and sit in His presence forever, and it will never be taken from you. But you must take it from here to where it is needed most."*

I knew he was right. I then looked past him to the Tree of Life. I had a compulsion to grab all of the fruit that I could before leaving. Knowing my thoughts, Wisdom gently shook me. *"No. Even this fruit, gathered in fear, would go bad. This fruit and this tree are within you because He is in you. You must believe."*

SEEING WITH EYES CLOSED

I closed my eyes and tried to see the Lord again, but I could not. When I opened my eyes, Wisdom was still staring at me. With great patience, he continued.

"You have tasted of the heavenly realm, and no one ever wants to go back to the battle once they do. No one ever wants to leave the manifest presence of the Lord. After the Apostle Paul came here, he struggled for the rest of his life as to whether he should continue to labor for the sake of the church or return here to enter into his inheritance. His inheritance was magnified the longer he stayed and served on earth. Now that you have the heart of a true worshiper, you will always

want to be here, and you can, whenever you enter into true worship. The more focused you are on Him, the more glory you will see, regardless of where you are."

Wisdom's words had finally calmed me. Again I closed my eyes just to thank the Lord for this wonderful experience and the life He had given to me. As I did, I started to see His glory again, and all of the emotion of the previous worship experience flooded my soul.

The Lord's words to me were so loud and clear that I was sure they were audible: *"I will never leave or forsake you."*

"Lord, forgive my unbelief," I responded. "Please help me never to leave or forsake *You."* This was both a wonderful and trying time. Here the "real world" was not real, and the spiritual realm was so much more real that I just could not imagine going back to the other. I was gripped both with wonder and a terrible fear that I might wake up at any moment and find it was all just a dream.

Wisdom understood what was going on inside of me. *"You are dreaming,"* he said. *"But this dream is more real than what you think of as real. The Father gave men dreams to help them see the door to His dwelling place. He will only dwell in men's hearts, and dreams can be a door to your heart, which will lead you to Him. This is why His angels so often appear to men in their dreams. In dreams they can bypass the fallen mind of man and go straight to his heart."*

As I opened my eyes, Wisdom was still gripping my shoulders. *"I am the primary gift that has been given to you for your work,"* he said. *"I will show you the way and keep you on it, but only love will keep you faithful. The fear of the Lord is the beginning of wisdom, but the highest wisdom is to love Him."*

Then Wisdom released me and started to walk toward the gate. I followed with ambivalence. I remembered the exhilaration of the battle and the climb up the mountain, and though it was compelling, there was no comparison to the presence of the Lord and the worship I had just experienced. Leaving this would be the greatest sacrifice I had ever made. Then I remembered how it was all inside of me, and I was amazed that I could forget this so quickly. It was as if a great battle was raging within me, between what I saw with my physical eyes and what I saw with my heart.

THE THIRD HEAVEN

Having moved forward so that I was walking beside Wisdom, I asked him: "I have prayed for twenty-five years to be caught up into the third heaven like the Apostle Paul. Is this the third heaven?"

"This is part of it," he replied, *"but there is much more."*

"Will I be allowed to see more?" I asked.

"You will see much more. I am taking you to see more now," he replied.

I started thinking of the Book of Revelation. "Was John's revelation part of the third heaven?" I asked.

"Part of John's revelation was from the third heaven, but most of it was from the second heaven. The first heaven was before the fall of man. The second heaven is the spiritual realm during the reign of evil upon the earth. In the third heaven the love and domain of the Father will again prevail over the earth through the King."

"What was the first heaven like?" I inquired, strangely feeling a cold chill as I asked.

"It is wisdom not to be concerned about that now," Wisdom responded with increased seriousness, as my question seemed to jolt him. *"Wisdom is to seek to know the*

[56]

third heaven just as you have. There is much more to know about the third heaven than you can know in this life, yet it is the third heaven, the kingdom, that you must preach. In the ages to come you will be told about the first heaven, but it is not profitable for you to know about it now."

When I resolved to remember the cold chill I had just felt, Wisdom nodded, which I knew to be an affirmation of that thought. "What a great companion you are," I had to say as I realized the valuable gift that this angel was. "You really will keep me on the right path."

"I will indeed," he replied.

THE OTHER HALF OF LOVE

I was sure I felt love coming from this angel, which was unique, since I had never felt it from the other angels. They usually showed their concern more out of duty than love. Wisdom responded to my thoughts as if I had spoken them out loud.

"It is wisdom to love, and I could not be Wisdom if I did not love you. It is also wisdom to behold the kindness and the severity of God. It is wisdom to love Him and to fear Him. You are in deception if you do otherwise. This is the next lesson that you must learn," he said with unmistakable earnestness.

"I do know that, and have taught it many times," I responded, feeling for the first time that maybe Wisdom did not fully know me.

"I have been your companion for a very long time, and I know your teachings," Wisdom replied. *"Now you are about to learn what some of your own teachings mean. As you have said many times, 'It is not by believing in your mind, but in your heart that results in righteousness.'"*

I apologized, feeling a bit ashamed at having questioned Wisdom. He graciously accepted my apology. It was then that I realized I had been questioning and challenging him most of my life, often to my harm.

"Just as there is a time to plant and a time to reap," Wisdom continued, *"there are times to adore the Lord, and there are times to honor Him with the greatest fear and respect. It is wisdom to know the time for each. True wisdom knows the times and seasons of God. I brought you here because it was time to worship the Lord in the glory of His love. This is what you need the most after such a battle. I am now taking you to another place because it is time for you to worship Him in the fear of His judgment. Until you know both, there is a danger that we can be separated from each other."*

"Do you mean that if I had stayed back there in that glorious worship I would have lost you?" I asked in disbelief.

"Yes. I would have always visited with you when I could, but we would have rarely crossed paths. Although it is hard to leave such glory and peace, that is not the whole revelation of the King. He is both a Lion and a Lamb. To the spiritual children, He is the Lamb. To the maturing, He is the Lion. To the fully mature, He is both the Lion and the Lamb. Again, I know you understand this, but you have known it primarily in your mind. Soon you will know it in your heart, for you are about to experience the judgment seat of Christ."

RETURNING TO THE BATTLE

Before leaving the gates to the Garden, I asked Wisdom if I could sit for a while to ponder all that I had just experienced. *"Yes, you should do this,"* he replied, *"but I have a better place for you to do it."*

I followed Wisdom out of the gates and we began to go down the mountain. To my surprise, the battle was still going on, but not as intensely as it was when we ascended. There were still arrows of accusation and slander flying about on the lower levels, but most of the enemy horde that remained was furiously attacking the great white eagles. The eagles were easily prevailing.

We kept descending until we were almost at the bottom. Just above the levels of "Salvation" and "Sanctification" was the level of "Thanksgiving and Praise." I remembered this level very well because one of the greatest attacks of the enemy came when I had first tried to reach it. Once we had arrived, the rest of the climb was much easier, and when an arrow penetrated our armor, healing came much faster.

As soon as my enemies spotted me on this level (they could not see Wisdom), a shower of arrows began to rain down on me. I knocked them down with my shield so easily that the enemies quit shooting. Their arrows were now almost gone, and they could not afford to waste them.

The soldiers who were still fighting from this level looked at me in astonishment with a deference that made me very uncomfortable. It was then I first noticed that the glory of the Lord was emanating from my armor and shield. I told these soldiers to climb to the top of the mountain without stopping, and they, too, would see the Lord. As soon as they agreed to go, they saw Wisdom. They started to fall down to worship him, but he restrained them and sent them on their way.

THE FAITHFUL

I was filled with love for these soldiers, many of whom were women and children. Their armor was a mess, and they were covered in blood, but they had not given up. In fact, they were still cheerful and encouraged. I told

[59]

them that they were deserving of more honor than I was because they had borne the greatest burden of the battle and had held their ground. They seemed to not believe me, but appreciated that I would say it. However, I really felt that it was true.

Every level on the mountain had to be occupied, or the vultures that were left would come and desecrate it with vomit and excrement until it was difficult to stand on. Most of the ledges were occupied by soldiers which I recognized to be from different denominations or movements that emphasized the truth of the level they were defending. I was embarrassed by the attitude I had maintained toward some of these groups. I had considered them out of touch and backslidden at best, but here they were fighting faithfully against a terrible onslaught of the enemy. Their defense of these positions had probably enabled me to keep climbing.

Some of these levels were situated so that there was a good view of the mountain and the battlefield, but some were so isolated that the soldiers on them could see only their own position. These seemed unaware of the rest of the battle that was raging or the rest of the army that was also fighting the battle. They were so wounded from the slander and accusations that they would resist anyone who came down to them from a higher level to encourage them to continue climbing.

However, when some came down from the top reflecting the glory of the Lord, the wounded warriors listened, most of them with great joy. Soon a number of them began to climb with courage and resolve. As I beheld all of this, Wisdom did not say much, but he seemed very interested in my reactions.

REALITY DISCOVERED

I watched as many soldiers who had been to the top began descending to all of the levels in order to relieve those who had been taking their stand on those truths. As they did, each level began to shine with the glory they carried. Soon the whole mountain was shining with a glory that was blinding to the vultures and demons that were left. After a time, there was so much glory on the mountain that it began to have the same feel as the Garden.

I started thanking and praising the Lord and immediately I was in His presence again. It was hard to contain the emotions and glory that I felt when I did this. The experience became so intense that I stopped. Wisdom was standing beside me. Putting his hand on my shoulder, he said, *"You enter His gates with thanksgiving, His courts with praise."*

"But that was so real!" I exclaimed. "I felt as if I was there again."

"You were there, indeed," replied Wisdom. *"It has not become more real, but you have. Just as the Lord told the thief on the cross, 'Today you will be with Me in Paradise,' you can enter Paradise at anytime. The Lord, His Paradise, and this mountain are all abiding in you, because He is in you. What were but foretastes are now a reality to you because you have climbed the mountain. The reason you can see me and others cannot is not because I have entered your realm, but because you have entered mine. This is the reality that the prophets knew which gave them great boldness even when they stood alone against armies. They saw the heavenly host that was for them, not just the earthly one arrayed against them."*

THE DEADLY TRAP

I then looked out over the carnage below and the slowly retreating demonic army. Behind me, more of the glorious warriors were constantly taking their places on the mountain. I knew that we were now strong enough to attack and destroy what was left of this enemy horde. *"Not yet,"* said Wisdom. *"Look over there."*

I looked in the direction he was pointing, but had to shield my eyes from the glory emanating from my own armor to see anything. Then I caught a glimpse of some movement in a small valley. I could not make out what I was seeing because the glory shining from my armor made it difficult to see into the darkness. I asked Wisdom if there was something that I could cover my armor with so I could see. He then gave me a very plain mantle to put on.

"What is this?" I inquired, a little insulted by its drabness.

"Humility," said Wisdom. *"You will not be able to see very well without it."*

Reluctantly I put it on, and immediately I saw many things that I could not see before. I looked toward the valley and the movement I had seen. To my astonishment, there was an entire division of the enemy horde that was waiting to ambush anyone who ventured from the mountain.

"What army is that?" I asked, "and how did they escape the battle intact?"

"That is Pride," explained Wisdom. *"It is the hardest enemy to see after you have been in the glory. Those who refuse to put on this cloak will suffer much at the hands of that most devious enemy."*

As I looked back at the mountain, I saw many of the glorious warriors crossing the plain to attack the remnant of the enemy horde. None of them were wearing the cloaks of humility, and they had not seen the enemy that was ready to attack them from their rear. I started to run out to stop them, but Wisdom restrained me.

"You cannot stop this," he said. *"Only the soldiers who wear this cloak will recognize your authority. Come with me. There is something else that you must see before you can help lead in the great battle that is to come."*

THE FOUNDATION OF GLORY

Wisdom led me down the mountain to the very lowest level, which was named "Salvation." *"You see this as the lowest level,"* declared Wisdom, *"but this is the foundation of the whole mountain. In any journey, the first step is the most important, and it is usually the most difficult. Without 'Salvation' there would be no mountain."*

I was appalled by the carnage on this level. Every soldier was very badly wounded, but none of them were dead. Multitudes were barely clinging to the edge. Many seemed ready to fall off, but none did. Angels were everywhere ministering to the soldiers with such great joy that I had to ask: "Why are they so happy?"

"These angels have beheld the courage that it took for these to hold on. They may not have gone any farther, but neither did they give up. They will soon be healed; then they will behold the glory of the rest of the mountain and they will begin to climb. These will be great warriors for the battle to come."

"But wouldn't they have been better off to climb the mountain with the rest of us?" I protested, seeing their present condition.

[63]

*"It would have been better for them, but not for you.
By staying here, they kept most of your enemies occupied
and that made it easier for you to climb. Very few from
the higher levels ever reached out to help others come to the
mountain, but these did. Even when barely clinging to the
mountain themselves, they would reach out to pull others
up. In fact, most of the mighty warriors were led to the
mountain by these faithful ones.*

*"These who stayed and faithfully fought on the level of
'Salvation' are no less heroes than the ones who made it to
the top. They brought great joy to heaven by leading others
to salvation. It was for this reason that all the angels in
heaven wanted to come to minister to them, but only the
most honored were permitted."*

Again I felt shame for my previous attitude toward
these great saints. Many of us had scorned them as
we climbed to the higher levels. They had made many
mistakes during the battle, but they had also displayed
more of the Shepherd's heart than the rest of us. The
Lord would leave the ninety-nine to go after the one who
was lost. These had stayed in the place where they could
still reach the lost, and they paid a dear price for it. I, too,
wanted to help but did not know where to start.

Wisdom then said, *"It is right for you to want to help,
but you will help most by going on to what you have been called
to do. These will all be healed and will climb the mountain.
They can now climb faster because of you and the others who
went before them, both destroying the enemy and marking the
way. They will join you again in the battle. These are fearless
ones who will never retreat before the enemy."*

THE POWER OF PRIDE

I was pondering how I was learning as much by
descending the mountain as I had by climbing it, when

[64]

the noise from the battlefield drew my attention. By now, thousands of the mighty warriors had crossed the plain to attack the remnant of the enemy horde.

The enemy was fleeing in all directions, except for one division—Pride. Completely undetected, it had marched right up to the rear of the advancing warriors and was about to release a hail of arrows. I then noticed that the mighty warriors had no armor on their backsides. They were totally exposed and vulnerable to what was about to hit them.

Wisdom remarked, *"You have taught that there is no armor for the backside, which means you are vulnerable if you run from the enemy. However, you never saw how advancing in pride also makes you vulnerable."*

I could only nod in acknowledgment, for it was too late to do anything. It was almost unbearable to watch, but Wisdom said that I must. I knew the kingdom of God was about to suffer a major defeat. Though I had felt sorrow before, I had never felt this kind of sorrow.

To my amazement, when the arrows of Pride struck the warriors they did not even notice. However, the enemy kept shooting. The warriors were bleeding and getting weaker fast, but they would not acknowledge it. Soon they were too weak to hold up their shields and swords; they cast them down, declaring that they no longer needed them. They started taking off their armor, saying it was not needed anymore either.

Then another enemy division appeared and moved up swiftly. It was called Strong Delusion. Its members released a hail of arrows and they all seemed to hit their marks. It only took a few of the demons of Delusion, who were all small and seemingly weak, to lead away this once great army of glorious warriors. They were taken to various prison camps, each named after a different doctrine of demons. I was astounded at how this great company of the righteous had been so easily defeated, and they still did not even know what had hit them.

I blurted out: "How could those who were so strong, who have been all the way to the top of the mountain, who have seen the Lord as they have, be so vulnerable?"

"Pride is the hardest enemy to see, and it always sneaks up behind you," Wisdom lamented. *"In some ways, those who have been to the greatest heights are in the greatest danger of falling. You must always remember that in this life you can fall at any time from any level."*

"Take heed when you think you stand, lest you fall," I replied. "How awesome such Scriptures seem to me now!"

"When you think you are the least vulnerable to falling is in fact when you are the most vulnerable. Most men fall immediately after a great victory," Wisdom lamented.

"How can we keep from being attacked like this?" I asked.

"Stay close to me, inquire of the Lord before making major decisions, and keep that mantle on. Then the enemy will not be able to easily blindside you as he did them."

I looked at my mantle. It looked so plain and insignificant. I felt that it made me look more like a homeless person than a warrior. Wisdom responded as if I had been speaking out loud.

"The Lord is closer to the homeless than to kings. You only have true strength to the degree that you walk in the grace of God, and 'He gives His grace to the humble.' No evil weapon can penetrate this mantle because nothing can overpower His grace. As long as you wear this mantle, you are safe from this kind of attack."

I then started to look up to see how many warriors were still on the mountain. I was shocked to see how few there were. I noticed, however, that they all had on the same mantle of humility. "How did that happen?" I inquired.

"When they saw the battle you just witnessed, they all came to me for help and I gave them their mantles," Wisdom replied.

"But I thought you were with me that whole time."

"I am with all who go forth to do the will of My Father," Wisdom answered.

"You're the Lord!" I cried.

"Yes," He answered. *"I told you that I would never leave you or forsake you. I am with all My warriors just as I am with you. I will be to you whatever you need to accomplish My will, and you have needed wisdom."* Then He vanished.

RANK IN THE KINGDOM

I was left standing in the midst of the great company of angels who were ministering to the wounded on the level of "Salvation." As I began to walk past these angels, they bowed on one knee and showed me great respect. I finally asked one of them why they did this, as even the smallest was much more powerful than I was. "Because of the mantle," he replied. "That is the highest rank in the kingdom."

"This is just a plain mantle," I protested.

"No!" the angel insisted. "You are clothed in the grace of God. There is no greater power than that!"

"But there are thousands of us all wearing the same mantle. How could it represent rank?" I asked.

[67]

"You are the dreaded champions, the sons and daughters of the King. He wore the same mantle when He walked on this earth. As long as you are clothed in that, there is no power in heaven or on earth that can stand before you. Everyone in heaven and hell recognizes that mantle. We are indeed His servants, but He abides in you, and you are clothed in His grace."

Somehow I knew that if I had not been wearing the mantle, and if my glorious armor had been exposed, the angel's statements and behavior toward me would have fed my pride. It was simply impossible to feel prideful or arrogant while wearing such a drab, plain cloak. However, my confidence in the mantle was growing fast.

Chapter III

The Return of the Eagles

On the horizon I saw a great white cloud approaching. Hope rose in me just from seeing it. Soon it had filled the whole atmosphere with hope, just as the rising sun chases away the darkness of night. As it grew closer, I recognized the great white eagles that had flown from the Tree of Life. They began landing on the mountain, taking their places on every level beside the companies of warriors.

I carefully approached the eagle that had landed near me because his presence was so awesome. When he looked at me with his penetrating eyes, I knew I could hide nothing from him. His eyes were so fierce and resolute that I trembled. Chills ran through me just from looking at him. Before I could even ask, he answered me.

"You want to know who we are. We are the hidden prophets who have been kept for this hour. We are the eyes of those who have been given the divinely powerful weapons. We have been shown all that the Lord is doing, and all that the enemy is planning against you. We have scoured the earth, and together we know all that needs to be known for the battle."

"Did you not see the battle that just took place?" I asked with as much irritation as I dared to express. "Couldn't you have helped those warriors who were just taken captive?"

"Yes," the eagle responded. "We saw it all, and we could have helped if they had wanted our help. We would have helped them by holding them back, telling them to sit and be still. But we can only fight in the battles that the Father commands, and we can only help those who believe in us. Only those who receive us as prophets can receive the prophets' reward, or the benefit of our services. Those who were ambushed did not yet have the mantle you are wearing, and those who do not have that mantle cannot understand who we are. We all need one another, including these here who are still wounded, and many others whom you do not yet know."

The Eagle's Heart

As I talked to the eagle, I started to think like him. After this short discussion I could see into the eagle's heart and I began to know him like he knew me. The eagle recognized this.

"You have some of our gifts," the eagle noted, "though they are not very well developed. You have not used them much. I am here to awaken these gifts in you, and in many others like you, and I will teach you how to use them. In this way, our communication will be sure. Unless we have sure communication, we will all suffer many unnecessary losses, not to mention missing many great opportunities for victory."

"Where did you just come from?" I asked.

"We eat snakes," the eagle replied. "The enemy is bread for us. Our sustenance comes from doing the

Father's will, which is to destroy the works of the devil. Every snake that we eat helps to increase our vision. Every stronghold of the enemy that we tear down strengthens us so we can soar higher and stay in the air longer. We have just come from a feast, devouring the serpents of Shame which have bound many of your brothers and sisters. They will be here soon. They are coming with the eagles we left behind to help them find the way and to protect them from the enemy's counterattacks."

These eagles were very sure of themselves, but not cocky. They knew who they were and what they were called to do. They also knew us and they knew the future. Their confidence was reassuring to me, but even more so to the wounded who were still lying all around us. Those who had recently been too weak to talk were actually sitting up, listening to my conversation with the eagle. They looked at him the same way lost children would look at their parents who had just found them.

THE WIND OF THE SPIRIT

When the eagle looked upon the wounded, his countenance changed as well. In place of the fierce resoluteness he had previously exhibited, he became like a soft, compassionate, old grandfather. The eagle opened his wings and began to gently flap them, stirring up a cool, refreshing breeze that flowed over the wounded. It was unlike any other breeze I had ever felt before. With each breath I was gaining strength and clarity of mind. Soon the wounded were standing and worshiping God with a sincerity that brought tears to my eyes.

Again I felt a profound shame at having scorned those who stayed on this level. They had seemed so weak and foolish to those of us who were ascending the mountain, but they had endured much more than we had and

[71]

remained faithful. God had kept them, and they loved Him with a great love.

I looked up at the mountain. The eagles were all gently flapping their wings. Everyone on the mountain was being refreshed by the breeze they were stirring up, and we all began to worship the Lord. At first there was some discord between the worship coming from the different levels, but soon everyone on every level was singing in perfect harmony.

Never on earth had I heard anything so beautiful. I never wanted it to end. Soon I recognized it as the same worship that we had known in the Garden, but now it sounded even richer and fuller. I knew this was because we were worshiping in the very presence of our enemies, in the midst of such darkness and evil surrounding the mountain.

I do not know how long this worship lasted, but eventually the eagles stopped flapping their wings and it ceased. "Why did you stop?" I asked the eagle I had been talking with.

"Because now they are whole," he replied, indicating the wounded who now were all standing and appeared to be in perfect condition. "True worship can heal any wound," he added.

"Please do it again," I begged.

"We will do this many times, but it is not for us to decide when. The breeze you felt was the Holy Spirit. He directs us; we do not direct Him. He has healed the wounded and has begun to bring about the unity that is required for the battles ahead. True worship also pours the precious oil upon the Head, Jesus. The oil then flows down over the entire body, making us one with Him and with each other.

"No one who comes into union with Him will remain wounded or unclean. His blood is pure life, and it flows through us when we are joined to Him. And when we are joined to Him we are also joined to the rest of the body, so that His blood flows through us all. A wound is healed by closing the wound so blood can flow to the wounded member and bring regeneration. When a part of His body is wounded, we must join in unity with that part until it is fully restored. We are all one."

In the euphoria still left from the worship, this brief teaching seemed almost esoteric. Yet I knew it was very basic. When the Holy Spirit moved, every word seemed glorious, regardless of how elementary it was. I was so filled with love that I wanted to hug everyone, including the fierce old eagles.

Then, like a jolt, I remembered the mighty warriors who had just been captured. The eagle sensed this but did not say anything. He just watched me intently. Finally, I spoke up, "Can we recover those who were just lost?"

"Yes. It is right for you to feel what you do," the eagle finally said. "We are not complete and our worship is not complete until the whole body is restored. Even in the most glorious worship, even in the very presence of the King, we will all feel this emptiness until all are one because our King also feels it.

"We all grieve for our brothers in bondage, but we grieve even more for the heart of our King. Though you love each of your children, you would be particularly concerned for the one who was sick or wounded. The King loves all of His children too, but the wounded and oppressed have most of His attention now. For His sake, we must not quit until all have been recovered. As long as any are wounded, He is wounded."

FAITH TO MOVE THE MOUNTAIN

Sitting down by the eagle, I pondered his words. Finally I remarked, "I know that Wisdom now speaks to me through you because I hear His voice when you speak. I was so sure of myself before that last battle, but I was almost carried away with the same presumption that they were carried away with. I could very easily have been captured with them if Wisdom had not stopped me.

"I was motivated more by hatred for the enemy than by the desire to set my brothers free. Since coming to this mountain and fighting in the great battle, I now think that most of the right things I did, I did for the wrong reasons, and many of the wrong things I did, I had good motives for. The more I learn, the more unsure of myself I feel."

"You must have been with Wisdom a long time," the eagle responded.

"He was with me a long time before I began to recognize Him, but I am afraid that most of that time I was resisting Him. Somehow I now know I am still lacking something very important, something I must have before I go into battle again, but I do not know what it is."

The great eagle's eyes became even more penetrating as he responded, "You also know the voice of Wisdom when He speaks to you in your own heart. You are learning well because you have the mantle. What you are feeling now is true faith."

"Faith?" I shot back. "I'm talking about serious doubts!"

"You are wise to doubt yourself. True faith depends on God, not on you and not even on your faith. You are close to the kind of faith that can move this mountain, and move it we must. It is time to carry it to places where it has not traveled before.

"However, you are right; you are still lacking something very important. You must yet have a revelation. Even though you have climbed to the top of the mountain and received from every truth along the way, and even though you have stood in the Garden of God, tasted of His unconditional love, and seen His Son many times now, you still understand only a part of the whole counsel of God, and that only superficially."

I knew this was true, and it was actually comforting to hear it. "I have judged so many people and so many situations wrongly!" I exclaimed. "Wisdom has saved my life many times now, but the voice of Wisdom is still a very small voice within me, and the clamor of my own thoughts and feelings is still far too loud. I hear Wisdom speaking through you much louder than I hear Him in my own heart, so I know I must stay very close to you."

"We are here because you need us," the eagle replied. "We are also here because we need you. You have been given gifts I do not have, and I have been given gifts you do not have. You have experienced things I have not experienced, and I have experienced things that you have not. The eagles have been given to you until the end, and you have been given to us. I will be very close to you for a time, and then you must receive other eagles in my place. Every eagle is different. It is together, not individually, that we have been given to know the secrets of the Lord."

THE DOORS OF TRUTH

The eagle then rose up from the rock on which he had perched and soared over to the edge of the level on which we stood. "Come," he said. As I approached him, I saw steps that led down to the very base of the mountain, and a small door.

"Why have I not seen this before?" I asked.

"When you first came to the mountain you did not stay on this level long enough to look around," he answered.

"How did you know that? Were you here when I first came to the mountain?"

"I would have known if I had not been here, because all who miss this door do so for the same reason, but in fact, I was here," he responded. "I was one of the soldiers you so quickly passed on your way up the mountain."

It was then that I recognized the eagle as a man I had met and had a few conversations with soon after my conversion. He continued, "I wanted badly to follow you then. I had been on this level for so long that I needed a change. I just could not leave all of the lost souls that I was still trying to lead here. When I finally committed myself to doing the Lord's will, whether it was to stay or go, Wisdom appeared to me and showed me this door. He said it was a shortcut to the top. That is how I was able to reach the top before you did. There I was changed into an eagle."

I then remembered that I had seen doors like this on a couple of the levels. I had even peeked into one of them and was amazed at what I saw. I did not venture very far into it because I was so focused on the battle and on trying to get to the top of the mountain. "Could I have entered one of those doors and gone right to the top?" I asked.

"It is not quite that easy," the eagle remarked, seeming a little irritated. "In every door there are passageways, one of which leads to the top." Anticipating my next question, he continued, "The other ones lead to the other levels on the mountain. The Father designed each passageway so that everyone would choose the one his level of maturity dictated."

"Incredible! How did He do that?" I thought to myself, but the eagle heard my thoughts.

"It was very simple," continued the eagle as if I had spoken my thoughts out loud. "Spiritual maturity is always determined by our willingness to sacrifice our own desires for the interests of the kingdom or for the sake of others. The door that requires the most sacrifice to enter will always take us to the highest level."

I was trying to remember all that the eagle was saying to me. I knew I must enter the door before me, and that it would be wise to learn all I could from someone who had preceded me and had obviously chosen the correct door to the top.

"I did not go directly to the top, and I haven't met anyone who has," the eagle continued. "But I went there much faster than most because I had learned so much about self-sacrifice while fighting here on the level of "Salvation." I have shown you this door because you wear the mantle and would have found it anyway, but time is short and I am here to help you mature quickly.

"There are doors on every level, and every one leads to treasures that are beyond your comprehension," he continued. "They cannot be acquired physically, but every treasure that you hold in your hands you will be able to carry in your heart. Your heart is meant to be the treasure house of God. By the time you reach the top again, your heart will contain treasures more valuable than all the treasures of the earth. They will never be taken from you; they are yours for eternity. Go quickly. The storm clouds are now gathering and another great battle is looming."

"Will you go with me?" I pleaded.

"No," he responded. "This is where I belong now. I must help these who were wounded. But I will see you here again. You will meet many of my brother and sister eagles before you return, and they will be able to help you better than I at the place where you meet them."

THE TREASURES OF HEAVEN

I already loved the eagle so much that I could hardly stand to leave him. I was glad to know I would see him again. Now the door was drawing me like a magnet. I opened it and entered.

The glory I beheld was so stunning that I immediately fell to my knees. The gold, silver, and precious stones were far more beautiful than can be described. They actually rivaled the glory of the Tree of Life. The room was so large that it seemed to be without end. The floor was silver, the pillars were gold, and the ceiling was a single pure diamond that reflected every color I had ever known and many that I had not known. Angels without number were all around, dressed in various robes and uniforms that were of no earthly origin.

As I began to walk through the room, the angels all bowed in salute. One stepped forward and welcomed me by name. He explained that I could go anywhere in the room and see anything I wanted. Nothing was withheld from those who came through the door.

I was so overwhelmed by the beauty that I could not even speak. I finally remarked that this was even more beautiful than the Garden had been. Surprised, the angel responded, "This is the Garden! This is one of the rooms in your Father's house. We are your servants."

As I walked, a great company of angels followed me. I turned and asked the leader why they were following. "Because of the mantle," he said. "We have been given to you, to serve you here and in the battle to come."

I did not know what to do with the angels so I just continued walking. I was attracted to a large blue stone that appeared to have the sun and clouds inside of it. When I touched it, the same feelings flooded over me as when I had eaten the fruit of the Tree of Life. I felt energy, unearthly mental clarity, and love for everyone and everything. I started to behold the glory of the Lord. The longer I touched the stone, the more the glory increased. I never wanted to take my hand off the stone, but the glory became so intense that I finally had to draw away.

Then my eyes fell on a beautiful green stone. "What does that one have in it?" I asked the angel standing nearby.

"All of these stones are the treasures of salvation. You are now touching the heavenly realm, and that one is the restoration of life," he continued.

As I touched the green stone, I began to see the earth in rich and spectacular colors. They grew in richness the longer I had my hand on the stone, and my love for all that I saw also grew. Then I began to see a harmony among all living things on a level that I had never seen before. I began to see the glory of the Lord in the creation. It began to grow until again I had to step away because of the intensity.

LOSING TRACK OF TIME

It occurred to me that I had no idea how long I had been there. I did know that my comprehension of God and His universe had grown substantially as I merely touched these two stones, and there were many, many more to touch. There was more in that one room than a person could have absorbed in a whole lifetime. "How many more rooms are there?" I asked the angel.

"There are rooms like this on every level of the mountain you climbed."

"How can one ever experience all that is in just one of these rooms, much less all of them?" I asked.

"You have forever to do this. The treasures contained in the most basic truths of the Lord Jesus are enough to last for more lifetimes than you can measure. No man can know all there is to know about any of them in just one lifetime, but you must take what you need and keep proceeding toward your destiny."

I started thinking about the impending battle again, and the warriors who had been captured. It was not a pleasant thought in such a glorious place, but I knew I would have forever to come back to this room. I had only a short time to find my way back to the top of the mountain and then back to the battlefront again.

I turned back to the angel and said, "You must help me find the door that leads to the top."

The angel looked perplexed. "We are your servants," he responded, "but you must lead us. This whole mountain is a mystery to us. We all desired to look into this great mystery, but after we leave this room we will be learning even more than you."

"Do you know where all the doors are?" I asked.

"Yes. But we do not know where they lead. There are some that look very inviting, some that are plain, and some that are actually repulsive. One is even terrible."

"In this glorious place there are doors that are repulsive?" I asked in disbelief. "And one that is terrible? How can that be?"

"We do not know, but I can show it to you," he responded.

"Please do," I said.

We walked for quite a while, passing treasures of unspeakable glory, all of which were difficult to bypass. There were also many doors with different biblical truths over each one. When the angel had called them "inviting," I felt that he had quite understated their appeal. I badly wanted to go through each one, but my curiosity about the "terrible door" kept me moving.

Then I saw it. "Terrible" had also been an understatement. Fear gripped me until I thought it would take my breath away.

GETHSEMANE

I turned away from that door and quickly retreated. There was a beautiful red stone nearby, which I almost lunged at to lay my hands on. Immediately I was in the Garden of Gethsemane beholding the Lord in prayer. The agony I beheld was even more terrible than the door I had just seen. Shocked, I jerked my hand away from the stone and fell to the floor in exhaustion.

I wanted so badly to return to the blue or green stones, but I had to regain my energy and my sense of direction. The angels were quickly all around me, serving me. I was given a drink that began to revive me. Soon I was feeling well enough to stand and begin walking back to the other stones. However, the recurring vision of the Lord praying finally compelled me to stop.

"What was that back there?" I asked.

"When you touch the stones we are able to see a little of what you see and feel a little of what you feel," said the angel. "We know that all these stones are great treasures, and the revelations they contain are priceless. We beheld for a moment the agony of the Lord before His crucifixion, and we briefly felt what He felt that terrible night. It is hard for us to understand how our God could ever suffer like that. It makes us appreciate much more what an honor it is to serve the men for whom He paid such a terrible price."

The angel's words were like lightning bolts straight to my soul. I had fought in the great battle. I had climbed to the top of the mountain. I had become so familiar with the spiritual realm that I hardly noticed angels anymore, and I could speak on nearly equal terms with the great eagles. Yet I could not bear to share even a moment of the sufferings of the Lord without wanting to flee to a more pleasurable experience. "I should not be here," I almost shouted. "I, more than anyone, deserve to be a prisoner of the evil one!"

"Sir," the angel said apprehensively, "we understand that no one is here because he deserves it. You are here because you were chosen before the foundation of the world for a purpose. We do not know what your specific purpose is, but we know that it is very great for everyone on this mountain."

"Thank you," I replied. "You are helpful. My emotions are being greatly stretched by this place, and they tend to overcome my understanding. You are right. No one is here because he is worthy. Truly, the higher we climb on this mountain, the more unworthy we are to be here and the more grace we need to stay. How did I ever make it to the top the first time?"

"Grace," my angel responded.

"If you want to help me," I said, "please keep repeating that word to me whenever you see me in confusion or despair. I am coming to understand that word better than any other.

"Now I must go back to the red stone," I continued. "I know now it is the greatest treasure in this room, and I must not leave until I am carrying that treasure in my heart."

THE TRUTH OF GRACE

The time I spent at the red stone was the most painful ordeal I have ever experienced. Many times I simply could not take any more and had to withdraw my hand. Several times I went back to the blue or green stone to rejuvenate my soul before I returned. It was harder to return to the red stone each time, but my love for the Lord was growing more through this than anything I had ever learned or experienced.

Finally, when I saw the presence of the Father depart from Jesus on the cross, I could stand it no longer. I quit. I could tell that the angels, who were also experiencing what I was to a degree, were in full agreement with me. The willpower to touch the stone again simply was no longer in me. I did not even feel like going back to the blue stone. I just lay prostrate on the floor, weeping over what the Lord had gone through. I also wept because I knew that I had deserted Him just like His disciples. I failed Him when He needed me the most, just as they did.

After what seemed like several days, I opened my eyes. Another eagle was standing beside me. In front of him were three stones: one blue, one green, and one red.

[83]

"Eat them," the eagle said. When I did, my whole being was renewed, and great joy and great soberness flooded my soul.

When I stood up, I caught sight of the same three stones set into the handle of my sword and on each of my shoulders.

"These are now yours forever," the eagle said. "They cannot be taken from you, and you cannot lose them."

"But I did not finish this last one," I protested.

"Christ alone will ever finish that test," he replied. "You have done well enough, and you must go on now."

"Where to?" I asked.

"You must decide, but with the time getting shorter I will suggest that you try to get to the top soon." The eagle then departed, obviously in a hurry.

I then remembered the doors. I started toward those that had been so appealing. But when I reached the first one, it did not appeal to me anymore. Then I went to another, and it felt the same. "Something seems to have changed," I remarked out loud.

"You have changed," the angels replied at once.

I turned to look at them and was amazed at how much they had changed. They no longer had a naive look about them, but were now more regal and wise-looking. I knew they reflected what had also taken place in me, but I now felt uncomfortable just thinking about myself.

"I ask for your counsel," I said to the leader.

"Listen to your heart," he said. "That is where these great truths now abide."

"I have never been able to trust my own heart," I responded. "It is subject to so many conflicts. I am too subject to delusions, deceptions, and selfish ambitions.

It is hard for me to even hear the Lord speaking to me above its clamor."

"Sir, with the red stone now in your heart, I do not believe that will continue to be the case," the leader offered with uncharacteristic confidence.

JUDGMENT'S DOOR

I leaned against the wall, thinking that the eagle was not here when I needed him the most. He had gone this way before and would know which door to choose. But I knew he would not come back, and I knew it was right that I choose. As I pondered my options, the "terrible door" was the only one I could think of. Out of curiosity I decided to go back and look at it. I had departed from it so fast the first time that I had not even noticed which truth it represented.

As I approached it, I could feel the fear welling up inside me, but not nearly as intensely as the first time. Unlike the other doors, it was very dark around this one, and I had to get very close to read the truth written over it. Mildly surprised, I read "THE JUDGMENT SEAT OF CHRIST."

"Why is this truth so fearful?" I asked aloud, knowing that the angels would not answer me. As I continued looking at it, I knew that it was the one I should go through.

"There are many reasons it is fearful," the familiar voice of the eagle responded.

"I'm very glad you came back," I replied. "Have I made a poor choice?"

"No! You have chosen well," the eagle assured me. "This door will take you back to the top of the mountain faster than any other. It is fearful because the greatest fear in the creation has its source through that door. The greatest wisdom that men can know in this life, or in the life to come, is also found through that door. Even so, very few will go through it."

"But why is this door so dark?" I asked.

"The light of these doors reflects the attention that the church is presently giving to the truths behind them. The truth behind that door is one of the most neglected of these times, yet it is one of the most important. You will understand when you enter. The greatest authority that men can receive will be entrusted only to those who will go through this door. When you see Christ Jesus sitting on this throne, you will be prepared to sit with Him on it, too."

"Then this door would not be so dark and foreboding if we had just given more attention to this truth?" I asked.

"That is correct. If men knew the glory that is revealed behind that door, it would be one of the most brilliant," the eagle lamented. "However, it is still a difficult door to pass through. I was told to return and encourage you because soon you will need it. You will see a greater glory, but also a greater terror than you have ever known.

"Because you have chosen the difficult way now, it will be much easier for you later. Because you are willing to face this hard truth now, you will not suffer loss later. Many love to know His kindness, but very few are willing to know His severity. If you do not embrace *both*, you will always be in danger of deception and of a fall from His great grace."

"I know that I would never come here if I had not spent the time I did at the red stone. How could I keep trying to take the easy way when that is so contrary to the nature of the Lord?" I asked.

"But now you have chosen, so go quickly," the eagle told me. "Another great battle is about to begin, and you are needed at the front," he said.

As I looked at the eagle and saw the great resoluteness in his eyes, my confidence grew. Finally, I turned toward the door.

CHAPTER IV

The White Throne

I gazed one last time around the huge room inside the mountain. The gems and treasures that represented the truths of salvation were breathtaking in their glory. It seemed that there was no end to their expanse and no way to fully comprehend their beauty.

I could not imagine that the rooms which contained the other great truths of the faith could be any more glorious. This helped me to understand why so many Christians never wanted to leave this level, being content to just marvel at the basic doctrines of the faith. I knew that I could stay here for eternity and never get bored.

Then the eagle who was standing next to me exhorted, "You must go on!" As I turned to look at him, he lowered his voice and continued, "There is no greater peace and safety than to abide in the Lord's salvation. You were brought here to know this because you will need this faith for where you are now going. But you must not stay here any longer."

The eagle's statement about peace and safety caused me to think about the courageous warriors who had fought in the battle from the first level of the mountain, "Salvation."

Although they had fought so well and delivered so many, they had also all been badly wounded. It did not seem that they had found peace and safety here.

The eagle interrupted my thoughts again as if he were listening to them. "God has a different definition of peace and safety than we do," he said. "To be wounded in the fight is a great honor. It is by the Lord's stripes that we are healed, and it is through our stripes that we, too, are given the authority for healing. Once we are healed, we are given the power to heal others in the very place where the enemy wounded us.

"Healing was a basic part of the Lord's ministry, and it is also a basic part of ours. One reason why the Lord allows bad things to happen to His people is so they can receive compassion for others, by which the power of healing operates. That is why the Apostle Paul told of his beatings and stonings when his authority was questioned. Every wound and other bad thing that happens to us can be turned into the authority to do good. Every beating that the great apostle took resulted in salvation for others. Every wound that a warrior receives will result in others being saved, healed, or restored."

The eagle's words were very encouraging. Standing here amid the glory of the treasures of salvation made this truth even clearer and more penetrating. I wanted to go shout it from the top of the mountain so that all who were still fighting would be encouraged.

Then the eagle continued, "There is another reason why the Lord allows us to be wounded. There is no courage unless there is real danger. The Lord said He would go with Joshua to fight for the Promised Land, but over and over He exhorted him to be strong and courageous. This was because he was going to have to fight, and there would be very real danger. It is in this way that the Lord proves those who are worthy of the promises."

THE GLORIOUS EAGLE

I looked at the old eagle, and for the first time I noticed the scars among his torn and broken feathers. However, the scars were not ugly. They were lined with gold that was somehow not metal, but rather flesh and feathers. I could see that this gold was giving off the glory that emanated from the eagle and made his presence so awesome.

"Why did I not see this before?" I inquired.

"Until you have beheld and appreciated the depths of the treasures of salvation, you cannot see the glory that comes from suffering for the sake of the gospel. Once you have seen it, you are ready for the tests that will release the highest levels of spiritual authority into your life. These scars are the glory that we will carry forever. This is why even the wounds our Lord suffered are with Him in heaven. You can still see His wounds and the wounds that all of His chosen ones have taken for His sake.

"These are the medals of honor in heaven. All who carry them love God and His truth more than their own lives. These are the ones who followed the Lamb wherever He went, willing to suffer for the sake of truth, righteousness, and the salvation of men. True leaders of His people, who carry genuine spiritual authority, must have first proven their devotion this way."

I looked at the leader of the company of angels that followed me. I had never witnessed deep emotion in an angel before, but these words were unquestionably moving him greatly, as well as the rest of the angels. I really thought they were about to cry.

Then the leader spoke: "We have witnessed many wonders since the creation. But the voluntary suffering of men for the Lord and for their fellow men is the greatest wonder of all. We, too, must fight and even suffer at times, but we dwell where there is such light and glory that it is very easy to do this.

"When we see men and women choose to suffer for a hope they can see only dimly in their hearts, it causes even the greatest angels to bow their knee and gladly serve these heirs of salvation. We marvel at the dedication of you who dwell with so little encouragement in a place of such darkness and evil.

"At first we did not understand why the Father decreed that men would have to walk by faith, suffering great opposition while not having the benefit of beholding the reality and the glories of the heavenly realm. But now we understand that through these sufferings He proves their worthiness to receive the great authority that they will be given as members of His own household.

"This walk of faith is now the greatest wonder in heaven. Those who pass this test are worthy to sit with the Lamb on His throne, for He has made them worthy and they have proven their love."

COURAGE

Then the eagle interjected, "Courage is a demonstration of faith. The Lord never promised that His way would be easy, but He has assured us that it would be worth it. The courage of those who fought from the level of "Salvation" moved the angels of heaven to esteem what God has brought about in fallen men. The faithful warriors took their wounds in the terrible onslaught, while only beholding darkness and a seeming defeat of the truth, just as our Lord did on His cross. Nevertheless, they did not quit, and they did not retreat."

I was again starting to regret that I had not remained on the level of "Salvation" and fought with those other brave souls. Once more, understanding my thoughts, the eagle interrupted them.

"By climbing the mountain, you were demonstrating faith and wisdom too. Your faith freed many souls so they could come to the mountain for salvation. You received some wounds, as the warriors on the level of "Salvation" did, but your authority in the kingdom has come more from acts of faith than from suffering. Because you have been faithful in a few things, you will now be given the great honor of going back to suffer, that you may be made a ruler over many more.

"But remember that we all work together for the same purposes regardless of whether we are building or suffering. If you go higher, many more souls will fill these rooms, to the great joy of heaven. You have now been called to climb and to build, but if you are faithful in this you will later be given the honor of suffering."

I then turned and looked at the dark and foreboding door over which was written, "THE JUDGMENT SEAT OF CHRIST." Just as warmth and peace had flooded my soul each time I looked at the great treasures of salvation, fear and insecurity gripped me when I looked at this door. Now it seemed that everything in me wanted to stay in this room, and nothing in me wanted to go through that door.

Again, the eagle answered my thoughts. "Before you enter the door to any great truth, you will have these same feelings. You even felt them when you entered into this room filled with the treasures of salvation. These fears are the result of the Fall. They are the fruit of the Tree of the Knowledge of Good and Evil. The knowledge from that tree made us all insecure and self-centered. The knowledge of good and evil makes the true knowledge of God seem fearsome, when in fact every truth from God leads to an even greater peace and security. Even the judgments of God are to be desired because all of His ways are perfect."

By now I had experienced enough to know that what seems right is usually the least fruitful path and is often the road to failure. Throughout my journey, the path of greatest risk was the path that led to the greatest reward. Even so, each time it seemed that more was at stake. Therefore, making the choice to go higher became more difficult each time. I started to sympathize with those who would stop at some point in their sojourn and refuse to go on, even though I knew more than ever that this was a mistake. The only true security came from continually moving forward into the realms that required more faith, which meant more dependence on the Lord.

"Yes, it takes more faith to walk in the higher realms of the Spirit," the eagle added. "The Lord gave us the map to His kingdom when He said, 'If you seek to save your life you will lose it, but if you will lose your life for My sake you will find it.' These words alone can keep you on the path to the top of the mountain and lead you to victory in the great battle ahead. They will also help you stand before the judgment seat of Christ."

THROUGH THE DOOR

I knew it was time for me to go. I resolved to always remember the glory of this chamber that contained the treasures of salvation, but I also knew that I had to move beyond them. I had to go on. I turned, and with all of the courage I could muster, opened the door to the judgment seat of Christ and stepped through it into terrifying darkness. The company of angels that had been assigned to me took positions all around the door, but did not enter.

"What's the matter? Aren't you coming?" I demanded.

"Where you are going now, you must go alone. We will be waiting for you on the other side."

Without responding, I turned and started walking before I could change my mind. Somehow I knew that I should not put my security in the company of angels. As I walked into the darkness, I heard the eagle's parting words, "After this you will not have your trust in anyone else, even yourself, but only in the Lord."

I immediately was in the most frightening darkness I had ever experienced. Each step became a terrible battle with fear. Soon I began to think I had stepped into hell itself. Finally I decided to retreat, but when I turned to go back, I could not see anything. The door was closed, and I could not even see where it was located. It was beginning to look as if everything that had happened to me, and everything the eagles and the angels had told me, had been a ruse to entrap me in this hell. I had been deceived!

I cried to the Lord to forgive me and help me. Immediately I began to see Him on the cross, just as when I had laid my hand on the red stone in the chamber I had just left. Again I beheld the darkness of His soul as He stood alone, bearing the sin of the world. Although in the chamber this had been a terrible darkness to behold, now it was a light. I resolved to go on, fixing my mind on Him. As I did, peace began to grow in my heart with each step, and it became easier than it had been just a few minutes earlier.

Soon I was not even aware of the chilly darkness, and I started to see a dim light. Gradually it became a glorious light. Then it became so wonderful that I felt I was entering into heaven itself. The glory kept increasing as I walked along, and I wondered how anything this magnificent could have an entrance so dark and foreboding. Now I was enjoying every step.

THE GREAT HALL

The path soon opened into a hall so large that I did not think the earth itself could contain it. Its beauty could not even be described by any reference to human architecture. This exceeded the wonder of anything I had yet experienced, including the Garden and the chamber that held the treasures of salvation.

By now I was as overwhelmed with joy and beauty as I had been overwhelmed by darkness and fear just minutes before. I then understood that every time I had experienced great pain or darkness of soul, it had been followed by a much greater revelation of glory and peace.

At the far end was the Source of the glory that was emanating from everything else in the room. I knew that it was the Lord Himself, and though I had now seen Him many times, I began to be a bit afraid as I walked toward Him. However, this fear was a holy fear that only magnified the great joy and peace that I also felt. Not only was the judgment seat of Christ a source of more security than I had ever experienced, but at the same time it was the source of a greater and purer fear.

I did not notice how great the distance was to the throne. It was so wonderful just to walk here that I did not care if it took me a thousand years to get there. In earthly terms, it did take me a very long time. In one sense I felt that it was days, and in another, years. But somehow earthly time had no relevance here.

My eyes were so fixed on the glory of the Lord that I walked a long time before I noticed that I was passing multitudes of people who were standing in ranks to my left (there were just as many to my right, but they were so far away that I could not see them until I reached the throne). As I looked at them, I had to stop. They were dazzling, more regal than anyone I had ever seen. Their countenances were captivating.

Never had such peace and confidence graced human faces. Each one was beautiful beyond any earthly comparison. As I turned toward those who were close to me, they bowed in a greeting as though they recognized me.

"How is it that you know me?" I asked, surprised at my own boldness in asking them a question.

"You are one of the saints fighting in the last battle," a man close by responded. "Everyone here knows you, as well as all those who are now fighting on the earth. We are the saints who have served the Lord in the generations before you. We are the great cloud of witnesses who have been given the right to behold the last battle. We know all of you, and we see all that you do."

To my surprise, I recognized someone I had known on earth. He had been a faithful believer, but I did not think he had ever done anything of significance. He was so unattractive physically on earth that it made him shy. Here he had the same features, but was somehow more handsome than any person I had known on earth. He stepped up to me with an assurance and dignity that I had never seen before in him, or in any man.

"Heaven is much greater than we could have dreamed while on earth," he began. "This room is but the threshold of realms of glory that are far beyond our ability to comprehend. It is also true that the second death is much more terrible than we understood. Neither heaven nor hell are like we thought they were. If I had known on earth what I know here, I would not have lived the way I did. You are greatly blessed to be able to come here before you die," he said, looking at my garments.

I then looked at myself. I still had the old mantle of humility on, and the armor was still under it. I felt both foul and crude standing before those who were so glorious. I began to think that I was in serious trouble if I was going to appear before the Lord like this. Like the eagles, my old acquaintance could understand my thoughts, and he responded to them.

"Those who come here wearing that mantle have nothing to fear. That mantle is the highest rank of honor, and it is why they all bowed to you when you passed."

"I did not notice anyone bowing to me," I replied, a bit disconcerted. "In fact, I didn't even notice anyone until just now."

"It is not improper for someone to bow down before you," he continued. "Here we show each other the respect that is due. Even the angels serve us here, but only our God and His Christ are worshiped. There is a marked difference between honoring others in love, and worshiping them. If we had understood this on earth, we would have treated others very differently. It is here in the light of His glory that we can fully perceive and understand each other, so we can relate properly."

FOOLISH VIRGINS

I was still ashamed. I had to restrain myself to keep from bowing down to those in the great hall, while at the same time wanting to hide myself because I felt so lowly. Then I began lamenting the fact that my thoughts were just as foolish here as they were on the earth, and here everyone knew them! I felt both stained and stupid standing before these who were so awesome and pure. Again my old acquaintance responded to these thoughts.

"We have our incorruptible bodies now, and you do not. Our minds are no longer hindered by sin. We are therefore able to easily comprehend what even the greatest earthly mind cannot fathom, and we will spend eternity growing in our ability to understand. This is so we can know the Father and understand the glory of His creation. On earth you cannot even begin to understand what the least of these knows here. In fact, we are the least of those here."

"How could you be the least?" I asked with disbelief.

"There is an aristocracy of sorts here," he answered. "The rewards for our earthly lives are the eternal positions that we will have forever. This great multitude are those whom the Lord called 'foolish virgins.' We knew the Lord and trusted in His cross for salvation, but we lived for ourselves more than we really lived for Him. We did not keep our vessels filled with the oil of the Holy Spirit. We have eternal life, but we wasted our lives on earth."

I was greatly surprised by what he was telling me, but I knew that no one could lie in this place.

"The foolish virgins gnashed their teeth in the *outer darkness*," I protested.

"And that we did. The grief that we experienced when we understood how we had so wasted our lives was beyond any grief possible on earth. The darkness of that grief can only be understood by those who have experienced it. Such darkness is magnified when it is revealed next to the glory of the One we failed.

"You are standing among those in the lowest rank of heaven. There is no greater folly than to know the great salvation of God, but to then go on living for yourself. To come here and learn the reality of that is a grief beyond what an earthly soul can experience. We are those who suffered outer darkness because of this greatest of follies."

I was still incredulous. "But you are more glorious and full of joy and peace than I ever imagined, even for those in heaven. I do not sense any remorse in you, and yet I know that here you cannot lie. This does not make sense to me."

Looking me straight in the eyes, he continued, "The Lord also loves us with a love greater than you can yet understand. Before His judgment seat I tasted the greatest remorse and darkness of soul that can be experienced. Though here we do not measure time as you do, it seemed to last for as long as my life on earth had lasted. All my sins and follies that I had not repented of passed before me and before all who are here.

"You cannot understand the grief of this until you have experienced it," he went on. "I felt that I was in the deepest dungeon of hell, even as I stood before the glory of the Lord. He was resolute until my life had been completely reviewed. When I said I was sorry and asked for the mercy of His cross, He wiped away my tears and took away the darkness. I no longer feel the bitterness that I knew as I stood before Him, but I remember it.

"Here you can remember such things without continuing to feel the pain. A moment in the lowest part of heaven is much greater than a thousand years of the highest life on earth. Now my mourning at my folly has been turned into joy, and I know that I will experience joy forever, even if I am in the lowest place in heaven."

I began to think again of the treasures of salvation. Somehow I knew that all this man had told me was revealed by those treasures. Every step I had taken up the mountain, or into it, had revealed that His ways are both more fearful and more wonderful than I had ever been able to comprehend before.

Looking at me intently, my former acquaintance continued: "You are not here just to gain understanding, but to be changed. The next level of rank has glory many times greater than what we have here. Each new level is that much greater than the previous one. It is not just that those on each level have an even more glorious spiritual body, but that each level is closer to the throne, from where all the glory comes.

"Even so, I no longer feel the grief of my failure. I really deserve nothing. I am here by grace alone, and I am so thankful for what I have. He is so worthy to be loved. I could be doing many wondrous things now in the different realms of heaven, but I would rather stay here and just behold His glory, even if I am on the outer fringes."

Then, with a distant look in his eyes, he added, "Everyone in heaven is now in this room to watch His great mystery unfold, and to watch those of you who will fight the last battle."

"Can you see Him from here?" I asked. "I see His glory far away, but I cannot see Him."

"I can see many times better than you can," he answered. "And yes, I can see Him and hear Him. I can see all that He is doing. He also gave us power to observe what is happening on earth. We are the great cloud of witnesses who are watching you and cheering you on."

He bowed and then returned to the ranks. I began walking again, trying to understand all that he had said to me. As I looked over the great host that he said were the foolish virgins, the ones who had spiritually slept away their lives on earth, I knew that if any one of them appeared on earth now they would be worshiped as gods.

Yet, they were the very least of those who were here!

I then began to think of all of the time that I had wasted in my own life. It was such an overwhelming thought that I stopped. Then parts of my life began to pass before me. I began to experience a terrible grief over my sin. I, too, had been one of the greatest of fools! I may have kept more oil in my lamp than others, but now I knew how foolish I had been to measure what was required of me by how others were doing. I, too, was one of the foolish virgins!

THE WOULD-BE MENTOR

Just when I thought I would collapse under the weight of this terrible discovery, a man I had known and esteemed as a great man of God came forward to steady me. As he greeted me warmly, his touch somehow revived me.

I had wanted to be discipled by this man, but we did not get along well. As had happened with a number of other men of God that I tried to get close to, I was an irritation to this man, and he had finally asked me to leave. For years I had felt guilty about this, convinced that I had missed a great opportunity because of some flaw in my character. Even though I had put it out of my mind, I still carried the weight of this failure. When I saw him it all surfaced and a sick feeling came over me. Now he was so regal that I felt even more repulsive and embarrassed by my poor condition. I wanted to hide, but there was no way I could avoid him here.

To my surprise, his warmth toward me was so genuine that he soon put me at ease. There did not seem to be any barriers between us. In fact, the love I felt coming from him almost completely took away my self-consciousness.

"I have waited eagerly for this meeting," he said.

"You were waiting for me?" I asked. "Why?"

"You are just one of many that I am waiting for. I did not understand until my judgment that you were one that I was called to help—to even disciple, but I rejected you."

"Sir," I protested, "it would have been a great honor to have been discipled by you, and I am very thankful for the time I did have with you. But I was so arrogant that I deserved the rejection. I know my rebellion and pride have prevented me from having a real spiritual father. This was not your fault, but mine."

"It is true you were prideful, but that is not why I was offended with you," he said. "I was offended because of my insecurity, which made me want to control everyone around me. I was offended that you would not accept everything I said without questioning it. I then started to look for anything that was wrong with you so I could justify rejecting you. I began to feel that if I could not control you, one day you would embarrass me and my ministry. I esteemed my ministry more than I did the people for whom it was given to me, so I drove you and many others like you away."

"I must admit that at times I thought you had turned into a..." I stopped myself, embarrassed by what I was about to say.

"And you were right," he said with a genuineness that is unknown in the realms of earth. "I had been given the grace to be a spiritual father, but I was a very poor one. All children are rebellious. They are all self-centered and think the world revolves around them. That is why they need parents to raise them. Almost every child will, at times, bring reproach on his family, but he is still a part of the family.

"I turned away many of God's own children—precious people He had entrusted to me so they could be brought to maturity. I failed with many of those who stayed with me. Most of them suffered terrible and unnecessary wounds and failures that I could have helped them avoid. Many of them are now prisoners of the enemy.

"I built a large organization," he continued, "and had considerable influence in the church. But the greatest gifts the Lord entrusted to me were the people who were sent to me for discipling, many of whom I rejected.

"Had I not been so self-centered and concerned with my own reputation, I would be a king here. I was called to sit on one of the highest thrones. All that you have and will accomplish would have been in my heavenly account as well. Instead, much of what I gave my attention to was of very little eternal significance."

"What you accomplished was astounding," I interjected.

"What looks good on earth looks very different here. What will make you a king on earth will often be a stumbling block to keep you from being a king here. What will make you a king here is lowly and unacclaimed on earth. I failed some of the greatest tests and greatest opportunities that were given to me, one of which was you. Will you forgive me?"

"Of course," I said, embarrassed. "But I am in need of your forgiveness too. I still think it was my awkwardness and rebellion that made it difficult for you. In fact, I, too, have failed to let some people get close to me who wanted to for the same reasons you did not want me around you."

"It is true that you were not perfect," he replied, "and I discerned some of your problems rightly, but that is never reason to reject someone. The Lord did not reject the world when He saw its failures. He did not reject me when He saw my sin. He laid down His life for me. It is always the greater who must lay down his life for the lesser. Even though I was more mature and had more authority than you, I became like one of the goats in the parable, rejecting the Lord by rejecting you and many others He sent to me."

As he talked, his words were striking me deeply. I, too, was guilty of everything he mentioned. Passing through my mind were the faces of many young men and women I had brushed off as not being important enough for my time. I desperately wanted to return and gather them together!

The grief I began to feel was even worse than how I had felt about wasting my time. I had wasted people! Now many of these were prisoners of the enemy, wounded and captured during the battle on the mountain. This whole battle was for the people, and yet people are often our least concern. We will fight for truths more than for the people for whom the truths are given. We will fight for ministries, while running roughshod over the people in them.

"And many people think of me as a spiritual leader! I am truly the least of the saints," I thought out loud.

THE ENEMY OF THE GOSPEL

"I understand how you feel," remarked another man. I recognized him as someone I had considered as one of the greatest Christian leaders of all time. "Paul the Apostle said near the end of his life that he was the least of the saints. Then, just before his death, he even called himself 'the greatest of sinners.' If he had not learned that lesson during his life on earth, he, too, would have been in jeopardy of becoming one of the least of the saints in heaven. Because he learned it on earth, he is now one of those closest to the Lord and will be one of the highest in rank for all of eternity."

Seeing this man in the company of the foolish virgins was the greatest surprise yet. "I cannot believe that you, too, are one of the foolish who slept away their lives on earth. Why are you here?"

"I am here because I made one of the gravest mistakes you can make as one entrusted with the glorious gospel of our Savior," he answered. "Just as the Apostle Paul progressed from not considering himself inferior to the greatest apostles, to being the greatest of sinners, I took the opposite course. I started out knowing that I had been one of the greatest of sinners who had found grace, but ended up thinking that I was one of the greatest apostles. It was because of my great pride, not insecurity like our friend here, that I began to attack everyone who did not see everything just the way I did.

"I stripped those who followed me of their own callings and even their personalities, pressuring them all to become just like me. No one around me could be himself. No one dared to question me because they knew I would crush them into powder. I thought by making others smaller I made myself greater. I thought that I was supposed to be the Holy Spirit to everyone.

"From the outside my ministry looked like a smooth running machine where everyone was in unity and there was perfect order, but it was the order of a concentration camp. I took the Lord's children and made them automatons. I molded them into my own image instead of His. In the end I was not even serving the Lord, but rather the idol I had built to myself. By the end of my life I was actually an enemy of the true gospel, at least in practice, even if my teachings and writings seemed impeccably biblical."

Coming from this person, such statements astounded me. I began to wonder if every meeting I had here was meant to give me a greater shock than the previous one.

"If it is true that you became an enemy of the gospel, how is it that you are still here?" I questioned.

"By the grace of God, I did trust in the cross for my own salvation. However, I actually kept other men from it, leading them to myself rather than to the Lord. Even so, the blessed Savior remains faithful to us even when we are unfaithful. It was also by His grace that the Lord took me from the earth sooner than He would have, just so those who were under me could find Him and come to know Him."

THROUGH A GLASS DARKLY

I could not have been more stunned to think that this particular man was guilty of such things. History had given us a very different picture of him.

Reading what was going on in my heart, he continued: "God does have a different set of history books than those on the earth. You have had a glimpse of this, but you do not yet know how different they are. Earthly histories will pass away, but the books that are kept here will last forever. If you can rejoice in what heaven is recording about your life, you are blessed indeed. Men see through a glass darkly, so their histories will always be clouded and sometimes completely wrong."

"How was it that so many other leaders esteemed you so?" I inquired, still having trouble absorbing what I was hearing.

"Very few Christians, even very few leaders, have the true gift of discernment. Without this gift it is impossible to accurately discern truth in those of the present or the past.

[106]

Even with this gift it is difficult. Until we have been here and been stripped, we will judge others through distorted prejudices, either positive or negative. That is why we were warned not to judge before the time.

"Until we have been here, we cannot really know what is in the hearts of others and whether they are performing good or evil deeds. There have been good motives in even the worst of men and evil motives in even the best of them. Only here can men be judged by both their deeds and their motives."

"When I return to earth, will I be able to discern history accurately because I have been here?"

"You are here because you prayed for the Lord to judge you severely, to correct you ruthlessly, so that you could serve Him more perfectly. This was one of the wisest requests you have ever made. The wise judge themselves lest they be judged. The even wiser ask for the judgments of the Lord because they realize they cannot even judge themselves well.

"Having come here, you will leave with far more wisdom and discernment, but on earth you will always see through a glass darkly, at least to some degree. Although your experience here will help you to know men better, only when you are fully here can you know them fully. When you leave here you will be more impressed by how little you know men rather than by how well you know them. This is just as true in relation to the histories of men. I have been allowed to talk with you because I have, in a sense, discipled you through my writings, and knowing the truth about me will help you," the famous Reformer concluded.

[107]

THE REFORMER'S WIFE

Then a woman I did not know stepped forward. Her beauty and grace were breathtaking, but they were not sensual or seductive in any way.

"I was his wife on earth," she began. "Much of what you know of him actually came from me. Therefore, what I am about to say is not just about him, but about us. You can reform the church without reforming your own soul. You can dictate the course of history and yet not do the Father's will or glorify His Son. If you commit yourself to making human history, you may do it, but it is a fleeting accomplishment that will evaporate like a wisp of smoke."

"But your husband's work, or your work, greatly impacted every generation after him for good. It is hard to imagine how dark the world would have been without him," I protested.

"True," she answered. "But you can gain the whole world and still lose your own soul. Only if you keep your own soul pure can you truly impact the world for the eternal purposes of God. My husband lost his soul to me, and he only regained it at the end of his life because I was taken from the earth so that he could.

"Much of what my husband did, he did more for me than for the Lord. I pressured him and even gave him much of the knowledge that he taught. I used him as an extension of my own ego because as a woman I could not be recognized at the time as a spiritual leader myself. In a sense, I took over his life so that I could live my life through him. Soon I had him doing everything just to prove himself to me."

"You must have loved her very much," I said, looking at him.

"No, I did not love her at all," he said to my amazement. "Neither did she love me. In fact, after just a few years of marriage we did not even like each other. But we both needed each other, so we found a way to work together. Our marriage was not a yoke of love, but of bondage. The more successful we became, the more unhappy we became, and the more deception we used to fool those who followed us. We were empty wretches by the end of our lives.

"The more influence you gain by your own self-promotion, the more you must strive to retain your influence, and the more your life will become dark and cruel. Kings feared us, but we feared everyone, from the kings to the peasants. We could trust no one because we were living in such deception ourselves that we did not even trust each other. We preached love and trust because we wanted everyone to love and trust us. But we, ourselves, secretly feared and despised everyone. If you preach the greatest truths but do not live them, you are only the greatest hypocrite and the most tormented soul."

Their words pounded me like a hammer. I could see that my life was already heading in the same direction. How much was I doing to promote myself rather than Christ? I began to see how much I did just to prove myself to others, especially those I felt in competition with or those who disliked or rejected me. I began to see how much of my own life was built on the facade of a projected image that belied who I really was. But here I could not hide. This great cloud of witnesses all knew who I was beyond the veil of my projected motives.

I looked again at this couple. They were now so guileless and so noble that it was impossible to question their motives. They were gladly exposing their most devious sins for my sake and were genuinely happy to be able to do it.

"I may have had a wrong concept of you from your history and your writings, but I have even more esteem for you now," I told them. "I pray that I can carry from this place the integrity and freedom that you now have. I am tired of trying to live up to projected images of myself. How I long for that freedom!" I lamented, wanting desperately to remember every detail of this encounter.

THE HIGH CALLING

Then the famous Reformer offered a final exhortation: "Do not try to teach others to do what you, yourself, are not doing. Reformation is not just a doctrine. True reformation only comes from union with the Savior. When you are yoked with Christ, carrying the burdens that He gives you, He will be with you and carry them for you. You can only do His work when you are doing it *with* Him, not just *for* Him.

"Only the Spirit can beget that which is Spirit. If you are truly yoked with Him, you will do nothing for the sake of politics or history. Anything you do because of political pressures or opportunities will only lead you to the end of your true ministry. The things that are done in an effort to make history will at best confine your accomplishments to history, and you will fail to impact eternity. If you do not live what you preach to others, you disqualify yourself from the high calling of God, just as we did."

"I do not think I could even consider seeking a high calling," I interrupted. "I don't even deserve to sit here in this place you say is for the *lowest* rank in heaven. How could I ever consider seeking a high calling?"

"The high calling is not out of reach for anyone that the Lord has called. I will tell you what will keep you on the path of life—love the Savior and seek His glory alone. Everything you do to exalt yourself will one day bring you the most terrible humiliation. Everything you do out of genuine love for the Savior, to glorify His name, will extend the limits of His eternal kingdom and ultimately result in a much higher place for yourself. Live for what is recorded here. Care nothing for what is recorded on earth."

The couple then parted with a cheerful embrace, yet I felt anything but cheerful. As they walked away, I was again overwhelmed by my own sin. Memories of the times I had used people for my own purposes, or even used the name of Jesus to further my own ambitions, or make myself look better, began to cascade down upon me. Here, in this place where I could behold the power and glory of the One I had so used, such memories became more repulsive than I could stand. I fell on my face in the worst despair I had ever known.

After what seemed like an eternity of seeing people and events pass before me, I felt the Reformer's wife lifting me to my feet again. I was overcome by her purity, especially as I now felt so evil and corrupt. I had the strongest desire to worship her because she was so pure.

"Turn to the Son," she said emphatically. "Your desire to worship me, or anyone else at this time, is only an attempt to turn the attention away from yourself and justify yourself by serving what you are not. I am pure now because I turned to Him. You need to see the corruption that is in your own soul, but then you must not dwell on yourself or seek to justify yourself with dead works, but turn to Him."

She said this with such genuine love that it was impossible to be hurt or offended by it. When she saw that I understood, she continued.

"The purity you see in me was what my husband first saw in me when we were young. I was relatively pure in my motives then, but I corrupted his love and my own purity

[111]

by allowing him to worship me wrongly. You can never become pure by worshiping those who are more pure than yourself. You must go beyond them to find the One who has *made them* pure, and in whom alone there is no sin.

"The more people praised us, and the more we accepted their praises, the further we drifted from the path of life. Then we started living for the praises of men and to gain power over those who would not praise us. That was our demise, and it is the same for many who are here in the lowest place."

PURIFIED LOVE

Simply wanting to prolong our conversation, I asked the next question that came to my mind: "Is it difficult for you and your husband to be here together?"

"Not at all," she responded. "All the relationships you have on earth are continued here. They are all purified by the judgment and by the fact that they are now spiritual, just as we are now spirit. The more you are forgiven, the more you love. After we forgave each other, we loved each other more. Now our relationship is continuing in much greater depth and richness because we are joint heirs of this salvation.

"As deep as the wounds were that we afflicted upon each other, that is how deep the love was able to reach when we were healed. We could have experienced this on earth, but we did not learn forgiveness in time. If we had learned forgiveness, the competition that entered our relationship and sidetracked our lives would not have been able to take root in us. If you truly love, you will truly forgive. The harder it is for you to forgive, the further you are from true love. Forgiveness is essential, or you will stumble and stray from the course chosen for you."

I realized that this woman, who had brought me into such confrontation with the pain of my own depravity, was also the most attractive person I could ever remember meeting. It was not romantic attraction, but I just did not want to leave her. Perceiving my thoughts, she withdrew a step, indicating that she was about to go. Before leaving, she offered me some final insights.

"The pure truth, spoken in pure love, will always attract," she said. "You will remember the pain you feel here, and it will help you through the rest of your life. Pain is good; it shows you where there is a problem. Do not try to reduce the pain until you find the problem. God's truth often brings pain as it highlights a problem that we have, but His truth will always show us the way to freedom too. When you know this, you will even begin to rejoice in your trials, which are all allowed to help keep you on the path of life.

"Your attraction to me is not out of order. It is the attraction between male and female that was given in the beginning, which is pure in its original form. When pure truth is combined with pure love, men can be the men they were created to be without having to dominate women out of insecurity. Such domination is nothing but lust, which is the lowest depth to which love falls because of our sin. With true love, men become true men. Women, likewise, can be the women they were created to be because their love has replaced their fear.

"Love will never manipulate or try to control out of insecurity because love casts out all fear. The very place where relationships can be the most corrupted is also where they can be the most fulfilling, after redemption has worked in them. True love is a taste of heaven, and lust is the enemy's ultimate perversion of the glory of heaven. To the degree that you are free of lust on earth, you will begin to experience heaven."

"But I do not think I have felt any lust for you or for *anyone* while I've been here," I mildly protested. "On the contrary, I was marveling that I could behold one with your beauty and not feel lust."

"That is because you are here. The light of His glory here casts out all darkness. But if you were not here, lust would be gripping you now," she said.

"I'm sure you are right. Can we ever be free from this terrible perversion on earth?" I begged.

"Yes. As your mind is renewed by the Spirit of Truth, you will not see relationships as opportunities to *take* from others, but to give. Giving provides the greatest fulfillment that we can ever know. The most wonderful human relationships are but fleeting glimpses of the ecstasy that comes when we give ourselves to the Lord in pure worship. What we experience in worship here, your frail, unglorified body could not endure. The true worship of God will purify the soul for the glory of true relationships.

"Therefore, you must not seek relationships, but true worship. Only then can relationships start to be what they are supposed to be. True love never seeks to be first or to be in control, but rather it takes the place of humble service. If my husband and I had kept this in our marriage, we would be sitting next to the King now, and this great hall would be filled with many more souls."

REMOVING MORE VEILS

With that, the Reformer's wife disappeared back into the ranks of the glorified saints. I looked again toward the throne and was taken aback because the glory appeared so much more beautiful than it had before. Another man standing close to me explained.

[114]

"With each encounter, a veil is being removed so that you can see Him more clearly. You are not changed just by seeing His glory, but by seeing it with an unveiled face. Those who come to the true judgments of God walk a corridor such as this to meet those who can help them remove whatever veils they are still wearing—veils that will distort their vision of Him."

I felt that I had already absorbed more understanding than my many years of ministry on earth had given me. All my study and seeking on earth had apparently only led me forward at a snail's pace. Even *many* lifetimes would not have prepared me to face the judgment! My life had already disqualified me more than all those I had met, and it seemed they had barely made it here!

"How could those who have not been given the grace of this experience have any hope at all?" I asked.

I heard a new voice say, "What you are experiencing here has been given to you on earth. Every relationship, every encounter with another person, could teach you what you are learning here if you keep that cloak of humility on and learn to always keep your attention fixed on His glory. You are being given this experience now because you will write the vision, and those who read it will understand it. Many will then be able to carry the glory and the power that they will need in the last battle."

I was amazed to recognize this man as a contemporary of mine, for I did not even know he had died. I had never met him on earth, but he had a great ministry which I respected very much. Through men that he had trained, thousands had been led to salvation, and many large churches had been raised up that were almost totally devoted to evangelism.

He asked if he could just embrace me for a minute, and I agreed, feeling quite awkward. When we embraced, I felt such love coming from him that a great pain deep within me stopped hurting. I had become so used to the pain that I did not even notice it until it stopped. After he released me, I told him that his embrace had healed me of something. His joy at this was profound. Then he began to tell me why he was in the lowest rank in heaven.

"I became so proud near the end of my life that I could not imagine that the Lord would do anything of significance unless He did it through me. I began to touch the Lord's anointed and to do His prophets harm. I was selfishly proud when the Lord used one of my own disciples, and I became jealous when the Lord moved through anyone who was outside of my ministry. I would search for anything that was wrong with them in order to expose them. I did not know that every time I did this I only demoted myself further."

"I never knew you had done anything like that," I said, surprised.

"I did not do it myself, but I incited men under me to investigate other ministers and do my dirty work. I had them scour the earth to find any error or sin in the lives of others so they could be exposed. I became the worst thing that a man can become on the earth—a stumbling block who produced other stumbling blocks. We sowed fear and division throughout the church, all in the name of protecting the truth. In my self-righteousness, I was headed for perdition.

"But in His great mercy, the Lord allowed me to be struck by a disease that would bring about a slow and humiliating death. Just before I died, I came to my senses and repented. I am thankful to be here at all. I may be one of the least of His here, but it is much more than I deserve. I just could not leave this room until I had a chance to apologize to those of you that I so wronged."

"But you never wronged me," I said.

"Oh, but I did indeed," he replied. "Many of the attacks that came against you were from those I had agitated and encouraged in their assaults on others. Even though I may not have personally carried out the attacks, the Lord holds me as responsible as those who did."

"I see. Of course I forgive you."

JUDGING THE STUMBLING BLOCKS

I was already beginning to remember how I had done this same thing, even though on a smaller scale. I recalled how I had allowed disgruntled former members of a nearby church to spread their poison about that church without stopping them. By allowing them to do this without correcting them, I had, in effect, encouraged them to continue. At the time I had rationalized that this was justified because of the errors of that church. I had even repeated many of their stories, justifying it under the guise of enlisting prayers for them.

Soon a great flood of memories of other such incidents began to arise in my heart. Again, I was starting to be overwhelmed by the evil and darkness of my own soul.

"I, too, have been a stumbling block!" I wailed. I knew that I deserved death and that I deserved the worst kind of hell. I had never seen such ruthlessness and cruelty as I was now seeing in my own heart.

"We actually comforted ourselves by thinking we were doing God a favor when we attacked His children," continued the understanding voice of this man. "It is good for you to see this here because you can go back. Please warn my disciples of their impending doom if they do not repent. Many of them are called to be kings

[117]

here, but if they do not repent they will face the worst judgment of all—the judgment of the stumbling blocks.

"My humbling disease was grace from God. When I stood before the throne, I asked the Lord to send such grace to my disciples. I cannot cross back over to them, but He has allowed me this time with you. Please forgive and release those who have attacked you. They really do not understand that they are doing the work of the accuser. Thank you for forgiving me, but please also forgive them. It is in your power to retain sins or to cover them with love. I entreat you to love those who are now your enemies."

I was so overwhelmed with my own sin that I could hardly hear this man. He was glorious and pure and obviously now had powers that were not known on the earth. Yet, he was entreating me with great humility. I felt such love coming from him that I could not imagine refusing him. But even without the impact of his love, I felt far more guilty than anyone attacking me could possibly be.

"Certainly I must deserve anything they have done to me and much more," I replied.

"That is true, but it is not the point here," he entreated. "Everyone on earth is deserving of the second death, but our Savior brought us grace and truth. If we are to do His work, we must do everything in both grace and truth. Truth without grace is what the enemy brings when he comes as an 'angel of light.'"

"If I can be delivered from this, maybe I will be able to help them," I replied. "But can't you recognize that I am far worse than they could possibly be?"

"I know that what just passed through your memory was bad," he answered, with profound love and grace. I knew that he had now become as concerned for me and my condition as he had been for his own disciples.

"This really is heaven," I blurted out. "This really is light and truth. How could we who live in such darkness become so proud, thinking we know so much about God?" Impulsively, I yelled in the direction of the throne, "Lord! Please let me go and carry this light back to earth!"

Immediately the entire host of heaven seemed to stand at attention, and I knew that I was the center of their gaze. I felt so insignificant before just one of these glorious ones, but when I knew they were *all* looking at me, fear came like a tidal wave. I felt there could be no doom like I was about to experience. Surely I was the greatest enemy of the glory and truth that so filled that place.

When I thought about my request to go back, I realized I was too depraved. I could never adequately represent such glory and truth. There was no way I could in my corruption convey the reality of that glorious place and His presence. I felt that even Satan had not fallen as far as I had. *This is hell!* I thought. There could be no worse pain than to be as evil as I was and to know that this kind of glory existed. To be banned from here would be a torture worse than I ever feared. "No wonder the demons are so angry and demented," I said under my breath.

Just when I felt that I was about to be banished to the deepest regions of hell, I simply cried, "JESUS!" Immediately, a deep peace came over me. I knew I had to move on toward the glory again, and somehow I had the confidence to do it.

THE WRITER'S REMORSE

I kept moving until I saw a man I considered to be one of the greatest writers of all time. I had counted his insights into the truth to be possibly the greatest I had encountered in all my studies.

"Sir, I have always looked forward to this meeting," I blurted out.

"As have I," he replied with genuine sincerity.

I was surprised by his comment, but I was so excited to meet him that I continued, "I feel that I know you, and in your writings I felt like you somehow knew me. I think I owe more to you than to anyone else who was not canonized in Scripture."

"You are very gracious," he replied. "But I am sorry that I did not serve you better. I was a shallow person, and my writings were shallow, filled more with worldly wisdom than divine truth."

"I know what you are saying must be true because you can only speak the truth here," I told him. "Yet it is hard for me to understand. I think your writings are some of the best that we have on earth."

"You are right," this famous writer admitted with sincerity. "It is so sad. Everyone here, even those who sit closest to the King, would live their lives differently if they had them to live over. But I think I would live mine even more differently than most. I was honored by kings, but failed the King of kings. I used the great gifts and insights that were given to me to draw men more to myself and my wisdom than to Him. Besides, I only knew Him by the hearing of the ear, which is the way I compelled other men to know Him. I made them dependent on me and on others like me. I turned them more to deductive reasoning than to the Holy Spirit, whom I hardly knew.

"I did not point men to Jesus," he continued, "but to myself and others like me who pretended to know Him. When I beheld Him here, I wanted to grind my writings into powder, just as Moses did with the golden calf. My mind was my idol, and I wanted everyone to worship my mind with me.

"Your esteem for me does not cause me to rejoice. If I had spent as much time seeking to know Him as I did seeking to know *about* Him in order to impress others with my knowledge, many of those who are in this lowest of companies would be sitting in the thrones that were prepared for them, and many others would be in this room."

"I know that what you are saying about your work must be true, but aren't you being a little too hard on yourself?" I questioned. "Your works fed me spiritually for many years, as I know they have multitudes of others."

"I am not being too hard on myself," he responded. "All that I have said is true, and it was confirmed when I stood before the throne. Even though I produced a lot, I was given more talents than almost anyone here, and I buried them beneath my own spiritual pride and ambitions. Just as we learn from the example of Adam, who could have carried the whole human race into a most glorious future, but by his failure led billions of souls into the worst of dooms instead—with authority comes responsibility.

"The more authority you are given, the more potential for both good and evil you have. Those who will rule with Him for the ages will know responsibility of the most profound kind. No man stands alone, and every human failure or victory resonates far beyond our comprehension, even to generations to come."

I could not help reflecting on the beautiful and articulate phrases that this man had written. He was the epitome of a wordsmith, a craftsman who turned words into works of art. But here, he was speaking as a common man, without the flair for which his writings were so well-known. Although he knew what I was thinking, as did everyone here, he continued with what he clearly thought was more important.

"Had I sought the Lord Himself instead of knowledge about Him, I could have successfully led many thousands, which would have resulted in many more millions being here now. Anyone who understands the true nature of authority would never seek it. They would only accept it when they knew they were yoked with the Lord, the only One who can carry authority without stumbling. Never seek influence for yourself, but only seek the Lord and be willing to take His yoke. My influence did not feed your heart, but rather your pride in knowledge."

"How can I know that I am not doing the same?" I asked as I began to think of my own writings.

"Study to show yourself approved unto God, not men," he replied as he walked back into the ranks. Before disappearing he turned, and with the slightest smile offered one last bit of advice: "And do not follow me."

HIGHER RANKS

In this first multitude I saw many other men and women of God, both from history and from my own time. I stopped and talked to many of them, and was shocked that so many I expected to be in the highest positions were instead in the lowest rank of the kingdom. Many shared the same basic story—they had fallen to the deadly sin of pride after their great victories, or fallen to jealousy when other men were anointed as much as they were. Others had fallen to lust, discouragement, or bitterness near the end of their lives and had to be taken before they crossed the line into perdition. They all gave me the same warning: The higher the spiritual authority that you walk in, the further you can fall if you are without love and humility.

As I continued toward the judgment seat, I began to pass those who were of higher rank in the kingdom. After many more veils had been stripped away from me by meetings with those who had stumbled over the same problems that I had, I began to meet some who had overcome. I met couples who had served God and each other faithfully to the end. Their glory here was unspeakable, and their victory encouraged me that it was possible to stay on the path of life and serve the Lord faithfully.

Those who stumbled did so in many different ways. But those who prevailed all did it the same way: They did not deviate from their devotion to the first and greatest commandment—loving the Lord. In this way, their service was done unto Him, not to men. These were the ones who worshiped the Lamb and followed Him wherever He went.

When I was still not even halfway to the throne, what had been the indescribable glory of the first rank now seemed to be outer darkness in comparison to the glory of those I was now passing. The greatest beauty on earth would not qualify to be found anywhere in heaven. And I was told that this room was just the *threshold* of indescribable realms of glory!

My march to the throne may have taken days, months, or even years. There was no way to measure time in that place. Everyone there showed respect to me, not because of who I was or anything I had done, but simply because I was a warrior in the battle of the last days. Somehow, through this last battle, the glory of God was to be revealed in such a way that it would be a witness to every power and authority, created or yet to be created, for all of eternity. During this battle the glory of the cross would be revealed, and the wisdom of God would be known in a special way. To be in that battle was to be given one of the greatest honors possible.

[123]

Near the judgment seat of Christ, those in the highest ranks were sitting on thrones that were all a part of His throne. Even the least of these thrones was many times more glorious than any earthly throne. Some of those on the thrones were rulers over cities on earth and would soon take their places. Others were rulers over the affairs of heaven, and still others ruled over the affairs of the physical creation, such as star systems and galaxies.

It was apparent that those who were given authority over cities were esteemed even above those who had been given authority over galaxies. The value of a single child surpasses that of a galaxy of stars because the Lord has chosen men as His eternal dwelling place. In the presence of His glory, the whole earth seemed as insignificant as a speck of dust. Yet, it was so infinitely esteemed that all of creation's attention was upon it.

HIS AWESOME PRESENCE

Now that I stood before the throne, I felt even lower than a speck of dust. Nevertheless, I felt the Holy Spirit upon me in a greater way than I ever had. It was by His power alone that I was able to stand. It was here that I truly came to understand His ministry as the Comforter. He had led me through the entire journey, even though for the most part I had been unaware of His presence.

The Lord was both more gentle and more terrible than I had ever imagined. In Him I saw Wisdom, who had accompanied me on the mountain. I somehow also felt the familiarity of many of my friends on earth, which I understood to be because He had often spoken to me through them. I also recognized Him as the One I had often rejected when He had come to me in others. I saw both a Lion and a Lamb, the Shepherd and the Bridegroom, but most of all I now saw Him as the Judge.

Even in the Lord's awesome presence, the Comforter was so mightily with me that I was comfortable. It was clear that the Lord in no way wanted me to be uncomfortable; He only wanted me to know the truth. Human words are not adequate to describe how awesome or how relieving it was to stand before Him. I had passed the point where I was concerned if the judgment was going to be good or bad; I just knew it would be right and that I could trust my Judge.

At one point the Lord looked toward the galleries of thrones around Him. Many were occupied, but many were empty. He then said, *"These thrones are for the overcomers who have served Me faithfully in every generation. My Father and I prepared them before the foundation of the world. Are you worthy to sit on one of these?"*

I remembered what a friend had once said, "When the omniscient God asks you a question, it is not because He is seeking information." I looked at those who were now seated on the thrones. I could recognize some of the great heroes of the faith, but realized most of those seated had not even been well-known on earth.

Many of those on the thrones had been missionaries who expended their lives in obscurity. They had never cared to be remembered on earth, but wanted only to be remembered by Him. I was a bit surprised to see some who had been wealthy, and rulers who had been faithful with what they had been given. However, it seemed that faithful, praying women and mothers occupied more thrones than any other single group.

There was no way I could answer "yes" to the Lord's question regarding whether I considered myself worthy to sit here. I was not worthy to sit in the company of any who were there. I knew I had been given the opportunity to run for the greatest prize in heaven or earth, and I had failed. I was desperate, but there was still one hope. Even though most of my life had been a failure, I was very glad that I was here before finishing my life on earth.

When I confessed that I was not worthy, the Lord asked, *"But do you want this seat?"*

"I do with all of my heart," I responded.

The Lord then looked at the galleries and said, *"Those empty seats could have been filled in any generation. I gave the invitation to sit here to everyone who has called upon My name. The seats are still available. Now the last battle has come, and many who are last shall be first. These seats will be filled before the battle is over. Those who will sit here will be known by two things: They will wear the mantle of humility, and they will have My likeness.*

"You now have the mantle. If you can keep it and do not lose it in the battle, when you return you will also have My likeness. Then you will be worthy to sit with these because I will have made you worthy. All authority and power have been given to Me, and I alone can wield it. You will prevail, and you will be trusted with My authority only when you have come to fully abide in Me. Now turn and look at My household."

I turned and looked back in the direction I had come from. Standing before His throne, I could see the entire room. The spectacle was glorious beyond description. Millions filled the ranks. Each individual in the lowest rank was more awesome than any army and had more power. It was far beyond my capacity to absorb such a panorama of glory. Even so, I could see that only a very small portion of the great room was occupied.

THE CUP OF TEARS

I then looked back at the Lord and was astonished to see tears in His eyes. He had wiped the tears away from every eye here except His own. As a tear ran down His cheek, He caught it in His hand. He then offered it to me.

"This is My cup. Will you drink it with Me?"

There was no way I could refuse Him. As the Lord continued to look at me, I began to feel His great love. Even as foul as I was, He still loved me. As undeserving as I was, He wanted me to be close to Him. Then He said:

"I love all of these with a love that you cannot now understand. I also love all who were supposed to be here but did not come. I left the ninety-nine to go after the one who was lost. My shepherds will not leave the one to go after the ninety-nine who are still lost. I came to save the lost. Will you share My heart to go and save the lost? Will you help to fill this room? Will you help to fill these thrones and every other seat in this hall? Will you take up this quest to bring joy to heaven, to Me, and to My Father?

"This is judgment for My own household, and My own house is not full. The last battle will not be over until My house is full. Only then will it be time for us to redeem the earth and remove the evil from My creation. If you drink My cup, you will love the lost the way that I love them."

He took a cup so plain that it seemed out of place in a room of such glory, and He placed His tear in it. He then gave it to me. I have never tasted anything so bitter! I knew that I could in no way drink it all, or even much of it, but I was determined to drink as much as I could. The Lord patiently waited until I finally erupted into such weeping that I felt like rivers of tears were flowing from me. I was crying for the lost, but even more, I was crying for the Lord.

I looked to Him in desperation, for I could not take any more of the great pain. Then His peace began to fill me, flowing together with the river of His love that erupted when I drank from His cup. Never had I felt anything so wonderful. This was the living water that I knew would spring up for eternity.

Then I felt as if the waters flowing within me caught on fire! I began to feel that this fire would consume me if I could not start declaring the majesty of His glory. I had never felt such an urge to preach, to worship Him, and to breathe every breath for the sake of His gospel.

"Lord!" I shouted, forgetting everyone but Him. "I now know that this throne of judgment is also the throne of grace, and I ask You now for the grace to serve You. Above all things, I ask You for grace! I ask You for the grace to finish my course. I ask You for the grace to love You like this, so I can be delivered from the delusions and self-centeredness that have so perverted my life.

"I call upon You for salvation from myself and the evil of my heart, so this love I now feel can flow in my heart continually. I ask You to give me Your heart, Your love. I ask for the grace of the Holy Spirit to convict me of my sin and to testify of You as You really are. Give me the grace to preach the reality of this judgment and testify of all You have prepared for those who come to You. I ask for the grace to share with those who are called to occupy these empty thrones, to give them words of encouragement that will keep them on the path of life and impart to them the faith to do what they have been called to do. Lord, I beg You for this grace!"

COMMISSIONED

The Lord then stood up, and all those who were seated upon the thrones for as far as I could see also stood up. His eyes burned with a fire I had not seen before.

"You have called upon Me for grace. This request I never deny. You shall return, and the Holy Spirit shall be with you.

Here you have tasted of both My kindness and My severity. You must remember both if you are to stay on the path of life. The true love of God includes the judgment of God. You must know both My kindness and severity or you will fall to deception. This is the grace that you have been given here, to know both. The conversations you had with your brethren here were My grace. Remember them."

He pointed His sword toward my heart, then my mouth, then my hands. When He did, fire came from His sword and burned me. The pain was very great. *"This, too, is grace,"* He said. *"You are but one of many who have been prepared for this hour. Preach and write about all that you have seen here. What I have said to you, say to My brethren.*

"Go and call My captains to the last battle. Go and defend the poor and the oppressed, the widows and the orphans. This is the commission of My captains, and it is where you will find them. My children are worth more to Me than the stars in the heavens. Feed My lambs. Watch over My little ones. Give the Word of God to them that they may live. Go to the battle. Go and do not retreat. Go quickly, for I will come quickly. Obey Me and hasten the day of My coming."

A company of angels then came and escorted me away from the throne. The leader walked beside me and began to speak.

"Now that He has stood, He will not sit again until the last battle is over. He has been seated until the time when His enemies are to be put under His feet. The time has now come. The legions of angels that have been standing ready since the night of His passion have now been released upon the earth. The hordes of hell have also been released.

"This is the time for which all of creation has been waiting," he continued. "The great mystery of God will soon be finished. We will now fight until the end. We will fight alongside you and your brethren."

[129]

CHAPTER V

The Overcomers

As I continued walking away from the judgment seat, I began to reflect on all that I had just experienced. It had been both terrible and wonderful. As challenging and heartrending as it had been, I felt more secure than I ever had. At first it had not been easy to be stripped so bare in front of so many, unable to hide even a single thought. But when I just relaxed and accepted it, knowing that it was cleansing my very soul, it became profoundly liberating. Having nothing to hide was like casting off the heaviest yoke and the strongest shackles. I began to feel as if I could breathe like I had never breathed before.

The more at ease I became, the more my mind seemed to increase in its capacity. Then I began to sense a communication going on which no human words could articulate. I thought of the Apostle Paul's comments about his visit to the third heaven, where he had heard inexpressible words—a spiritual communication that greatly transcends any form of human communication. It is more profound and meaningful than human words are able to convey. Somehow it is a pure communication of the heart and mind together, so pure that there is no possibility of misunderstanding.

As I looked at someone in the room, I began to understand what he was thinking, just as he had been able to understand me. When I looked at the Lord, I began to understand Him in the same way. We continued to use words, but the meaning of each one had a depth that no dictionary could have ever captured. My mind had been freed so that its capacity was multiplied many times over. It was exhilarating beyond any previous experience.

THE SPIRIT'S COMMUNICATION

It was also obvious that the Lord was enjoying being able to communicate this way with me as much as I was with Him. Never before had I understood so deeply what it meant for Him to be the Word of God. Jesus is the Communication of God to His creation. His words are spirit and life, and their meaning and power greatly exceed our present human definitions.

Human words are a very superficial form of the communication of the Spirit. God created us with the ability to communicate on a level that far transcends human words, but because of the Fall and the debacle at the Tower of Babel, we lost this capacity. We cannot be who we were created to be until we regain this, and we can only attain it when we are freed in His presence.

I began to understand that when Adam's transgression caused him to hide from God, it was the beginning of a most terrible distortion of what man was created to be. It brought about a severe reduction of our intellectual and spiritual capacities. These can only be restored when we "come out of hiding" and are genuinely transparent. This means opening ourselves to God and to each other. It is as we behold the glory of the Lord with an "unveiled face" that we are changed into His image. The veils, caused by our hiding, must be discarded.

[131]

The Lord's first question to Adam after his transgression was, "Where are you?" In the same way, it is the first question that we must answer if we are to be fully restored to Him. Of course, the Lord knew where Adam was. The question was for Adam's sake. That question was the beginning of God's quest for man.

The story of redemption is God's pursuit of man, not man's pursuit of God. When we can fully answer this question, knowing where we are in relation to God, we will have been fully restored to Him. But we can only know the answer to this question when we are in His presence.

That was the essence of my entire experience at the judgment seat. The Lord already knew all there was to know about me. The whole experience was for my sake, so I would know where I was. It was all to bring me out of hiding, to bring me out of darkness and into the light.

I also began to understand just how much the Lord desired to be one with His people. Through the entire judgment, He was not trying to get me to see something as good or bad as much as to see it in union with Him. The Lord was seeking me more than I was seeking Him. His judgments set me free, and His judgment of the world will set the world free.

The darkness in the world has been perpetuated by our compulsion to hide, which began immediately after the Fall. "Walking in the light" is more than just knowing and obeying certain truths—it is *being* true and being free from the compulsion to hide. When judgment day comes, it will bring the final deliverance of Adam from his hiding place. Not only will it be the final liberation of Adam, but it will also begin the final liberation of the creation, which was subject to bondage because of Adam.

"Walking in the light" means no more hiding from God or anyone else. The nakedness of Adam and Eve before the Fall was not just physical, but spiritual as well. When our salvation is complete, we will know this kind of transparency again. To be completely open to others will unlock realms we do not presently even know exist. This is what Satan is attempting to counterfeit through the New Age movement.

WISDOM RETURNS

As I walked, pondering all that I had learned, the Lord suddenly appeared by my side again in the form of Wisdom. He now appeared far more glorious than I had ever seen Him, even when He was on the judgment seat. I was both stunned and overjoyed.

"Lord, are You returning with me like this?" I asked.

"I will always be with you like this. However, I want to be even more to you than the way you see Me now. You have seen My kindness and My severity here, but you still do not fully know Me as the Righteous Judge."

This surprised me. I had just spent a considerable amount of time before His judgment seat and felt that all I had been learning pertained to His judgment. He paused to let this sink in, and then continued.

"There is a freedom that comes when you perceive truth, but whomever I set free is free indeed. The freedom of My presence is greater than just knowing truth. You have experienced liberation in My presence, but there is yet much more for you to understand about My judgments. When I judge, I am not seeking to condemn or to justify, but to bring forth righteousness. Righteousness is only found in union with Me. That is the righteous judgment—bringing men into unity with Me.

[133]

"My church is now clothed with shame because she does not have judges. She does not have judges because she does not know Me as the Judge. I will now raise up judges for My people who know My judgment. They will not only decide between people or issues; they will make things right, which means bringing them into agreement with Me.

"When I appeared to Joshua as the Captain of the Host, I declared that I was neither for him nor his enemies. I never come to take sides. When I come, it is to take over— not to take sides. I appeared as the Captain of the Host before Israel could enter her Promised Land. The church is now about to enter her Promised Land, and I am again about to appear as the Captain of the Host. When I do, I will remove all who have been forcing My people to take sides against their brothers.

"My justice does not take sides in human conflicts, even those involving My people. What I was doing through Israel, I was doing for their enemies, too—not against them. It is only because you see from the earthly, temporal perspective that you do not see My justice. You must see My justice in order to walk in My authority because righteousness and justice are the foundation of My throne.

"I have imputed righteousness to the people I have chosen. But like Israel in the wilderness, even the greatest saints of the church age have only aligned themselves with My ways a small portion of the time, or with a small part of their minds and hearts. I am not for them or against their enemies, but I am coming to use My people to save their enemies. I love all men and desire for all to be saved."

BRETHREN USED BY THE ENEMY

I could not help thinking about the great battle we had fought on the mountain. We had wounded many of our own brethren as we fought against the evil controlling them. Many of them were still in the camp of the enemy, either being used by him or kept as his prisoners. I started to wonder if the next battle would be against our own brothers again. The Lord was watching me ponder all of this, and then He continued.

"Until the last battle is over, there will always be some of our brothers who are being used by the enemy. But that is not why I am telling you this now. I am telling you this to help you see how the enemy gets into your own heart and mind, and how he uses you! Even now, you still do not see everything the way I do.

"This is common with My people. At this time, even My greatest leaders are seldom in harmony with Me. Many are doing good works, but very few are doing what I have called them to do. This is largely the result of divisions among you. I am not coming to take sides with any one group, but I am calling for those who will come over to My side.

"You are impressed when I give you a 'word of knowledge' about someone's physical illness, or some other knowledge that is not known to you. This knowledge comes when you touch My mind to just a small degree. I know all things. If you were to fully have My mind you would be able to know everything about everyone you encounter, just as you have begun to experience here. You would see all men just the way I see them. But even then, there is more to fully abiding in Me. To know how to use such knowledge rightly, you must have My heart. Only then will you have My judgment.

"I can only trust you with My supernatural knowledge to the degree that you know My heart. The gifts of the Spirit that I have released to My church are but small tokens of the powers of the age to come. I have called you to be messengers of that age, and you must therefore know its powers. You should earnestly desire the gifts because they

are a part of Me, and I have given them to you so that you can be like Me. You are right to seek to know My mind, My ways, and My purposes, but you must also earnestly desire to know My heart. When you know My heart, then the eyes of your heart will be opened. Then you will see as I see, and you will do what I do.

"I am about to entrust much more of the powers of the age to come to My church. However, there is a great deception that often comes upon those who are trusted with great power. If you do not understand what I am about to show you, you, too, will fall to this deception.

"You have asked for My grace, and you shall have it. The first grace that will keep you on the path of life is to know the level of your present deception. Deception involves anything that you do not understand as I do. Knowing the level of your present deception brings humility, and I give My grace to the humble.

"That is why I said, 'Who is blind but My servant?' And that is why I told the Pharisees, 'It is for judgment that I came into the world . . . to give sight to those who do not see and to make blind those who see . . . If you were blind you would not be guilty, but because you claim to see, your guilt remains.' That is also why My light struck Paul blind when I called him. My light only revealed his true condition. Like him, you must be struck blind in the natural so that you can see by My Spirit."

THE APOSTLE'S ADVICE

I then felt compelled to look at those who were sitting on the thrones we were passing. As I did, my gaze fell upon a man I knew was the Apostle Paul. As I looked back at the Lord, He motioned for me to speak to him.

"I have so looked forward to this," I said, feeling awkward but excited by this meeting. "I know you are aware of how much your letters have guided the church, and they are probably still accomplishing more than all the rest of us put together. You are still one of the greatest lights on earth."

"Thank you," he said graciously. "But you do not understand just how much we have looked forward to meeting all of you. You are soldiers in the last battle; you are the ones everyone here is waiting to meet. We only saw these days dimly through our limited prophetic vision, but you have been chosen to live in them. You are soldiers preparing for the last battle. You are the ones we have all been waiting for."

Still feeling awkward, I continued, "But there is no way that I can convey the appreciation we feel for you and for the others who helped set our course with their lives and their writings. I also know we will have an eternity for exchanging our appreciation, so please, while I am here, let me ask: What would you say to my generation that will help us in this battle?"

"I can only say to you now what I have already said to you through my writings," Paul stated, looking me resolutely in the eyes. "However, you will understand them better if you realize that I fell short of all that I was called to do."

"But you are here, on one of the greatest thrones!" I protested. "You are still reaping more fruit for eternal life than any of us could ever hope to reap."

"By the grace of God I was able to finish my course, but I still did not walk in all that I was called to. I fell short of the highest purposes that I could have walked in—everyone has. I know that some would practically consider it blasphemy to think of me as anything less than the greatest example of Christian ministry, yet I was being honest when I wrote near the end of my life that I was the greatest of sinners. I was not saying that I *had been* the greatest of sinners, but rather that I was the greatest of sinners *then*. Even though I had been given so much understanding, I walked in comparatively little of it."

"How could that possibly be?" I asked. "I thought you were just being humble."

"True humility is agreement with the truth. Do not fear. My letters were true, and they were written by the anointing of the Holy Spirit. However, I was given so much, and I did not use all that I was given. I, too, fell short. Everyone here has fallen short, except One. The reason you must see this particularly about me is that many are still distorting my teachings because they have a distorted view of me.

"As you saw the progression in my letters, I went from feeling that I was not inferior to even the most eminent apostles to acknowledging that I was the least of the apostles. I then saw that I was the least of the saints, and finally that I was the greatest of sinners. I was not just being humble; I was speaking sober truth. I was entrusted with much more than I used. There is only One here who fully believed, who fully obeyed, and who truly finished all that He was given to do. But you can walk in much more than I did."

REDISCOVERING THE FOUNDATION

Rather feebly, I replied, "I know what you are saying is true, but are you sure this is the most important message you could give to us for the last battle?"

"I am sure!" he replied with utter conviction. "I so appreciate the grace of the Lord to use my letters as He has, but I am concerned with the way many of you are using them improperly. They are the truth of the Holy Spirit and they are Scripture. The Lord did give me great stones to set into the structure of His eternal church, but they are not foundation stones. The foundation stones were laid by Jesus alone. My life and ministry are not the example of what you are called to be; Jesus alone is that.

"If what I have written is used as a foundation, it will not be able to hold the weight of that which needs to be built upon it. What I have written must be built upon the only Foundation that can withstand what you are about to endure; it must not be used as the foundation. You must see my teachings through the Lord's teachings, not try to understand Him from my perspective. His Words are the foundation. I have only built upon them by elaborating on His Words. The greatest wisdom and the most powerful truths are His Words, not mine.

"It is important for you to know that I did not walk in all that was available to me. There is much more available for every believer to walk in than I did. All true believers have the Holy Spirit in them. The power of the One who created all things lives within them. The least of the saints has the power to move mountains, to stop armies, or to raise the dead.

"If you are to accomplish all that you are called to do in your day, my ministry must not be viewed as the ultimate, but merely as a starting place. Your goal must not be to be like me, but to be like the Lord. You can be like Him and do everything that He did, and even more, because He saved His best wine for last."

I reminded myself that only truth could be spoken here. I knew that Paul was right concerning the wrong use of his teachings as a foundation, rather than building upon the foundation of the Gospels. But it was still hard for me to accept that Paul had fallen short of his calling.

[139]

I looked at Paul's throne and the glory of his being. It was much more than I ever dreamed the greatest saints in heaven would have. He was every bit as forthright and resolute as I had expected him to be. It struck me how obvious it was that he still carried his great concern for all of the churches. I had idolized him, and that was a transgression he was trying to set me free from. Even so, he was much greater than the Paul I had idolized. Knowing what I was thinking, he put both hands on my shoulders and looked at me even more resolutely in the eyes.

"I am your brother. I love you as everyone here does. But you must understand that our course is now finished. We can neither add to nor take away from what we planted on the earth, but you can. We are not your hope. You are now *our* hope. Even in this conversation I can only confirm what I have already written, but you still have much writing to do. Worship only God, and grow up in all things into Him. Never make any man your goal, but only Him.

"Many will soon walk the earth who will do much greater works than we did. The first shall be last, and the last first. We do not mind this. It is the joy of our hearts because we are one with you. The Lord used my generation to lay and begin building upon the foundation, and we will always have the honor of participating in that. But every floor built upon the foundation should go higher. We will not be the building we are supposed to be unless you go higher."

THE MINISTRY AND THE MESSAGE

As I pondered this, he watched me closely. Then he continued, "There are two things we attained in our time that were lost very quickly by the church. They have not yet been recovered, but you must recover them."

"What are they?" I inquired, feeling that what he was about to say was more than just an addendum to what he had already shared with me.

"You must recover the *ministry* and the *message*," he said emphatically.

I looked at the Lord, and He nodded His affirmation, adding, *"It is right that Paul should say this to you. Until this time he has been the most faithful with both of these."*

"Please explain," I implored Paul.

"All right," he replied. "Except for a few places in the world where there are great persecutions or difficulties, we can hardly recognize either the ministry or the message that is being preached today. Therefore, the church is now but a phantom of what it was even in our time, and we were far from all we were called to be. When we served, being in ministry was the greatest sacrifice that one could make, and this reflected the message of the greatest sacrifice that was made—the cross.

"The cross is the power of God, and it is the center of all we are called to live by. You now have so little power to transform the minds and hearts of believers because you do not live or preach the cross. Therefore, we have difficulty seeing much difference between the church and the heathen. That is not the gospel or the salvation that we were entrusted with. You must return to the cross."

With those words, he squeezed my shoulders like a father and then returned to his seat. I felt as if I had received both an incredible blessing and a profound rebuke. As I walked away, I began thinking about the level of "Salvation" on the mountain, and the treasures of salvation I had seen inside the mountain. I began to see that most of my own decisions—even the decision to enter the door that led me here—were based mainly on what would get me further, not on a consideration of the will of the Lord.

I was still living for myself, not for Him. Even in my desire to embrace the judgments here, I was motivated by what would help me make it back in victory without suffering loss. I was still walking much more in self-centeredness than in Christ-centeredness.

THE LAST-DAY CHURCH

I knew the short talk with Paul would have consequences that would take a long time to fully understand. In a way, I felt that I had received a blessing from the entire eternal church. We really were being cheered on by the great cloud of witnesses. They looked at us like proud parents who wanted better things for their children than they themselves had known. Their greatest joy would be to see the church in the last days become everything the church in their day had failed to attain. I also knew I was still falling far short of what they had prepared for us to walk in.

"The last-day church will not be greater than Paul's generation, even if she does greater works," the Lord interjected. *"All that is done is done by My grace. However, I will make more of My grace and power available to the last-day church because she must accomplish more than the church in any age has yet accomplished.*

"Last-day believers will walk in all the power that I demonstrated, and more, because they will be the final representatives of all who have gone before them. The church will demonstrate My nature and My ways as they have never been demonstrated before by men. It is because I am giving you more grace, and to whom much is given much will be required."

This just made me think even more about Paul. "How could we even become as dedicated and faithful as he was?" I thought to myself.

[142]

"I am not asking you to attain that," the Lord answered. *"I am asking you to abide in Me. You cannot continue to measure yourself by others—not even Paul. You will always fall short of the one you look to, but if you are looking to Me you will go far beyond what you would have otherwise accomplished. As you yourself have taught, it was when the two on the road to Emmaus saw Me break the bread that their eyes were opened. When you read Paul's letters, or anyone else's writings, you must hear Me. Only when you receive your bread directly from Me will the eyes of your heart be opened.*

"You can be distracted the most by those who are the most like Me if you do not see through them to see Me. There is also another trap for those who come to know more of My anointing and power than others. They are often distracted by looking at themselves. As I was saying before you talked to Paul, My servants must become blind so that they can see. I let you talk to him then because he is one of My best examples of this. It was because of My grace that I allowed him to persecute My church. When he saw My light, he understood that his own reasoning had led him into direct conflict with the very truth he claimed to be serving.

"Your reasoning will always do that. It will lead you to do that which is exactly contrary to My will. Greater anointing brings greater danger of this happening to you, if you do not learn what Paul did. If you do not take up your cross every day, laying down all that you are and all that you have before it, you will fall because of the authority and power that I will give you. Until you learn to do all things for the sake of the gospel, the more influence you have, the greater the danger of this you will face.

"Sometimes My anointed ones are deceived into thinking that because I give them a little supernatural knowledge or power, their ways must therefore be My ways and everything they think must be what I think. This is a great deception,

[143]

and many have stumbled because of it. You think like Me when you are in perfect union with Me. Even with the most anointed who have yet walked the earth, such as Paul, this union has only been partial and for brief periods of time.

"Paul walked with Me as close as any man ever has. Even so, he was also beset by fears and weaknesses that were not from Me. I could have delivered him from these, as he requested several times, but I had a reason for not delivering him. Paul's great wisdom was to embrace his weaknesses, understanding that if I had delivered him from them, I would not have been able to trust him with the level of revelation and power that I did.

"Paul recognized his own weaknesses and learned to distinguish between them and the revelation of My Spirit. When he was beset with weakness or fear, he knew he was not seeing from My perspective, but from his own. This caused him to seek Me and depend on Me even more. He was also careful not to confuse what came from his own mind and heart with the thoughts of My mind and heart. Therefore I could trust him with revelations that I could not entrust to others."

THE QUEST

I began to think about how clear all of this was here, but how very often, even after I have had a great experience like this, I still forget it so easily. It is easy to understand and to walk in the light here, but back in the battle it becomes cloudy again. I also thought about how I was not so much beset with fears, as Paul was, but my tendencies were impatience and anger, which were just as much a distortion of the perspective we should have by abiding in the Holy Spirit.

Wisdom stopped and turned to me. *"You are an earthen vessel, and that is all you will be while you walk the earth. However, you can see Me just as clearly there as you do here, if you will look with the eyes of your heart. You can be just as close to Me there as anyone has ever been to Me, and even more so.*

"I have made the way for everyone to be as close to Me as they truly desire to be. If you really desire to be even closer to Me than Paul was, you can. Some will want this, and they will want it badly enough to give themselves fully to it, laying aside anything that hinders their intimacy with Me. They will have what they seek.

"If it is your quest to walk on earth just as you can walk with Me here, I will be just as close to you there as I am now. If you seek Me, you will find Me. If you draw near to Me, I will draw near to you. It is My desire to set a table for you right in the midst of your enemies. This is not just My desire for My leaders, but for all who call upon My name. I want to be much closer to you, and to everyone who calls upon Me, than I have yet been able to be with anyone who has lived on earth. You determine how close we will be, not I. I will be found by those who seek Me.

"You are here because you asked for My judgment in your life. You sought Me as the Judge, and now you are finding Me. But you must not think that just because you have seen My judgment seat, now all of your judgments will be My judgments. You will only have My judgments as you walk in unity with Me and seek the anointing of My Spirit. This can be gained or lost every day.

"I have let you see angels and given you many dreams and visions because you kept asking for them. I love to give My children the good gifts that they ask for. For years you asked Me for wisdom, so you are receiving it. You have asked Me to judge you, so you are receiving My judgment. But these experiences do not make you fully wise, nor do they make you a righteous judge. You will only have wisdom and judgment as you abide in Me.

[145]

"Do not ever stop seeking Me. The more you mature, the more you will know your desperate need for Me. The more you mature, the less you will seek to hide from Me or others for your desire will be to always walk in the light.

"You have seen Me as Savior, Lord, Wisdom, and Judge. When you return to the battle, you can still see My judgment seat with the eyes of your heart. When you walk in the knowledge that all you think and do are fully revealed here, you will have the freedom to live there just as you do here. It is only when you hide from Me or others that the veils return to hide Me from you. I am Truth, and those who worship Me must do so in Spirit and Truth.

"Truth is never found hiding in the darkness, but always seeks to remain in the light. Light exposes and makes manifest. Only when you seek to be exposed, and allow who you are in your heart to be exposed, will you walk in the light as I am in the light. True fellowship with Me requires complete exposure. True fellowship with My people requires the same.

"When you stood before the judgment seat, you felt more freedom and security than you have ever felt because you did not have to hide anymore. You felt more security because you knew that My judgments were true and righteous. The moral and spiritual order of My universe is just as sure as the natural order established upon the natural laws. You trust My law of gravity without even thinking about it. You must learn to trust My judgments in the same way. My standards of righteousness are unchanging and are just as sure. To live by this truth is to walk in faith. True faith is to have confidence in who I am."

THE POWER OF HIS WORD

"You seek to know and walk in My power so that you can heal the sick and perform miracles, but you have

not even begun to comprehend the power of My Word. To resurrect all the dead who have ever lived on earth will not even cause Me to strain. I uphold all things by the power of My Word. The creation exists because of My Word, and it is held together by My Word.

"Before the end, I will reveal My power on earth. Even so, the greatest power that I have ever revealed on the earth, or ever will, is still a very small demonstration of My power. I do not reveal My power to cause men to believe in My power, but to cause men to believe in My love.

"If I had wanted to save the world with My power when I walked the earth, I could have moved mountains by pointing a finger. Then all men would have bowed to Me, not because they loved Me or loved the truth, but because they feared My power. I do not want men to obey Me because they fear My power, but because they love Me and love the truth.

"If you do not know My love, then My power will corrupt you. I do not give you love so you can know My power, but I give you power so you can know My love. The goal of your life must be love, not power. Then I will give you power with which to love people. I will give you the power to heal the sick because you love them, and I love them, and I do not want them sick.

"So you must seek love first, and then faith. You cannot please Me without faith. But faith is not just the knowledge of My power; it is the knowledge of My love and the power of My love. Faith must first be exercised in order to receive more love. Seek faith to love more and to do more with your love. Only when you seek the faith to love can I trust you with My power. Faith works by love.

"My Word is the power that upholds all things. To the degree that you believe My Word is true, you can do all things. Those who really believe that My Words are true will also be

true to their own words. It is My nature to be true, and the creation trusts My Word because I am faithful to it.

"Those who are like Me are also true to their own words. Their word is sure, and their commitments are trustworthy. Their 'yes' means 'yes,' and their 'no' means 'no.' If your own words are not true, you will also begin to doubt My Words because deception is in your heart. If you are not faithful to your own words, it is because you do not really know Me. To have faith, you must be faithful. I have called you to walk by faith because I am faithful. It is My nature.

"That is why you will be judged because of the careless words you speak. To be careless is to care less. Words have power, and those who are careless with words cannot be trusted with the power of My Word. It is wisdom to be careful with your words and to keep them as I do Mine."

The Lord's words were rolling over me like great waves from the sea. I felt like Job before the whirlwind. I thought that I was getting smaller and smaller and then realized that He was getting larger. I had never felt so presumptuous. How could I have been so casual with God? I felt like an ant staring up at a mountain range. I was less than dust, yet He was taking the time to speak to me. I could not stand it any more and turned away.

After a few moments, I felt a reassuring hand on my shoulder. It was Wisdom. His glory was even greater now, but He was again my size. *"Do you understand what happened just then?"* He asked.

Knowing very well that when the Lord asks a question He is not seeking information, I began to ponder what had happened. I knew it was reality. Compared to Him, I am less than a speck of dust would be to the earth, and for some reason He wanted me to experience that realization in a profound way.

Answering my thoughts, He elaborated:

"What you are thinking is true, but this comparison of man to God is not just in size. You began to experience the power of My Words. To be entrusted with My Words is to be entrusted with the power by which the universe is held together. I did not do this to make you feel small, but to help you understand the seriousness and the power of that with which you have been entrusted—the Word of God.

"In all of your endeavors, remember that the importance of a single Word from God to man is of more value than all of the treasures on earth. You must understand and teach My brethren to respect the value of My Word. As one who is called to carry My Words, you must also respect the value of your own words. Those who will carry the truth must be true."

MEETING THE EVANGELIST

While hearing these words, I felt compelled to look up toward one of the thrones beside me. Immediately I saw a man I recognized. He had been a great evangelist when I was a child, and many felt that he had walked in more power than anyone since the early church. I had read about him and had listened to some of his recorded messages. It was hard not to be touched by his genuine humility and the obvious love he had for the Lord and people. Even so, I also felt that some of his teachings had gone seriously awry. I was surprised, but also relieved, to see him sitting on a great throne. I was captured by the humility and love that still exuded from him.

As I turned to ask the Lord if I could talk with this man, I could see how much the Lord loved him. However, the Lord motioned for me to continue walking and would not permit me to speak with the evangelist.

"I just wanted you to see him here," the Lord explained, *"and to understand the position that he has with Me. There is much for you to understand about him. He was a messenger to My last-day church, but the church could not hear him for reasons that you will understand in due time. He did fall into discouragement and delusion for a time, and his message was distorted. It must be recovered, as well as the parts that I have given to others which were also distorted."*

Knowing everything here happened in perfect timing with all I was meant to learn, I began to think about how seeing this man must be related to what we had just talked about—the potential of power to corrupt.

"Yes. There is great danger in walking in great power," the Lord responded. *"Many of My messengers have fallen subject to this danger, and that is part of the message they are to give to My last-day church. You must walk in My power, even much greater power than these experienced. But if you ever start to think the power is My endorsement of you or even of your message, you will open the door to the same delusion. The Holy Spirit is given to testify only of Me. If you are wise, like Paul, you will learn to glory more in your weaknesses than in your strengths.*

"True faith is the true recognition of who I am. It is nothing more and nothing less. But you must always remember, even if you abide in My presence and see Me as I am, you can still fall if you turn from Me to look at yourself. That is how Lucifer fell. He dwelt in this room and beheld My glory and the glory of My Father. However, he began to look at himself more than he looked to Us. He then began to take pride in his position and power.

"Many of My servants who have been allowed to see My glory and be entrusted with My power have fallen in the same way as Lucifer. If you begin to think that it is because of your wisdom, your righteousness, or even your devotion to pure doctrine, you will stumble too."

[150]

CONFIDENCE

I knew this was as severe a warning as anything that I had been told here. I wanted to go back and fight in the last battle, but I was having serious questions about being able to do so without falling into the traps that now seemed to be everywhere. I looked back at the Lord. He was Wisdom, and I thought of how badly I needed to know Him as Wisdom when I returned.

"It is good for you to lose confidence in yourself. I cannot trust you with the powers of the age to come until you do. The more confidence you lose in yourself, the more power I will be able to trust you with, if...."

I waited a long time for the Lord to continue, but He didn't. Somehow I knew He wanted me to continue the sentence, but I did not know what to say. However, the more I looked at Him, the more confidence I felt. Finally I knew what to say.

"If I put my confidence in You," I added.

"Yes. You must have faith to do what you are called to do, but it must be faith in Me. It is not enough for you to just lose confidence in yourself. That only leads to insecurity if you do not fill the void with confidence in Me. That is how many of these men fell to their delusions.

"Many of these men and women were prophets. But some of them out of insecurity would not let men call them prophets. Yet that was not the truth because they were. False humility is also a deception. If the enemy could deceive them into thinking that they were not really prophets, he could also deceive them into thinking that they were greater prophets than they were just by nurturing their self-confidence. False humility will not cast out pride. It is just another form of self-centeredness, which the enemy has a right to exploit.

[151]

"All of your failures will be the result of this one thing: self-centeredness. The only way to be delivered from this is to walk in love. Love does not seek its own."

As I was thinking about all of this, a wonderful clarity began to come. I could see the whole experience from beginning to end, having as its focus a single, simple message. "How easily I am beguiled from the simplicity of devotion to You," I lamented.

THE SMILE OF THE LORD

The Lord then stopped and looked at me with an expression I pray that I will never forget. He smiled. I did not want to abuse this opportunity, but I somehow felt when He smiled like that I could ask Him anything and He would give it to me. So I took the chance.

"Lord, when You said, 'Let there be light,' there was light. You prayed in John 17 that we would love You with the same love that the Father loved you with. Will You please say to me now, 'Let there be love in you' so that I will love You with the Father's love?"

He did not quit smiling, but rather put His arm around me like a friend. *"I already said that to you before the creation of the world when I called you. I have also said it to your brethren who will fight along with you in the last battle. You will know My Father's love for Me. It is a perfect love that will cast out all of your fears. This love will enable you to believe Me so you can do the works that I did, and even greater works, because I am with My Father. You will know His love for Me, and the works you will be given to do will glorify Me. Now, for your sake, I say again, 'Let there be My Father's love in you.'"*

I was overwhelmed with appreciation for this whole experience. "I love Your judgments," I said. I then started to turn and look back at the judgment seat, but the Lord stopped me.

"Don't look back. I am not there for you now; I am here. I will lead you from this room and on to your place in the battle, but you must not look back. You must see My judgment seat in your own heart because that is where it is now."

"Just like the Garden and like the treasures of salvation…" I thought to myself.

"Yes. Everything that I am doing, I am doing in your heart. That is where the living waters flow. That is where I am."

He then gestured toward me, so I looked at myself, pulling back the cloak of humility. I was stunned by what I saw. My armor contained the same glory that surrounded Him. I quickly covered it again with my cloak.

"I also prayed to My Father on the night before My crucifixion that the glory I had with Him in the beginning would be with My people, so that you will be one. It is My glory that unifies. As you come together with others who love Me, My glory will be magnified. The more My glory is magnified by the joining of those who love Me, the more the world will know that I was sent by the Father. Now the world really will know that you are My disciples because you will love Me, and you will love each other."

As I kept looking at Him, my confidence continued to grow. It was like being washed on the inside. Soon I was feeling ready to do anything He asked.

ANGELO

"There is still someone you must meet before you return to the battle," He said as we walked. I continued to be astonished by how much more glorious He had become than even a few minutes before.

[153]

"Every time you see Me with the eyes of your heart, your mind is renewed a little bit more," He proceeded to say. *"One day you will be able to abide in My presence continually. When you do that, all you have learned by My Spirit will be readily available to you, and I will be available to you."*

I could hear and understand everything He said, but I was so captured by His glory that I just had to ask Him, "Lord, why are You so much more glorious now than when You first appeared to me as Wisdom?"

"I have never changed, but you have. You are changed as you behold My glory with an unveiled face. The experiences you have had are removing the veils from your face so that you can see Me more clearly. Yet nothing removes them as quickly as when you behold My love."

He then stopped and I turned to look at those on the thrones next to us. We were still in the place where the highest kings were sitting. Then I recognized a man who was close by.

"Sir, I know you from somewhere, but I simply cannot remember where."

"You once saw me in a vision," he replied.

I immediately remembered and was shocked! "So you were a real person?"

"Yes," he replied.

I remembered the day when, as a young Christian, I had become frustrated with some issues in my life. I went out into the middle of a battlefield park near my apartment and determined that I would wait until the Lord spoke to me. As I sat reading my Bible, I was caught up into a vision, one of the first ones I ever had.

In the vision I saw a man who was zealously serving the Lord. He was continually witnessing to people, teaching the Bible, and visiting the sick to pray for them. He was very zealous for the Lord and had a genuine love for people. Then I saw another man, named Angelo, who was obviously a tramp or a homeless person. When a small kitten wandered onto his path, he started to kick it but restrained himself, though he still shoved it out of the way rather harshly with his foot. Then the Lord asked me which of these men pleased Him the most.

"The first," I said without hesitating.

"No, the second," He responded, and began to tell me their stories.

He shared that the first man had been raised in a wonderful family, which had always known the Lord. He grew up in a thriving church and then attended one of the best Bible colleges in the country. He had been given one hundred portions of His love, but he was using only seventy-five.

The second man had been born deaf. He was abused and kept in a dark, cold attic until he was found by the authorities when he was eight years old. He had then been shifted from one institution to another, where the abuse continued. Finally, he was turned out onto the streets. The Lord had only given him three portions of His love to help him overcome all of this, but he had mustered every bit of it to fight the rage in his heart and keep from hurting the kitten.

I now looked at that man, a king sitting on a throne far more glorious than Solomon could have even imagined. Hosts of angels were arrayed about him, waiting to do his bidding. I turned to the Lord in awe. I still could not believe he was real, much less one of the great kings.

"Lord, please tell me the rest of his story," I begged.

"Of course, that is why we are here. Angelo was so faithful with the little I had given to him that I gave him three more portions of My love. He used all of that to quit stealing. He almost starved, but he refused to take anything that was not his. He bought his food with what he could make collecting bottles, and occasionally he found someone who would let him do yard work.

"Angelo could not hear, but he had learned to read, so I sent him a gospel tract. As he read it, the Spirit opened his heart, and he gave his life to Me. I again doubled the portions of My love to him, and he faithfully used all of them. He wanted to share Me with others, but he could not speak. Even though he lived in such poverty, he started spending over half of everything he made on gospel tracts to give out on street corners."

"How many did he lead to You?" I asked, thinking that it must have been multitudes for him to be sitting with the kings.

"One," the Lord answered. *"In order to encourage him, I let him lead a dying alcoholic to Me. It encouraged him so much that he would have stood on that corner for many more years just to bring another soul to repentance. But all of heaven was entreating Me to bring him here quickly, and I, too, wanted him to receive his reward."*

A DIFFERENT KIND OF MARTYR

"But what did Angelo do to become a king here?" I asked.

"He was faithful with all that he was given. He overcame all until he became like Me, and he died a martyr."

"But what did he overcome, and how was he martyred?"

[156]

"He overcame the world with My love. Very few have overcome so much with so little. Many of My people dwell in homes with conveniences that kings would have envied just a century ago, yet they do not appreciate them. Angelo, on the other hand, would so appreciate even a cardboard box on a cold night that he would turn it into a glorious temple of My presence.

"Angelo began to love everyone and everything. He would rejoice more over an apple than some of My people do over a great feast. He was faithful with all that I gave him, even though it was not very much compared to what I gave others, including you. I showed him to you in a vision because you passed by him many times. Once you even pointed him out to one of your friends and spoke of him."

"I did? What did I say?"

"You said, 'There is another one of those Elijahs who must have escaped from the bus station.' You said he was 'a religious nut' who was sent by the enemy to turn people off of the gospel."

This was the worst blow that I had yet suffered in this whole experience. I was more than shocked, I was appalled. I tried to remember the specific incident, but could not—simply because there were so many others like it. I had never had much compassion for filthy street preachers, considering them tools of Satan.

"I'm sorry, Lord. I'm really sorry."

"You are forgiven," He quickly responded. *"And you are right that there are many who try to preach the gospel on the streets for wrong or even perverted reasons. Even so, there are many who are sincere, even if they are untrained and unlearned. You must not judge by appearances. There are as many true servants who look like he did as there are among the polished professionals in the great cathedrals and organizations that men have built in My name."*

[157]

He then motioned for me to look up at Angelo. When I had turned, he had descended the steps to his throne and was now right in front of me. Opening his arms, he gave me a great hug and kissed my forehead like a father. Love poured over me and through me until I felt that it would overload my nervous system. When he finally released me, I was staggering as if I was drunk, but it was a wonderful feeling. It was love like I had never felt before.

"He could have imparted that to you on earth," the Lord continued. *"He had much to give to My people, but they would not come near him. Even My prophets avoided him. He grew in the faith by buying a Bible and a couple of books that he read over and over. He tried to go to churches, but he could not find one that would receive him. If they would have taken him in, they would have taken Me in. He was My knock upon their door."*

I was learning a new definition of grief. "How did he die?" I asked, remembering that he had been martyred. Based on what I had seen so far, I was half expecting that I somehow was even responsible for that.

"He froze to death trying to keep alive an old wino who had passed out in the cold."

THE UNLIKELY OVERCOMER

As I looked at Angelo, I could not believe how hard my heart had been. Even so, I did not understand how dying in this way made him a martyr, which I thought was a title reserved for those who died because they would not compromise their testimony of the lordship of Christ.

"Lord, I know that he is truly an overcomer," I remarked. "And it truly is warranted for him to be here.

But are those who die in such a way actually considered martyrs?"

"Angelo was a martyr every day that he lived. He would only do enough for himself to stay alive, and he gladly sacrificed his life to save a needy friend. As Paul wrote to the Corinthians, even if you give your body to be burned, but do not have love, it counts as nothing. But when you give yourself with love, it counts for much.

"Angelo died every day, because he did not live for himself, but for others. Even though he always considered himself the least of the saints, he was truly one of the greatest. As you have already learned, many of those who consider themselves the greatest, and are considered by others to be the greatest, end up being the least here. Angelo did not die for a doctrine, or even for his testimony, but he did die for Me."

"Lord, please help me to remember this. When I return, please do not let me forget what I am seeing here," I begged.

"That is why I am with you here, and I will be with you when you return. Wisdom is to see with My eyes and to not judge by appearances. I showed you Angelo in the vision so that you would recognize him when you passed him on the street. If you had shared with him the knowledge of his past that I had shown you in the vision, he would have given his life to Me then. You could have then discipled this great king and he would have had a great impact on My church.

"If My people would look at others the way I do, Angelo and many others like him would have been recognized. They would have been paraded into the greatest pulpits. My people would have come from the ends of the earth to sit at their feet, because by doing this they would have sat at My feet. He would have taught you to love and how to invest the gifts that I have given to you so that you could bear much more fruit."

I was so ashamed that I did not want to even look at the Lord, but finally I turned back to Him as I felt the pain driving me toward self-centeredness again. When I looked at Him, I was virtually blinded by His glory. It took a while, but gradually my eyes adjusted so that I could see Him.

"Remember that you are forgiven," He said. *"I am not showing you these things to condemn you, but to teach you. Always remember that compassion will remove the veils from your soul faster than anything else."*

As we began to walk again, Angelo entreated me, "Please remember my friends, the homeless. Many will love our Savior if someone will go to them."

His words had such power in them that I was too moved to answer, so I just nodded. I knew that those words were the decree of a great king and a great friend of the King of kings.

"Lord, will You help me to help the homeless?" I asked.

"I will help any who help them," He responded. *"When you love those whom I love, you will always know My help. You will be given the Helper by the measure of your love. You have asked many times for more of My anointing; that is how you will receive it. Love those whom I love. As you love them, you love Me. As you give to them, you have given to Me, and I will give more to you in return."*

LIVING LIKE A KING

My mind drifted to my nice home and all the other possessions I had. I was not wealthy, yet I knew by earthly standards I lived much better than kings had lived just a century before. I had never felt guilty about it before, but I did now. Somehow it was a good feeling, but at the same time it did not feel right. Again I looked back to the Lord, for I knew He would help me.

"Remember what I said about how My perfect law of love made light and darkness distinct. When confusion such as you are now feeling comes, you know what you are experiencing is not My perfect law of love. I delight in giving My family good gifts, just as you do yours. I want you to enjoy them and appreciate them. Nevertheless, you must not worship them, and you must freely share them when I call you to.

"I could wave My hand and instantly remove all poverty from the earth. There will be a day of reckoning when the mountains and high places are brought down and the poor and oppressed are raised up, but I must do it. Human compassion is just as contrary to Me as human oppression. Human compassion is used as a substitute for the power of My cross. I have not called you to sacrifice, but to obey. Sometimes you will have to sacrifice in order to obey Me, but if your sacrifice is not done in obedience, it will separate us.

"You are guilty for the way you misjudged and treated this great king when he was My servant on earth. Do not judge anyone without inquiring of Me. You missed more of the encounters I set up for you than you have ever imagined, simply because you were not sensitive to Me. However, I did not show you this just to make you feel guilty, but rather to bring you to repentance so you will not continue to miss such opportunities.

"If you just react in guilt, you will begin to do things to compensate for your guilt, which is an affront to My cross. My cross alone can remove your guilt. And because I went to the cross to remove your guilt, whatever is done in guilt is not done for Me.

"I do not enjoy seeing men suffer," Wisdom continued.

[161]

"But human compassion will not lead them to the cross, which alone can relieve their real suffering. You missed Angelo because you were not walking in compassion. You will have more when you return, but your compassion must still be subject to My Spirit. Even I did not heal all those for whom I had compassion, but I only did what I saw My Father doing. You must not do things out of compassion, but in obedience to My Spirit. Only then will your compassion have the power of redemption.

"I have given you the gifts of My Spirit. You have known My anointing in your preaching and writing, but you have known it much less than you realize. Rarely do you really see with My eyes or hear with My ears or understand with My heart. Without Me, you can do nothing that will benefit My kingdom or promote My gospel.

"You have fought in My battles, and you have even seen the top of My mountain. You have learned to shoot arrows of truth and hit the enemy. You have learned a little about using My sword. But remember, love is My greatest weapon. Love will never fail. Love will be the power that destroys the works of the devil. And love will be what brings My kingdom. Love is the banner over My army, and under this banner you must now fight."

With this, we turned into a corridor and were no longer in the great hall of judgment. The glory of Wisdom was all around me, but I could no longer see Him distinctly. Suddenly, I came to a door. My first impulse was to turn because I did not want to leave, but I knew that I must. This was the door Wisdom had led me to. I had to go through it.

To be continued...

THE CALL

INTRODUCTION

This is the second book in *The Final Quest* series. Though it begins where the first book ends, it is possible to read this one and generally understand it without having read the first book. However, if you do this, some of the material may seem disconnected. This is a continuing spiritual saga, and there are some foundations laid in the first book that are built upon in this one.

As I explained in the introduction to *The Final Quest*, this book is the result of a series of "prophetic experiences." I have been counseled many times that this book would be received by many more people if I had written it as a fictional allegory. That may be true; however, it is not my goal to have this read by more people, but to simply be faithful to what I have been entrusted with, conveying it as accurately as I can. For me to claim that this is the result of my own creativity would be dishonest, which would therefore be an affront to the Spirit of Truth.

Even so, because *The Final Quest* has been widely received across the spectrum of Christian denominations and movements and has found remarkable favor with conservative evangelicals, I do feel that I should explain a little more about what I mean by "prophetic experiences," how I received these in particular, and just a little about the biblical basis for these in our own time.

Biblical prophetic experiences are very diverse in nature, as were those which I received and are included in this unfolding series. Some came in dreams, others in visions, and other parts in what the Bible calls trances.

These all have biblical precedents and are established ways that the Lord speaks to His people. Because there is an increasing number of Christians who are having such experiences today, it is regarded by some to be a fulfillment of Peter's prophecy on the Day of Pentecost, which he quoted from the prophet Joel:

> **"And it shall be in the last days," God says, "That I will pour forth of My Spirit upon all mankind; and your sons and your daughters shall prophesy, and your young men shall see visions, and your old men shall dream dreams;**
>
> **"Even upon My bondslaves, both men and women, I will in those days pour forth of My Spirit and they shall prophesy" (Acts 2:17-18).**

As this text declares, prophetic revelations through visions, dreams, and prophecies will be prevalent in the last days. Because there is such a dramatic increase in prophetic revelation being given to Christians in these times, it is understandable why it is regarded as a sign that we are indeed in the **"last days."**

DISCERNING THE TRUE FROM THE FALSE

Jesus also warned that in the last days there would be many **"false prophets" (see Matthew 24:24).** This is to be expected because, as the Lord also taught, whenever He sows wheat in a field, the enemy comes along and sows tares in the same field (see Matthew 13:24-30). Tares look like wheat and may even taste like wheat, but they are noxious. Satan will immediately try to counterfeit everything that God is doing, creating confusion and, if possible, deceiving even the elect. However, Satan could not do this if God did not allow it. Obviously, the Lord wants us to learn to distinguish the real from the false and to allow the real to be tested by the false in order to purify that which is true.

That false prophets are also becoming more prevalent should not surprise us, but rather encourage us to seek the real with greater determination. If we do not want to be deceived by the false, the answer is not to reject all prophecy, but rather to know the true. Those who cannot discern true prophecy in the time to come will become increasingly subject to the false. If God is planting something, it is because we will need it. If you do not plant a field, but neglect it, the only harvest that you will reap will be weeds. Those who do not receive what God is doing today will end up reaping that which grows wild.

From the beginning the Lord has been committed to allowing men to choose between the real and the false, the good and the evil. That is why He put the Tree of the Knowledge of Good and Evil in the Garden along with the Tree of Life. He did not put the Tree of Knowledge there in order to cause men to stumble, but rather so they could prove their obedience and love for Him. There could be no true obedience from the heart unless there was the freedom to disobey.

Likewise, true teachers and teaching will always be shadowed by false teachers and false teaching. True prophets and prophecy will always be shadowed by the false. The Lord allows the enemy to sow tares among the wheat in order to test our hearts. Those who love the truth will discern what is true, and those who are pure will discern what is pure.

The Lord's warning that there will be false prophets at the end of the age implies there will be true ones, or He would have just said that at the end all prophets will be false. Some do believe that all prophets at the end will be false, but this conflicts with the biblical prophecy that at the end He will be pouring out His Spirit, and there will be visions, dreams, and prophecy.

There is danger in being open to prophetic revelations such as dreams, visions, and prophecy. However, there is much greater danger if we are not open to them. These revelations are not given to us for our entertainment, but because we need them for the time in which we live. The Lord also declared the following:

> **"Truly, truly, I say to you, he who does not enter by the door into the fold of the sheep, but climbs up some other way, he is a thief and a robber.**
>
> **"But he who enters by the door is a shepherd of the sheep.**
>
> **"To him the doorkeeper opens, and the sheep hear his voice, and he calls his own sheep by name, and leads them out.**
>
> **"When he puts forth all his own, he goes before them, and the sheep follow him because they know his voice.**
>
> **"And a stranger they simply will not follow, but will flee from him, because they do not know the voice of strangers"** (John 10:1-5).

The Lord's sheep know His voice. They are not deceived by others because they know His voice so well that they can distinguish it from the voice of others. One of the ways the Lord has spoken to His people from the earliest times has been prophetically. Because we also know that He never changes, and because the Scriptures are so clear about the visions, dreams, and prophecies that He will be giving at the end, it is imperative for us to be able to distinguish those which come from Him and then to interpret them correctly. After they are interpreted correctly, we must then have the wisdom to apply them correctly.

THE PURPOSE OF PROPHECY

Prophecy is given for encouragement, but it is also given for edification. To edify means to build. Much of my life and ministry has been built on fulfilled prophetic words. Almost every major aspect of our ministry, even the places where I go to minister or speak, is foretold prophetically. I do not consider doing something or going somewhere to minister unless the Lord has spoken to me in advance. Jesus did the same. He did not respond to human needs; He only did what He saw the Father doing (see John 5:19). We do not have time to go places or start things that God is not leading us to do. I think that our devotion to hearing from the Lord before we do things has enabled us to be quite fruitful with the resources and time entrusted to us.

I know of others who have successfully built a ministry or church on prophetic words. I also know of some who have been wrecked and others who suffered serious diversions because they did not know how to judge prophecy. Many of these problems happened because they received genuine revelation from the Lord, but misinterpreted or misapplied it. For some this may sound too complicated, but it is the process clearly established by the Scriptures, and we will pay a dear price if we deviate from sound biblical wisdom in regard to prophetic revelation.

Jesus said in Matthew 22:29: **"Ye do err, not knowing the Scriptures, nor the power of God" (KJV).** Many today make errors because they know the Scriptures, but they do not know the power of God. Those who know His power often make mistakes because they do not know the Scriptures as they should. If we are going to keep from making mistakes, we must know both the Scriptures and the power of God. Prophecy was never intended to replace the Scriptures, and the Scriptures were never intended to replace prophecy.

I have spent many hours with conservative, evangelical leaders of major ministries that God has begun speaking to through dreams, visions, and prophecies. In many cases He began to do this even when it violated their theology. This has become so widespread that I wondered if there were any conservative, evangelical leaders whom God was not dealing with in this way. There is almost a steady stream of contacts from those who are seeking help in understanding what is happening to them. What they may not understand at this point is that prophetic people need their help every bit as much as they need the help of those who have some experience with the prophetic gifts. For the church to come to the maturity to which she is called, there must be a union between those who know the Scriptures and those who know the power of God. This is now happening at a fast pace.

I have searched the Scriptures to establish that the teachings which are given in my experiences are biblical, and I am confident that they are. I do admit that some of them caused me to view certain Scriptures in a way that I had not seen them before. Even so, I believe this is consistent with the purpose of such prophetic revelations. *Prophecy should never be used to establish doctrine.* We were given the Bible for that, and the doctrine of the Bible is complete and should never be added to. However, the Bible itself has many examples of how prophetic experiences were given to individuals for the purpose of illuminating or confirming the Scriptures.

A prominent New Testament example of this would be the trance that Peter fell into which led him to go to the house of Cornelius, opening the door of faith to the Gentiles (see Acts 10). This experience, and the fruit it bore, clarified to the church that the Lord also intended for the gospel to be preached to the Gentiles. This did not establish a new doctrine, but illuminated what the Scriptures said and also what the Lord Himself had taught when He was with them, but it seems they had forgotten.

Many of the experiences that are included in *The Final Quest Series* did the same for me. They constantly reminded me of my own teachings, and sometimes teachings I had heard from others, that at best had only superficially been implemented in my life. In this way, these experiences were a constant challenge to me, bringing essential correction and even judgment to my life and teachings. As I was the one having the experiences, I took them personally, and I do not presume that the same corrections are needed by everyone. However, I do believe that many of them, if not most of them, are common to the church in our time.

[171]

There are a number of recurring themes in this discourse. Not only are there repetitious statements, but some of these themes are repeated from different perspectives or are worded differently in different situations. I realize this may have been done because of my own dullness, just as it seemed that the Lord had to repeat Himself over and over to Peter. I also realize that such repetition is not good literary style, but style is not my goal here. Each time something is repeated, the probability that it will be retained is increased. I have therefore tried to repeat everything just as it was repeated to me.

PROPHETIC EXPERIENCES

I also understand how the nature of some of these revelations would cause theological problems for some. One of these would certainly be the way that I met and talked with many Old and New Testament characters, as well as prominent people in church history who are now dead. There are biblical precedents for this, such as when the Lord talked to Moses and Elijah. Even though Elijah was carried up without dying, Moses had died. We also have the example when the Apostle John fell down to worship the angel in Revelation 22:9. The angel rebuked John, declaring that he was a fellow servant of his brethren. Many have understood this to indicate that he was one of the saints who had gone on to be with the Lord.

Even so, I can understand how some would still have a problem with this, and there is another explanation. There is a difference between prophetic experiences and actually doing something. For example, when Ezekiel was caught up in the Spirit and carried to Jerusalem, it is obvious that he was not taken to the actual Jerusalem, even though it seemed very real to him. Much of what he experienced did not actually exist, but was meant to convey a message to the exiles. Likewise, even though some of these experiences and the people seemed very real to me, I question very much whether I was talking to the actual people in heaven. I believe that these were prophetic experiences meant to convey a message.

In the same way, I do not know if the places I saw in heaven were the actual places, or if they appeared to me the way that they did for the purpose of conveying a message. However, I am open to the fact that I saw the real places and met the real people and see no conflict with the Scriptures which would prohibit this, though I could understand how some would. Even so, just as Abel still speaks though he is dead, certainly the lives of all of the characters in the Bible are messages, and these experiences helped to illuminate this to me more than ever before.

One reason I lean toward the belief that these were prophetic experiences, and that I was not talking with the real people, is because of how they lasted, or did not last. For example, most people have probably had dreams which were so real that when they woke up, for a brief time, they thought that they were real. However, even the most realistic dreams usually begin to fade so that in just a couple of hours they are forgotten. Real experiences are not this way. I have had real encounters with the Lord and with angels that are almost as real to me now as they were years ago when I had them. I have had many dreams and visions in which I saw the Lord or angels, but they would fade very fast. The experiences I had that are included in these books, except for a very few, faded like revelations rather than enduring like real encounters.

[173]

For this reason, I tried to write down these experiences as quickly as I could after having them. In some cases I was not able to do this. When I was able to get to a place where I could write them down, my memory of them had faded. I did feel the Holy Spirit helping to bring things to my remembrance, but the more time that elapsed between the experience and the time that I was able to write them, the more concerned I was that they may have not been conveyed exactly as I received them.

In such cases I was concerned that my own pet doctrines or prejudices could easily creep into my writing, and though I sincerely tried not to let this happen, I know it could have in some instances. For this reason, my continual prayer for this book has been for the Holy Spirit to lead me in writing it and also lead everyone who reads it. He was given to lead us to the truth and to Jesus. My prayer is that you will discern that which is truth and that which is from Jesus, holding fast to that which is and discarding anything that is not.

INFALLIBILITY OF SCRIPTURE

Though there are many places where I tried to write the exact words of the Lord as they were spoken to me, this is not Scripture, and I do not believe that any prophetic experience is intended to carry the weight of Scripture. Even so, prophecy is very important for the church or we would not have been exhorted by the Scripture to: **"Pursue love, yet desire earnestly spiritual gifts, but especially that you may prophesy" (I Corinthians 14:1).** We are told **"one who prophesies speaks to men for edification and exhortation and consolation. One who speaks in a tongue edifies himself; but one**

who prophesies edifies the church" (see I Corinthians 14:3-4). Again, we do not use prophecy to establish doctrine because we have the Scriptures for this. Never are we told that prophecy is infallible, which is why we must judge prophecy. However, prophecy does edify. Because prophecy is a gift of the Holy Spirit, we must treat everything which comes from Him as holy. But because it comes through men, it must not be considered infallible.

The Scriptures, as they were originally written, are infallible. They are the rock of truth and pure revelation of God and His ways which we can build our lives on and be sure that they will stand. I view prophecy more like the manna that the Lord served in the wilderness. It is from the Lord and will help to sustain us in our day-by-day walks, but if you try to keep it longer than intended, it will become foul. The Scriptures are permanent and are given so we can build our lives upon truth. Prophecy is given for edification and encouragement, strategically keeping us in the day-to-day will of the Lord. The quality of any relationship will be determined by the quality of the communication, and any relationship that does not have continuing communication is a dying relationship. Prophecy does help to keep our day-to-day relationship with the Lord fresh, which is why I believe that the Scripture encourages us to **"especially"** seek this gift.

I have sought the gift of prophecy for many years. I did this out of obedience to the Scripture that exhorts us to do this, and I did it because I do love the prophetic gifts. I love prophetic experiences even though all but a couple I have received have been a rebuke to me. Even so, I have prayed much more for wisdom and the gift of a word of wisdom than I have any of the others. That is why I think that the Lord almost always appears to me in these experiences personified as Wisdom. I also think that a truly wise man loves rebukes because **"reproofs for discipline are the way of life" (see Proverbs 6:23).** In every one of these experiences, I felt that I received a profound and badly needed correction in my life.

In this book there are also some very general corrections for the church as a whole. Except for the churches for which I have personal responsibility, I try not to see problems that the church has. The church is the Lord's bride, and I am very cautious about any way that I would presume to bring correction to the King's wife! Just as Paul explained to the Corinthians, we have spheres of authority that we must stay within. I do not think it is right for me to correct someone else's children, but as a friend I may speak to the parents and hope that they would feel at liberty to speak to me if they see things that need correcting in my kids. However, in the experiences included in this book, the Lord began to show me that the church today is headed for some terrible catastrophes if we do not make some very basic course corrections. I am still seeking more revelation, a greater understanding in the interpretation, and the wisdom to apply this all correctly.

I encourage you to keep in mind that even though these prophetic experiences were very real when I received the messages, they would often seem unreal to me only hours later. This was sometimes a problem when I tried to record these experiences. I did my best to write them as faithfully as I could, but by no means could I claim that these are the exact words spoken to me or that I wrote everything about these experiences exactly as they occurred. However, even though I may have forgotten some of the details or did not always get the wording right, the message is true, it is from the Lord, and the time is near.

Rick Joyner
1999

CHAPTER 1

The Glory

I stood looking at the door that I was to enter next. It was plain and uninviting. As I turned to view once again the Great Hall of Judgment, I was overwhelmed by its glory and expanse. I did not want to leave here, even though the evil of my own heart was continually exposed. Although the process was painful, it was so liberating that I did not want it to stop. I actually yearned for more conviction.

"And you shall have more," Wisdom interjected, knowing my thoughts. *"What you have found here will go with you. However, you do not have to come here to be changed. The power of the cross is enough to change you. What you have experienced here, you can experience every day. The Holy Spirit was sent to convict you of sin, to lead you to truth, and to testify of Me. He is with you continually. You must get to know the Holy Spirit better.*

"Many believe in the Holy Spirit, but few make room for Him in their lives. As the end of this age approaches, that will change. The Holy Spirit is about to move over the earth as He did in the beginning. He will take the chaos and confusion

that is spreading across the earth, and He will bring forth the glorious new creation right in the midst of it. You are about to enter the time when He will do wonders continually, and the whole world will be in awe of His works.

"He will do all of this through My people. When the Holy Spirit moves, the sons and daughters of God will prophesy. From the old to the young, they will dream dreams and see visions. The works that I did, and greater works, will they do in My name, that I might be glorified in the earth. The whole creation groans and travails for what the Holy Spirit is about to do.

"What you will find through that door will help you to prepare for what is to come. I am the Savior, but I am also the Judge. I am about to reveal Myself to the world as the Righteous Judge. First I must reveal My judgment to My own household. My people are about to know the fellowship of the Holy Spirit. Then they will know His power to convict of sin. They will also know that He will always lead them to the truth that will set them free. This is the truth that testifies of Me. When My people have come to know Me as I AM, then I will use them to testify of Me.

"I am the Judge, but it is better for you to judge yourself so that I will not have to judge you. Even so, My judgments are about to be restored to My people. I will judge My own household first. After that I will judge the whole earth."

The glory of Wisdom was overshadowing everything around me. I had never seen such splendor before, even here. It increased as He talked about His judgments. I knew by this that there was a glory to be seen by knowing Him as the Judge which was greater than I had seen before. I started feeling so small and insignificant in His presence that it was hard for me to concentrate on what He was saying.

Just when I thought I would be overwhelmed by His glory, He reached out and touched me on the forehead, gently but firmly. When He did this, my mind became focused and clear.

"You began to look at yourself. This will always bring confusion, making it harder for you to hear Me. Every time you experience My touch, your mind will become clearer. Every time you feel My presence, know that I have come to touch you in order that you may see Me and hear Me. You must learn to abide in My presence without becoming self-conscious and self-absorbed. This causes you to turn from the truth that is in Me and turn to the deception that is in your fallen nature.

"Many people fall when My Spirit touches them. The time for falling is over. You must learn to stand when My Spirit moves. If you do not stand when My Spirit moves, He cannot use you. The heathen should fall before Me, but I need for My people to stand so that I can use them."

THE PRIDE OF FALSE HUMILITY

I heard irritation in the Lord's voice when He said this. I felt that it was like the irritation He seemed to have in the Gospels with His disciples. Immediately I understood that this usually came when they started looking at their inadequacies or failures.

"Lord, I'm sorry," I pleaded, "but Your presence is so overwhelming. How do I keep from feeling so small when I'm close to You like this?"

"You are small, but you must learn to abide in My presence without looking at yourself. You will not be able to hear from Me or speak for Me if you are looking at yourself. You will always be inadequate. You will always be

[181]

unworthy for what I call you to do, but it will never be your adequacy or worthiness that causes Me to use you. You must not look at your inadequacy, but look to My adequacy. You must stop looking at your own unworthiness and look to My righteousness. When you are used, it is because of who I am, not who you are.

"You did feel My anger as you began to look at yourself. This is the anger I felt toward Moses when he started to complain about how inadequate he was. This only reveals that you are looking to yourself more than to Me, which is the main reason why I am able to use so few of My people for what I desire to do. This false humility is actually a form of the pride that caused the fall of man. Adam and Eve began to feel inadequate and that they needed to be more than I had made them to be. They took it upon themselves to make themselves into who they should be. You can never make yourself into who you should be, but you must trust Me to make you into who you should be."

Although I had never related false humility to the fall of man in the Garden, I knew that this was a major stumbling block preventing many from becoming useful to the Lord, and I had taught on this many times. Now in His presence, my own false humility was revealed in me and looked even worse than I had ever seen it in anyone else. This form of pride was repulsive, and I could understand why it caused the anger of the Lord to burn. In His presence, all that we are is soon revealed, and even after all of the judgment I had just endured, I still had some of the most basic flaws that kept me from knowing Him and serving Him as I was called to do. As shocking as this was, I did not want to dwell on myself any longer, so I turned to look at Him, desiring to see as much of His glory as I could endure while He was with me in this way. Immediately, my gloom turned into ecstasy. My knees wanted to buckle, but I was determined to stand as long as I could.

Soon after, I awoke. I felt an energy surging through me for days afterward, making everything look glorious. I loved everything that I saw. A doorknob seemed wonderful beyond comprehension. Old houses and cars were so beautiful to me that I was sorry I was not an artist so I could capture their beauty and nobility. I could not look at anything without seeing magnificence, hardly believing that I had walked through my life missing so much. Trees and animals all seemed like very special, personal friends. Every person I saw was like a library of revelation and meaning. I was so thankful for eternity to get to know them all.

Yet, for all of this wonderful emotion and revelation I felt flowing through me, I did not know what to do with it. I knew if I did not learn how to use it for good that it would fade, which it did in just a few days. It was as if the meaning of life was slipping from me, and I knew that I had to recover it. What I had experienced was more wonderful than any drug, and I was addicted. This was the result of seeing His glory, and I had to see more. I desired to learn how to *abide* in His presence and to let this life flow through me in order to touch others. I had to abide in the Holy Spirit and let Him use me. This was my call.

Chapter II

Two
Witnesses

F or days I had been in a deep depression. Everything
seemed so bleak. Even the very sound of people
irritated me, and any disruption of what I wanted
to do angered me. I thought the worst of everyone and
had to fight to contain the black thoughts which arose in
me toward them. I felt as if I had slipped into hell and was
sliding deeper into it each day. Finally, I cried out to the
Lord, and almost immediately, I found myself standing in
front of the door with Wisdom standing next to me.

"Lord, I'm sorry. I slipped from Your presence all the
way into hell it seems."

"The whole world still lies in the power of the evil one," He
replied, *"and you walk on the edge of hell every day. Through
the midst of it there is a path of life. There are deep ditches on
either side of the path of life, so you must not deviate from the
narrow way."*

"Well, I fell into one of the ditches, and I could
not find my way out."

"No one can find his own way out of those ditches.

[184]

Following your own way is how you fall into them, and your own way will never lead you out. I am the only way out. When you fall, do not waste your time trying to figure everything out, for you will only sink deeper into the mire. Just ask for help. I am your Shepherd, and I will always help you when you call on Me."

"Lord, I don't want to waste time trying to figure everything out, but I would really like to understand how I fell so far so fast. What caused me to turn from the path of life and fall into the ditch like that? You are Wisdom, and I know that it is wisdom to ask."

"It is wisdom to know when to ask for understanding and when to just ask for help. Here, it is wisdom for you to ask. Only when you are in My presence can you understand. Your understanding will always be twisted when you are depressed, and you will never accurately see truth from that place. Depression is the deception that comes from seeing the world from your perspective. Truth comes from seeing the world through My eyes from where I sit, at the right hand of the Father. Like the cherubim in Isaiah 6:3, those who abide in My presence will say, 'The whole earth is filled with His glory.'"

I remembered how as a new believer I had read this text and actually thought that these cherubim were deceived. I could not understand how they could say *"The whole earth is filled with His glory,"* when the whole earth seemed to be filled with wars, disease, child abuse, treachery, and evil on every side.

Then the Lord had spoken to me one day and said, *"The reason these cherubim say that the whole earth is filled with My glory is because they dwell in My presence, and when you dwell in My presence you will not see anything but glory."*

"Lord, I remember You teaching me that, but I have not lived it very well. I have spent much of my life seeing things from the dark side. I guess I have spent much of my life sitting in one of those ditches beside the path of life rather than walking on it."

"That is true," the Lord responded. *"Every now and then you would get up and take a few paces, but then slide off into the ditch on the other side. Even so, you have made some progress, but now it is time for you to stay on the path. You do not have any more time to waste in those ditches."*

The Lord's kindness and patience seemed overwhelming as He continued.

"What caused you to slide into the ditch this last time?" He began.

After thinking about it, I could see that I had become consumed with maintaining the feeling rather than knowing the Source of the feeling.

"I took my eyes off of You," I confessed.

"I know it seems too simple, but this is all you did, and taking your eyes off of Me is all that you have to do to drift from the path of life. When you abide in Me, you will see nothing but glory. This does not mean that you will not see the conflicts, confusion, darkness, and deception in the world, but when you see them, you will always see My answer to them. When you abide in Me, you will always see how truth prevails over deception, and you will see the manner in which My kingdom will come."

"Lord, when I am here, this is all more real to me than anything I have experienced on earth, but when I am on the earth, all that is here seems like an unreal dream. I know this is the true reality and that earth is temporary. I also know that if this place were more real to me when I am on the earth, I would be able to walk in Your wisdom more and be able to stay on the path of life. You have said it is always wisdom to ask. I ask You to make this realm more real to me when I am on the earth. Then I will be able to walk more perfectly in Your ways. I also ask You to help me to convey this reality to others. The darkness is growing great on the earth, and there are few who have vision. I ask You to give us more of Your power, let us see more of Your glory, and let us know the true judgment that comes from Your presence."

"When you start to live by what you see with the eyes of your heart, you will walk with Me and you will see My glory. The eyes of your heart are your window into this realm of the Spirit. Through the eyes of your heart, you may come to My Throne of Grace at any time. If you will come to Me, I will be more real to you. I will also trust you with more power."

As He spoke, I was compelled to turn and look at the multitudes of kings, princes, friends, and servants of the Lord who were all standing in that great room. The wonder and glory of all that occurred there was so great that I would have been satisfied to stay forever. Again, I was astounded to think that this place was just the beginning of heaven. But even with all of its wonders, the real wonder of heaven was the presence of the Lord. Here, in the beginning of heaven, He was Wisdom and He was the Judge, which are the same.

"Lord," I inquired, "here You are Wisdom and the Judge, but how are You known in the other realms of heaven?"

"I AM Wisdom and I AM the Judge in every realm, but I AM also much more. Because you have asked, I will show

[187]

you who I AM. Even so, you have only begun to know Me as Wisdom and Judge. In due time, you will see more of Me, but there is more for you to learn about My judgments first."

THE FIRST WITNESS

"God's judgments are the first step into the heavenly realm," a voice which I had not heard before said, "When the Judgment Day comes, the King will be known to all, and His judgments will be understood. Then the earth will be set free. You asked for His judgments to come to your own life; now begin asking for them to come to the world."

I turned to see who had spoken. He was of great stature and brilliance, but a little less than the others I had met in the Hall of Judgment. I assumed that he was an angel, but then he said:

"I am Lot. You have been chosen to live in difficult times just as I was chosen. Just as Abraham lived and interceded for Sodom, you must do the same. During the time when great perversion is being released upon the earth, men and women of great faith will also arise. Like Abraham, you must use your faith to intercede for the wicked, and you must also witness the judgment of God coming upon the earth. The Lord cannot abide the increasing evil of man much longer. I was silent and many perished. You must not be like me—you must not be silent."

"Tell me more. How do I warn them?" I asked.

"I thought that I would be a warning just by being different. Being different is not enough! The power of the Holy Spirit to convict of sin is released by the spoken word. What the Lord did to Sodom, He did as an example so that others would not have to be destroyed in that way. You can warn those who are headed for destruction by telling them my story. There are now many cities whose evil He will not abide much longer. If those who know the Lord do not arise, there will be many more like Sodom very soon.

"The Judgment Day is coming. All of creation will then know the wisdom of His judgments, but you must not wait for that day. You must seek His judgments every day, and you must make them known on the earth. If His people will walk in His judgments, many on the earth will know of them before the great Day of Judgment. By this many more will be saved. It is His desire that none should be lost and that none of His people suffer loss on that day.

"The people of the earth are blind. They will not see if you simply try to be a witness. The message of judgment must go forth in *words*. The Holy Spirit anoints words, but the words must be spoken in order for Him to anoint them.

"Righteousness and justice are the foundation of His throne. His people have come to know something of His righteousness, but few know His justice. His throne will abide in His house; therefore judgment must begin with His own house.

"You must live by the truth that you have learned here, and you must teach it. His judgments are coming. If His people will walk in His judgments before the Judgment Day, then that day will be glorious for them. If they do not live by them, they, too, will know the sorrow the world is about to know. His judgments would not be true if they were not the same for all. Through you and others He will entreat His people again to judge themselves lest they be judged. Then you must entreat the world."

Then Lot directed me to look at the door before which I was standing. It still seemed dark and uninviting, like the doctrines of God's judgment, I thought. The glory of the Lord which surrounded us made it seem even more bleak. Even so, I now knew how glorious His judgment really is. I had also come to understand that almost every door that He leads us through looks bleak at first, and then becomes glorious. It almost seems that the bleaker the door looks, the more glorious it will be on the other side. Just passing through His doors takes faith, but then they always lead to more glory.

Lot continued with my train of thought. As I had already learned in this place, thoughts are broadcast to all.

"Through that door, you will experience more of His glory. His glory is not just the brilliance that you see around Him or in this place; nor is it just the feelings that you have while abiding in Him. His glory is also revealed through His judgments. This is not the only way that it is revealed, but it is in this way that you were called here to understand. Through that door, you will learn of another way to see His glory. It is by seeing His glory that His people will be changed, and He is about to show them His glory. When they see His glory, they will rejoice in all of His ways, even in His judgments."

The Second Witness

Then a second voice spoke: "I, too, confirm this truth. The judgment of God is about to be revealed on the earth. Even so, 'Mercy triumphs over judgment.' The Lord always extends mercy before judgment. If you will warn the people that His judgments are near, His mercy will save many."

I did not recognize the one speaking, but he was another man of great stature and nobility, with a brilliance that indicated a high rank.

"I am Jonah," he said. "When you understand the Lord's judgments, you understand His ways. However, even if you understand them, it does not mean that you agree with them. Understanding is necessary, but it is not enough. The Lord also wants you to agree with Him.

"You have often asked for the Lord's presence to go with you. That is wisdom. I was a prophet, and I knew Him, yet I tried to flee from His presence. That was a great folly but not as foolish as you may think. I had come to understand the great burning that comes with His presence. I had come to understand the responsibility that comes from being close to Him. In His presence, all wood, hay, and stubble is consumed. When you draw close to Him with hidden sin in your heart, it will drive you to insanity, as many have learned through the ages. I was not trying to flee from the will of the Lord as much as I was fleeing from His presence.

"When you ask for the reality of His presence, you are asking for the reality that you have seen here to be with you. Heaven is your true home, and it is right for you to yearn for this. Even so, He is a holy God, and if

[191]

you will walk closely with Him, you, too, must be holy. The closer you get to Him, the more deadly hidden sin can be."

"I understand this," I replied. "That is why I asked for the Lord's judgments in my own life."

"Now I must ask you this," Jonah continued. "Will you seek Him? Will you come to Him?"

"Of course," I responded. "I desire His presence more than anything. There is nothing greater than being in His presence. I know that many of my motives for wanting to be with Him are selfish, but being with Him helps to set me free from that kind of selfishness. I do want to be with Him. I will come to Him."

"Will you?" Jonah continued. "Until now you have been even more foolish than I was. You can come boldly before His Throne of Grace at any time and for any need, but rarely do you come. Yearning for His presence is not enough. You must come to Him. If you draw near to Him, He will draw near to you. Why do you not do this? You are always as close to Him as you want to be.

"Many have come to know His ways and follow His ways, but they do not come to Him. In the times that you will soon enter, they will depart from His ways because they did not come to Him. You have laughed at my folly, which was great, but yours is even greater than mine. However, I do not laugh at your folly—I weep for you. Your Savior weeps for you; He intercedes for you continually. When He weeps, all of heaven weeps. I weep because I know how foolish His people are. I know you because you are just like me, and like me, the church has run to Tarshish, desiring to trade with the world even more than sitting before His glorious throne. At the same time, the sword of God's judgments is hanging over the earth. I weep for the church because I know you so well."

"I am guilty!" I pleaded. "What can we do?"

"Great storms are coming upon the earth," Jonah continued. "I slept when the storm came upon the ship that I was in while running from the Lord. The church is also sleeping. I was the prophet of God, but the heathen had to wake me up. So it is with the church. The heathen have more discernment than the church at this time. They know when the church is going the wrong way, and they are shaking the church, trying to wake you up so that you will call on your God.

"Soon the leaders of the world will cast you overboard, just as the men in that ship had to do to me. They will not let you keep going in the way you are headed. This is the grace of God to you. He will then discipline you with a great beast that comes up out of the sea. It will swallow you for a time, but you will be vomited out of it. Then you will preach His message."

"Is there no other way?" I asked.

"Yes, there is another way," Jonah replied, "although this has come and is coming. Some are already in the belly of the beast. Some are about to be cast overboard, and some are still sleeping, but almost all have been on the ship going the wrong way, seeking to trade with the world. However, you can judge yourself, and He will not have to judge you. If you will wake yourself up, repent, and go the way that He sends you, you will not have to be swallowed by the beast."

"Is the beast which you are referring to the one in Revelation 13?" I asked.

[193]

"It is the same. As you read in that chapter, this beast is given to make war with the saints and to overcome them. This will happen to all who do not repent. But know that those who are overcome by this first beast will be vomited out of it before the next beast comes, the one who comes up out of the earth. Even so, it will be much easier for you if you repent. It is much better not to be swallowed by the beast.

"Just as Lot's story is a warning to those who are given over to perversion, my story is a warning to the Lord's prophet, the church. The church is running from the presence of the Lord. It is running to activity in place of seeking the Lord's presence. You may call your activity 'ministry,' but it is actually running from the presence of the Lord. As I have said, the church is running to Tarshish so that it can trade with the world and seek the treasures of the sea, while the greater treasures—the treasures of heaven—few are seeking.

"The sin of wanting to trade with the world has entangled the church, just as I was entangled in the belly of the beast with the weeds wrapped around my head. The weeds, the cares of the world, have wrapped themselves around the mind of the church. It took me three days to turn to the Lord because I was so entangled. It is taking Christians much longer. Their minds are so entangled with the world, and they have fallen to such depths, that many have no hope of getting free. You must turn to the Lord instead of away from Him. He can untangle any mess, and He can bring you up from the greatest depths. Run *from* Him no longer! Run *to* Him!"

Then Lot added, "Remember the mercy that the Lord had for Nineveh. He had mercy because Jonah preached. He did not live among them and try to be a witness: He preached the Word of God. Power is in the Word. There is no darkness so dark that His Word cannot penetrate it. Many will repent

[194]

and be saved if you will go to those to whom the Lord sends you and give His warning."

Then Jonah continued, "When you fall short of the Lord's grace and sin entangles you, it is hard for you to come to Him. You must learn to always run to the Lord at such times, not away from Him. When you go through that door, you will enter the times when the Lord's power and glory will be released on the earth such as He has not done since the beginning of time. All of heaven has been waiting for the things that you are about to see. It will also be the time of the greatest darkness. You cannot endure either the glory or the darkness without His grace. You will not walk in His ways without coming to Him daily. You must not only seek His presence, but abide in His presence continually.

"Those who have tried to follow Him by just seeking Him once a week in a church service, while they spend the rest of the week seeking the world, will soon fall away. Those who call upon His name, thinking that He is their servant, also will soon fall away. He is the Lord of all, and all will soon know this! First, His own people must know it, so the judgment is going to begin with His own household.

"It is presumption to only call upon the Lord when you want something. You should call on Him to ask what He wants, not what you want. Many of those who have some faith also have great presumption; the line between the two can be very thin. When God's judgments come to His own household, His people will learn the difference between faith and presumption. Those who try to do His work without Him will fall away. Many have faith in the Lord but only know Him from a distance. These do great works in His name, but He does not know them.

Those who have known Him from afar will soon weep over their folly.

"God does not exist for the sake of His house—His house exists for Him. In His patience, He has been waiting outside of His own house, knocking, calling, but few have opened to Him. Those who hear the Lord's voice and open to Him will sit with Him at His table. They will also sit with Him on His throne, and they will see the world as He sees it. Presumption cannot sit with Him at His table, nor on His throne. Presumption is the pride that caused the first fall, and all of the darkness and evil that is about to be reaped on the earth has come because of it.

"When Satan saw God's glory, he turned to the way of presumption. Satan dwelt in His presence and still turned from Him. This is the greatest danger for those who see His glory and know His presence. Do not become presumptuous because of what you have seen. Never become proud because of your visions: This will always lead to a fall."

MERCIFUL JUDGMENT

As Jonah spoke, each word was like a hammer blow. I was appalled at my sin. I was ashamed of the way I had thought of him, but, even more, I was ashamed of the way that I was so much like all of his ways which I had mocked. Even though I tried desperately to stand, my knees could not hold me up any longer, and I fell to my face. His words were like being flailed by a whip, but at the same time, the pain was welcome. I knew I needed to hear them, and I did not want Jonah to stop teaching me until all of my evil ways were exposed. The exposing power of the words was great, but it was much more than that. There was a power on them that made any excuse seem appalling. They passed every barrier and went straight to my heart. As I lay on the ground, I felt as if I were being operated on.

Then Lot interjected, "Many believers have made falling down in the Lord's presence frivolous and meaningless, but the church is about to fall under the same power that felled you—conviction. If you fall when you cannot stand, then your falling will result in your standing for truth."

Still, I did not want to move. I did not want to do anything until I had firmly grasped what Jonah had said. I did not want the conviction to go away until it had done its work. They seemed to understand because there was silence for a time, and then Lot continued.

"Jonah had the greatest preaching anointing yet given to a man. Without miracles or signs, when he preached, one of the most wicked cities that ever existed repented. If Jonah had preached in Sodom, that city would have remained until this day. The power of Jonah's preaching is a sign. When he awakened and was vomited out of the beast, he had this power. This is the power of preaching that will be given to the church in the last days. This is the power of conviction that the Lord is waiting to give His church. When she is vomited out of the beast who has swallowed her, even the most evil will listen to her words. This is the sign of Jonah that will be given to the church. The words of those who experience resurrection from the deep will have power."

I was still stunned. Even so, I was determined to run to the Lord and not away from Him, so I turned to look directly at Wisdom.

"Lord, I, too, can fall away in what is coming! I am guilty of all of these things. I have seen so much of Your glory, and still I fall to the traps and diversions that keep me from drawing close to You. Please help me in this. I desperately need Your wisdom, but I also need Your mercy. Please send mercy and help us before You send the judgment that we deserve. I ask for the mercy of the cross."

Wisdom answered, *"You will be given mercy because you have asked for it. I will give you more time. My mercy to you is time. Use this time wisely, for soon there will be no more. The time is near when I can delay no longer. Every day that I delay My judgment is mercy. See it as that and use it wisely.*

"I would always rather show mercy than judgment, but the end is near. The darkness is growing, and the time of great trouble will be upon you soon. If you do not use the time I give you, the coming troubles will overtake you. If you use the time I give you wisely, you will overcome and prevail. There is one characteristic common to the overcomers in every age—they did not waste their time!

"In My mercy, I am giving you this warning. Warn My people that in My mercy, I will no longer let them presume on My mercy. In My mercy, My discipline will be upon them. Warn them not to harden their hearts, but to repent and turn to Me.

"It is true that you, too, can fall away. Your love will grow cold, and you will deny Me if you do not deny yourself and take up your cross every day. Those who seek to save their own lives will lose them, but those who lose their lives for My sake will find true life. What I will give to My people will be a life of even more abundance than they have asked for, even in their presumption.

"When I have finished judging My own household, I will then send My judgments upon the whole earth. In My righteous judgment, I will show a distinction between My people and those who do not know Me. Now the whole world lies in the power of the evil one, and he rewards unrighteousness and resists the righteous. When the Judgment Day comes, the whole world will know that I reward righteousness and resist the proud.

"Righteousness and justice are the foundation of My throne. It is because of My justice that I discipline more severely those who know the truth but do not live by it. I have brought you here to see My judgments. You have gained understanding here, but this will be an even greater judgment to you if you do not walk in what you have seen. To whom much is given, much will be required. Here you have known the mercy of My judgments. If you continue to allow sin to entangle you, you will know the severity of My judgment. Many of My people still love sin. Those who love sin and their own comfort and prosperity more than Me will soon know My severity. These will not stand in the time that is coming.

"I will show severity to the proud and mercy to the humble. The greatest distraction of My people has not been the difficulties, but the prosperity. If My people would seek Me during times of prosperity, I could trust them with even more of the true wealth of My kingdom. I desire for you to have an abundance for every good deed. I want your generosity to overflow. My people will prosper in earthly riches in the time ahead, even in the times of trouble, but the riches will be from Me and not the prince of this present evil age. If I cannot trust you with earthly riches, how can I trust you with the powers of the age to come? You must learn to seek Me as much in prosperity as when you are in poverty.

[199]

All that I entrust to you is still Mine. I will only entrust more to those who are more obedient.

"Know that the prince of darkness also gives prosperity. He continues to make the same offer to My people as he made to Me. He will give the kingdoms of this world to those who bow down and worship him, who will serve him by living according to his ways. There is a prosperity of the world and there is the prosperity of My kingdom. The coming judgments will help My people to know the difference. The riches of those who have prospered by serving the prince of this evil age and using the ways of this evil age will be a millstone that hangs about their necks when the floods come. All will soon be judged by the truth. Those who prosper by Me do not compromise truth in order to prosper.

"My judgment begins with My household to teach you discipline so that you will walk in obedience. The wages of sin is death, and the wages of righteousness are peace, joy, glory, and honor. All are about to receive their worthy wages. This is the judgment, and it is justice that it begins with My own household."

Then Lot and Jonah spoke together, "Behold now the kindness and the severity of God. If you are going to know Him more, you are going to know both of these more."

Conviction was coming upon me like a cascade, but it was a cascade of living water. It was cleansing and refreshing, and it was difficult. I also knew that His correction would preserve me through what I was about to encounter after entering through the door. I desperately wanted all of the correction I could get before I entered it. I knew I would need His correction, and I was right.

CHAPTER III

The Path
of Life

I was pondering the things that had been spoken by
Lot and Jonah when the Lord began to speak.

*"You asked to know the reality of this place even as
you walk in the earthly realm. This is the reality for which
you asked—to see as I see. It is not this place that is the
reality. Reality is wherever I am. My presence gives any
place true reality and makes everything you look at seem
so alive because I am Life. My Father made Me the Life of
all creation, both in the heavens and on the earth. All of
creation exists through Me and for Me, and apart from Me,
there is no life and there is no truth.*

*"I am the Life that is in creation. I am even the Life
in My enemies. I AM. All that exists does so through Me. I
AM the Alpha and the Omega; I AM the Beginning and I
AM the End of all things. There is no truth or reality apart
from Me. It is not just the reality of this place that you seek,
but the reality of My presence. You seek the true knowledge
of Me, and this knowledge gives life. This reality is just as
available to you in the earthly realm as it is here, but you
must learn not to just look for Me, but at Me.*

[201]

"I am the power of God. I am the revelation of His glory. I am Life, and I am Love. I am also a Person. I love My people, and I want to be with them. The Father loves Me, and He also loves you. He loves you so much that He gave Me for your salvation. We want to be close to you. We love mankind and Our eternal dwelling place will be with them. Wisdom is knowing Me, knowing the Father, and knowing Our love. The light, the glory, and the power that I am about to reveal in the earth will be released through those who have come to know My love.

"My Father has entrusted Me with all power. I can command the heavens and they obey Me, but I cannot command love. Love commanded is not love at all. There will be a time when I demand obedience from the nations, but then the time to prove your love will have passed. While I am not demanding obedience, those who come to Me obey Me because they love Me and they love the truth. These are the ones who will be worthy to reign with Me in My kingdom, those who love Me and serve Me in spite of persecution and rejection. You must want to come to Me. Those who become Our dwelling place will not come because of a command or just because they know My power—they will come because they love Me and they love the Father.

"Those who come to the truth will come because they love Us and want to be with Us. It is because of the darkness that this is the age of true love. True love shines the brightest against the greatest darkness. You love Me more when you obey Me, even though your eyes do not see Me as they do now. Then you see Me with your heart. Love and worship will be greatest in the great darkness that is coming upon the earth. Then all of creation will know that your love for Me is true and why We desire to dwell with men.

"Those who come to Me now, fighting through all the forces of the world that now rebel against Me, come because they have the true love of God. They want to be with Me so much that even when it all seems unreal, even when I seem like a vague dream to them, they will risk all for the hope that the dream is real. That is love. That is the love of the truth. That is the faith that pleases My Father. All will bow the knee when they see My power and glory, but those who bow the knee now when they can only see Me dimly through the eyes of faith are the obedient ones who love Me in Spirit and in truth. These I will soon entrust with the power and glory of the age to come, which is stronger than any darkness.

"As the days grow darker upon the earth, I will show more of My glory. You will need this for what is coming. Even so, remember that those who serve Me even when they do not see My glory are the faithful, obedient ones to whom I will entrust My power. Obedience in the fear of God is the beginning of wisdom, but the fullness of wisdom is to obey because of your love for God. Then you will see the power and the glory.

"You are not here because of your faithfulness. Even the humility that caused you to pray for My judgments was a gift. You are here because you are a messenger. Because I have called you for this purpose, I gave you the wisdom to ask to know My judgments. It is wisdom for you to be faithful to what you see here, but the greatest wisdom is for you to come to Me every day. The more you come to Me, the more real I will be to you. I can be as real to you on the earth as I am to you now, and when you know the reality of My presence, you are walking in truth."

I AM

"Now you see Me as the Lord of Judgment. You must also see Me as the Lord of the Sabbath. I AM both. You must know Me as the Lord of Hosts and behold My armies, and you must see Me as the Prince of Peace. I AM the Lion of Judah, and I AM also the Lamb. To know My wisdom is also to know My times. You are not walking in wisdom if you are proclaiming Me to be the Lion when I want to come as the Lamb. You must know how to follow Me as the Lord of Hosts into battle, and you must know when to sit with Me as the Lord of the Sabbath. To do this you must know My times, and you can only know My times by staying close to Me.

"The coming judgment for those who call upon My name but do not seek Me will be that they will increasingly fall out of timing with Me. They will be at the wrong place, doing the wrong things and even preaching the wrong message. They will try to reap when it is time to sow, and sow when it is time to reap. Because of this they will bear no fruit.

"My name is not I WAS, nor is it I WILL BE, but I AM. To really know Me, you must know Me in the present. You cannot know Me as I AM unless you come to Me every day. You cannot know Me as I AM unless you abide in Me.

"Here you have had a taste of My judgments. You are about to see Me in other ways. You will not be able to fully know Me as I AM until you live in eternity. Here the different aspects of My nature all fit together perfectly, but they are hard to see when you are in the realm of time. This Great Hall reflects a part of Me that the world is about to see. This will be an important part of your message, but it will never be all of it. In one city, I will send My judgment, but in the next, I may send mercy. I will send famine to one nation and abundance to another. To know what I am

doing, you must not judge by appearances, but from the reality of My presence.

"In the times that are now coming upon the earth, if your love for Me is not growing stronger, it will grow cold. I AM Life. If you do not stay close to Me, you will lose the life that is in you. I AM the Light. If you do not stay close to Me, your heart will grow dark.

"All of these things you have known in your mind, and you have taught them. Now you must know them in your heart, and you must live them. The springs of life issue from the heart, not the mind. My wisdom is not just in your mind nor just in your heart. My wisdom is the perfect union of both mind and heart. Because man was made in My image, his mind and heart can never agree apart from Me. When your mind and heart agree, I will be able to trust you with My authority. Then you will ask what you will, and I will do it because you will be in union with Me.

"Because of the difficulty of the time in which you are called to walk, I have given you the experience of beholding My judgment seat before the appointed time of your judgment. Now your prayer has been answered. What you did not understand was that during the time when you were waiting for Me to answer this prayer, I was answering it every day through all that I allowed to happen in your life.

"It is better to learn of My ways and My judgments through the experiences of life than to learn of them in this way. I have given you this experience because you are a messenger and the time is short. You already knew what you have learned here, but you did not live by that knowledge. I have given you this experience as mercy, but you must choose to live by it.

[205]

"I will use many messengers to teach My people to live in righteous judgment so that they do not perish when My judgments come upon the earth. You must hear My messengers and obey their words that are from Me without delay, for the time is now short. To hear them without obeying will only bring a more severe judgment upon you. This is righteous judgment. To whom much is given, much will be required. .

"These are the times when knowledge increases. Knowledge of My ways is also increasing with My people. Your generation has been given more understanding than any other generation, but few are living by their understanding. The time has come when I will no longer tolerate those who say they believe Me but do not obey Me. The lukewarm are about to be removed from among My people. Those who do not obey Me do not really believe in Me. By their lives, they teach My people that disobedience is acceptable.

"Solomon wrote, **'Because the sentence against an evil deed is not executed quickly, therefore the hearts of the sons of men among them are given fully to do evil'** (Ecclesiastes 8:11). This has happened to many of My own people, and their love has been growing cold. My judgments are going to come more swiftly as grace to keep My own people's hearts from giving themselves fully to evil. My people are about to know that the wages of sin is death. They cannot continue to call on Me to deliver them from their troubles when they still love sin. I will give a little more time to judge yourself so that I will not have to judge you, but that time is short.

"Because you have been here, even more will be required of you. I will also impart more grace to you to live by the truth that you know, but you must come to My Throne of Grace *every day to get it. I say to you again, the time has come upon the earth when no one will be able to stand in truth without coming to My Throne of Grace each day. What I am about to tell you is so that you and those who are with you do not only live, but stand and prevail. As My people stand and prevail over the time of darkness that is coming, the creation will know that light is greater than darkness.*

"Life and death have been planted on the earth, and life and death are about to be reaped. I came to give you life. The evil one comes to give death. In the time ahead, both will be seen in their fullness. I will, therefore, give those who obey Me an abundance of life such as has never been seen on earth before. There will be a distinction between My people and those who serve the evil one. Choose life that you may live. Choose life by obeying Me. If you are choosing Me and the light that is in you is My true light, it will grow brighter every day. By this you will know that you are walking in My light. The seed that is planted in good soil always grows and multiplies: You will be known by your fruit."

Chapter IV

Truth
and Life

As the Lord spoke, His glory seemed to increase. It was so great that at times, I thought I was going to be consumed by it. His glory burned, but it was not like a fire; it burned from the inside out. I somehow knew that I would either be consumed by His glory or by the evil I would face after I went through the door. His words were penetrating and gripping, but I knew that it was even more important to behold His glory, so I was determined to do just that for as long as I could.

He appeared more brilliant than the sun. I could not see all of His features because of the brightness, but as I continued to look, my eyes adjusted some to His brilliance. His eyes were like fire but not red; they were blue, like the hottest part of the fire. They were fierce, yet they had the attraction of an endless wonder.

His hair was black and sparkled with what I thought at first were stars; I then realized that it glistened with oil. I knew this was the oil of unity, which I had seen in a vision before. This oil radiates like precious stones but is more beautiful and more valuable than any earthly treasure. As I looked at His face, I felt the oil begin to cover me, and as it did, the pain of the fire of His glory was more bearable. It seemed to impart peace and rest and only came upon me as I looked at His face. When I looked away from His face, it would stop.

I felt compelled to look at His feet. They also were like flames of fire but were more of a bronze or golden flame. They were beautiful but also fearsome, as if they were about to walk with the most fearful of strides. As I looked at His feet, I felt like an earthquake was going off inside of me, and I knew that as He walked, everything that could be shaken would be shaken. I could only stand it for a moment, and then I had to fall on my face.

When I looked up, I was looking at the door. Now it was even less attractive than before. At the same time, I felt a desperation to go through it before I would choose not to. It was my calling to go through the door, and to not go would be to disobey. In His presence, even the *thought* of disobedience seemed to be such a base selfishness, more repulsive than the thought of returning to the battle of the earthly realm.

As I looked at the door, I heard another voice begin to speak which I did not recognize. I turned to see who was speaking. He was one of the most naturally attractive people I had seen yet, regal and strong.

"I am Abel," he said. "The authority that the Lord is about to give His people is the anointing for true unity. When there were just two brothers on the earth, we could not live in peace with one another. From my time until yours, man has walked in the way of increasing darkness. Murder will be released on the earth as never before. Even your world wars were but birth pangs leading to what is to come. But remember this: Love is stronger than death. The love that the Father is about to give to those who serve Him will overcome death."

"Please, tell me everything that you have been given to tell me," I responded, knowing that he had much to say.

"My blood still speaks. The blood of every martyr still speaks. Your message will live on if you trust in the life that you have in God more than you trust in the life that you have on earth. Do not fear death, and you will overcome it. Those who do not fear death will have the greatest message during the time you are entering when death is released on the earth."

I thought of all of the wars, famine, and plagues that had come upon the earth just in my century. "How much more can death be released?" I asked.

Abel continued without answering me, which I understood to be the answer. "The blood sacrifice has already been made for you. Trust the power of the cross, for it is greater than life. When you trust the cross, you cannot die. Those on earth have power for a time to take your earthly life, but they cannot take your life if you have embraced the cross.

"A great unity will come to the Lord's people who dwell on the earth. This will take place when His judgments come upon the earth. Those who are in unity will not only endure His judgments but will prosper because of them. By this He will use His people to warn the earth. After the warnings, He will then use His people as a sign. Because of the discord and conflict that rises in the darkness, the unity of His people will be a sign that the whole earth will see. His disciples will be known by their love, and love does not fear. Only true love can bring true unity. Those who love will never fall. True love does not grow cold, but true love does grow."

LOVE RELEASES LIFE

Another man who looked almost exactly like Abel came and stood beside him.

"I am Adam," he said. "I was given authority over the earth, but I gave it to the evil one by obeying evil. He now rules in my place and your place. The earth was given to man, but the evil one has taken it. The authority I lost was restored by the cross. Jesus Christ is 'the last Adam,' and He will soon take His authority and rule. He will rule through mankind because He gave the earth to mankind. Those who live in your time will prepare the earth for Him to rule."

"Please tell me more," I asked, a little surprised to see Adam but wanting to hear everything he had to say. "How do we prepare for Him?"

"Love," he said. "You must love one another. You must love the earth and you must love life. My sin released the death that now flows as rivers upon the earth. Your love will release rivers of life. When evil reigns, death is stronger than life, and death prevails over life. When righteousness reigns, life prevails, and life is stronger than death. Soon the life of the Son of God will swallow up the death that was released through my disobedience. It is not just living that you must love, but life. Death is your enemy. You are called to be a messenger of life.

"When the Lord's people begin to love, He will use them to release His judgments. His judgments are to be desired. The whole world is groaning and travailing

[211]

as it waits for His judgments, and when they come, the world will learn righteousness. What He is about to do, He will do through His people, and His people will stand as Elijah in the last days. Their words will shut up the heavens or bring rain; they will prophesy earthquakes and famines, and they will come to pass; they will stop famines and earthquakes.

"When they release armies in the heavens, armies will march on the earth. When they hold back armies, there will be peace. They will decide where He shows mercy and where He shows His wrath. They will have this authority because they will love, and those who love will be one with Him. What you will see through that door is to help prepare you for what He is about to do through His people.

"I know authority. I also know the responsibility of authority. Because of the great authority that I was given, I am responsible for what has happened to the earth. Even so, the grace of God began to cover me, and God's great redemption will soon swallow up my mistake. Peace will be taken from the earth, but you are called to help restore it. Peace prevails in heaven, and you are called to bring heaven to earth. Those who abide in His presence will know peace and will spread peace.

"The earth itself will shake and tremble. Times of trouble greater than have ever been known will begin to move across the earth like great waves of the sea. Even so, those who know Him will not be troubled. They will stand before the raging of the seas and say, 'Peace, be still,' and the seas will be calm. Even the least of His little ones will be like great fortresses of peace that will stand through all that is coming. His glory will be revealed to His people first and then through them. Even the creation will recognize Him in His people and will obey them as it does Him.

"This is the authority that I had, and it will be given to mankind again. I used my authority to turn Paradise into a wilderness. The Lord will use His authority to turn the wilderness into Paradise again. This is the authority that He is giving to His people. I used mine wrongly and death came. When His authority is used in righteousness, it will release life. Be careful how you use authority. With authority comes responsibility. You, too, can use it wrongly, but you will not do this if you love. All of heaven knows, **'Love never fails'** **(see I Corinthians 13:8)**."

"What about the earthquakes, famines, and even wars that you said we would release on the earth? Won't this be releasing death?" I asked.

"All the death that is coming upon the world is being allowed to prepare the way for life. Everything that is sown must be reaped, unless those who have sown evil call upon the cross in Spirit and truth. The army of the cross is about to be released, and it will march in the power of the cross, carrying the offer of mercy to all. Those who reject the mercy of God have rejected life."

"That is a great responsibility," I said. "How do we know when they have rejected His mercy?"

"Disobedience brought death, and obedience will bring life. When I walked with God, He taught me His ways. As I walked with Him, I began to know Him. You must walk with God and learn of His ways. Your authority is His authority, and you must be one with Him in order to use it. The weapons of His army are not carnal—they are spiritual and much more powerful than any earthly weapons. Your most powerful weapons are truth and love. Even the final judgment of destruction is God's love extended in mercy.

"When truth spoken in love is rejected, death has been chosen over life. You will understand this as you walk with Him. You will come to understand the Spirit that He has given to you to bring life and not death. There is a time to give men over to reap what they have sown, but you must do all things in obedience. Jesus came to give *life*. He does not desire for any to perish, and this must be your desire also. For this reason, you must even love your enemies if you are to be trusted with the authority that He wants to give to His people.

"The time is at hand for the fulfillment of what has been written. His people have prayed for more time, and He gave it to them. However, few have used it wisely. You have a little more time, but soon the time can no longer be delayed. The time is near when time itself will seem to speed up. As it is written, when He comes, He will come quickly. However, you are not to fear the times. If you fear Him, you do not need to fear anything that is coming upon the earth.

"All that is about to happen is coming so that His wisdom can again prevail on earth just as it does in heaven. All of the evil that was sown in man is about to be reaped. Even so, the good that He has sown will also be reaped. Goodness is stronger than evil. Love is stronger than death. He walked the earth to destroy the works of the devil, and He will finish what He has begun."

POWER AND LOVE

As Adam talked, I was captured by his grace and dignity. I began to wonder if he had possibly lived his whole life after the Fall without sinning again because he seemed to be so pure. Knowing my thoughts, he changed the subject briefly to answer them.

[214]

"I lived long on the earth because sin did not have a deep root in me. Even though I had sinned, I was created to walk with God, and my desire was still for Him. I did not know the depths of sin that the following generations knew. As sin grew, life was shortened. But in every generation, those who walk with God touch the life that is in God. Because Moses walked so closely with God, he would have lived on had the Lord not taken him. Enoch walked with Him so closely that the Lord had to take him as well. That is why Jesus said, **'I am the resurrection and the life; he who believes in Me shall live even if he dies, and everyone who lives and believes in Me shall never die'** (see John 11:25-26).

"What you are seeing in me is not just the lack of sin, but the presence of life that I had on the earth. What we were on earth will remain a part of who we are forever. I can look at all of the others who are here that are a part of the great cloud of witnesses and know much about their lives on earth."

"So you are a part of the great cloud of witnesses?"

"Yes. My story is a part of the eternal gospel. My wife and I were the first to taste sin and the first to see our children reap the consequences of disobedience. We have beheld the death that spread through each generation, but we have also beheld the cross and seen the victory over sin.

"Satan has boasted since the cross that Jesus could redeem men but He could not change them. During the times of the greatest darkness and evil that are about to come, His people will stand as a testimony for all time that He not only redeemed His people from sin, but He also removed sin from them. Through them He will remove sin from the whole earth. He will now display to the whole creation the power of His new creation. He did not come just to forgive sin, but to save mankind from sin, and He is returning for a people who are without stain from the world. This will come to pass in the most difficult of times.

"I was created to love the Lord and to love the earth, as were all people. I have loathed the sight of the world's rivers becoming sewers. Even more have I loathed the sight of what has happened to the human mind. The philosophies of the human mind now filling the streams of human thought are as loathsome as the sewage filling the rivers. But the rivers of human thought will one day be pure again, just as the rivers of the earth. By this, for all time to come, it will be proven that good is stronger than evil.

"The Lord did not go to the cross just to redeem, but also to restore. He walked the earth as a man to show mankind how to live. He will now reveal Himself through His chosen ones to show them what they were created to be. This demonstration will not just come through power, but through love. He will give you power because He is all-powerful, and power is also a revelation of Him. Even so, He uses His power because of love, and so must you. Even His judgments come because of love. When you send them forth, it must be because of love. Even His final judgment of the earth will be His final mercy."

I looked at Adam, Abel, Lot, and Jonah as they stood together. I knew that it would take forever to understand the depths of the revelation of the great gospel of God that each of their lives represented. Adam's disobedience made the way for Abel's obedience, whose blood still speaks as a harbinger of salvation. Righteous Lot could not save his city, while an unrighteous Jonah could. Like the four Gospels, there seemed to be no end to the understanding that could be learned from them. This, too, was my call.

CHAPTER V

The Door

I tried desperately to absorb every word these men had spoken to me. Never had Wisdom said so much to me at once, yet I felt that every sentence was crucial, and I did not want to forget anything. I thought about how good it would be to have His words carved in stone like Moses had and to carry the words of the Lord to His people in such a way that they could be preserved untainted by me. Again knowing my thoughts, Wisdom answered them.

"That is the difference between the Old Covenant and the New. You will write My words in a book, and they will inspire My people. Even so, the true power of My words can only be seen when they are written in the hearts of My people. Living epistles are more powerful than letters written on paper or stone. Because you are not writing Scripture, the words you write will have you in them. Even so, your books will be as I desire them to be because I prepared you for this task. They will not be perfect because perfection will not come to the earth until I come. For perfection, men will have to look to Me. Even so, My people are the book that I am writing, and the wise can see Me in My people and in their works.

[217]

"My Father sent Me into the world because He loves the world, and I am sending My people into the world because I love the world. I could have judged the world after My resurrection, but the course of the world was allowed to continue so that My righteous ones could be proven and the power of what I did on the cross would be seen in man. I did this because of love. You are the witnesses of My love. This is My commandment to you: Love Me and love your neighbors. Only then will your witness be true. Even when I command you to speak of My judgments, it must be in love.

"The life of every person is in My book, and their life is a book that will be read by all of creation for all of eternity. The history of the world is the library of God's wisdom. My redemption is the demonstration of Our love, and the cross is the greatest love that the creation will ever know. Even the angels who stand before My Father so love the story of redemption that they, too, long to dwell with men. They marveled when We made man in our image. They marveled when men chose evil, even in the midst of the Paradise We made for man. Now, because of redemption, the marred image of God is restored and is now revealed even more gloriously in mankind. The glory is still in earthen vessels, which makes the glory easier to see for those who have eyes to see.

"This is the new creation that is greater than the first creation. Through My new creation, We are making a new Paradise that is greater than the first Paradise. Every man, woman, and child that embraces My redemption is a book that I am writing which will be read forever. Through the new creation, We will also restore the former creation, and it will be a Paradise again. I will restore all things, and all evil will be overcome with good.

"My church is the book that I am writing, and the whole world is about to read it. Until now, the world has wanted to read the book that the evil one has written about My church, but soon I will release My book.

"I am about to release My last-day apostles. I will have many like Paul, John, Peter, and the others. To prepare them, I am sending many like John the Baptist who will teach them devotion to Me and lay the foundation of repentance in their lives. These apostles will also be like the Baptist. Just as the chief joy of John's life was to hear the voice of the Bridegroom, these will have one devotion—to see My bride made ready for Me. Because of this, I will use them to build highways through the wilderness and rivers through the deserts. They will bring down the high places and raise up the lowly. When you go through that door, you will meet them.

"I am about to release My last-day prophets. They will love Me and walk with Me, even as Enoch did. They will demonstrate My power and prove to the world that I am the One true God. Each will be a pure well from which only living waters flow. At times, their water will be hot for cleansing; at times, it will be cold for refreshing. I will also give them lightning in one hand and thunder in the other. They will soar like eagles over the earth, but they will descend upon My people like doves because they will honor My family. They will come upon cities like whirlwinds and earthquakes, but they will give light to the meek and lowly. When you go through that door, you will also meet them.

"I am about to release My last-day evangelists. I will give them a cup of joy that will never run out. They will heal the sick and cast out devils; they will love Me and love righteousness; they will carry their crosses every day, not living for themselves but for Me. Through them, the world will know that I live and that I have been given all authority and power. These are the fearless ones who will attack the gates of the enemy and raid the dark places of the earth, leading many to My salvation. These, too, are just beyond that door, and you will meet them.

"I am about to release shepherds who will have My heart for the sheep. These will feed My sheep because they love Me. They will care for each of My little ones as if they were their own, and they will lay down their own lives for My sheep. This is the love that will touch men's hearts—when My people lay down their lives for one another. Then the world will know Me. I have given them choice food to serve My household. These are the faithful ones that I will trust to watch over My own house. These, too, are beyond that door, and you will meet them.

"I am about to release My last-day teachers upon the earth. They will know Me and teach My people to know Me. They will love the truth. They will not retreat before the darkness, but they will expose it and drive it back. They will unstop the wells that your fathers dug and serve the pure waters of life. They will also carry out the treasures of Egypt and use them to build My dwelling place. You will meet these, too, just beyond that door."

As the Lord spoke, I looked at the door. Now, for the first time, I wanted to go through it. Each word that He spoke brought a rising expectation in my heart, and I badly wanted to meet these last-day ministries.

"You have known in your heart for many years that these are coming. I have brought you here to show you how to recognize them and how to help them on their way."

I went through the door.

Chapter VI

The Prison

S uddenly, I was in another place. I was standing in a large prison yard. There were huge walls such as I had never seen before. They extended for as far as I could see, hundreds of feet high and very thick. There were other fences and razor wire in front of the wall. Every few hundred feet there were guard towers along the top of the wall. I could see guards in each one, but they were too far away for me to see much about them.

It was gray, dark, and dreary, which seemed to perfectly reflect the mass of people who stood in the prison yard. All over the yard, different people sat in groups of their own kind. Old black men were in one group, young black men in another. Old and young white men also stayed apart, and the women were also separated. With every race, this seemed to be the same. Those with any distinguishing characteristic were separated, except for the youngest children.

Between the groups, many people seemed to be milling around. As I watched, I could tell that they were trying to find their own identity by finding the group which they were the most like. However, it was obvious that these groups did not let anyone join them easily.

As I looked more closely at these people, I could see that they all had deep wounds and many scars from previous wounds. Except for the children, they all seemed to be nearly blind. They could only see well enough to stay in their own group. Even with their own groups, they were constantly trying to see the differences that others might have. When they found even a small difference, they would attack the one who was different. They all seemed hungry, thirsty, and sick.

I approached an older man and asked him why they were all in prison. He looked at me in astonishment, declaring emphatically that they were not in prison and that he wondered why I would ask such a stupid thing. I pointed at the fence and the guards, and he replied, "What fence? What guards?" He looked at me as if I had insulted him terribly, and I knew that if I asked him anything else, I would be attacked.

I then asked a young woman the same question and received the same response. I then realized that they were so blind that they could not even see the fence or the guards. These people did not know that they were in prison.

THE GUARD

I decided to ask a guard why these people were in prison. As I walked toward the fences, I could see holes in them that would be easy to climb through. When I reached the wall itself, I found it so irregularly built that it was easy for me to climb. Anyone could easily escape, but no one was trying because they did not know that they were captives.

When I got to the top of the wall, I could see for a great distance. I could also see the sun shining beyond the walls. It did not shine in the prison yard because of the height of the wall and the clouds that hung over it. I saw fires far off in the prison yard toward the end where the children were gathered. The smoke from these fires formed a thick cloud over the yard that turned what would have been just shade from the walls into a choking, dreary haze. I wondered what was burning.

I walked along the top of the wall until I reached the guard post. I was surprised to find the guard dressed in a fine suit with a collar indicating that he was some kind of minister or priest. He was not shocked to see me, and I think he assumed that I was another guard.

"Sir, why are these people in prison?" I asked.

That question shocked him, and I watched fear and suspicion come over him like a blanket.

"What prison?" he replied. "Who are you talking about?"

"I'm talking about those people in this prison yard," I said, feeling a strange boldness. "You're obviously a prison guard because you're in a guardhouse, but why are you dressed like that?" I continued.

"I am not a prison guard! I am a minister of the gospel. I am not their guard—I am their spiritual leader. Son, if you think your questions are funny, I'm not laughing! This is not a guardhouse—it is the Lord's house!" He grabbed his gun and seemed ready to shoot at me.

[223]

"Please excuse me for disturbing you," I replied, sensing that he would definitely use his gun.

As I walked away, I expected to hear shots at any moment. The man was so insecure I knew he would shoot before thinking if he felt threatened. I could also tell that he was sincere. He really did not know that he was a guard.

THE SCHOOL TEACHER

I walked along the wall until I felt I was a safe distance away and turned to look back at the minister. He was pacing back and forth in his guardhouse, greatly agitated. I wondered why my questions disturbed him so much. It was obvious that my questions did not open him to seeing anything differently, but rather made him even more insecure and more deadly.

As I walked, I felt a desperation to find out what was going on and I thought about how I could rephrase my questions so as not to offend the next guard I tried to talk to. As I approached the next guardhouse, I was again surprised by the appearance of the guard. It was not another minister, but a young lady who was about twenty-five years old.

"Miss, may I ask you some questions?" I inquired.

"Certainly. What can I help you with?" she said with a condescending air. "Are you the parent of one of these children?"

"No," I responded. "I'm a writer," which I somehow knew was the answer I should give to her. As I expected, this got her attention.

Not wanting to make the same mistake I had made with the minister by calling what he was standing in a "guardhouse," I asked the young lady why she was standing in that "place." Her response was immediate, and she seemed surprised that I did not know.

"I'm a school teacher, so don't you think it quite natural that I should be in my school?"

"So this is your *school?*" I replied, indicating the guardhouse.

"Yes. I've been here for three years now. I may be here the rest of my life. I love what I'm doing so much." This last remark was so mechanical that I knew I would discover something if I pressed her.

"What do you teach? It must be interesting for you to consider spending the rest of your life doing it."

"I teach general science and social studies. It is my job to shape the philosophy and worldview of these young minds. What I teach them will steer them for the rest of their lives."

"What do you write?" she inquired.

"Books," I responded, "I write leadership books," anticipating her next question. I also somehow knew that if I had said, "Christian leadership books," our conversation would have been over. She seemed even more interested after this answer.

"Leadership is an important subject," she stated, still with a slightly condescending air. "Changes are happening so quickly that we must have the right leadership tools to steer these changes in the right direction."

"What direction is that?" I asked.

"Toward the prosperity that can only come through peace and security," she replied, as if she were surprised that I would even ask such a question.

"I don't mean to offend you," I replied, "but I'm interested in your views on this. What do you feel is the best way for this peace and security to be achieved?"

"Through education of course. We are all together on this spaceship earth, and we have to get along. Through education, we are helping deliver the masses from their caveman, tribal mentality to understand that we are all the same and that if we all do our part for society, we will all prosper together."

"That's interesting," I replied, "but we are not all the same. It's also interesting that all of the people down there are becoming even more divided and separated than ever. Do you think that it may be time to possibly modify your philosophy a bit?"

She looked at me in both amazement and agitation but obviously not because she even considered for a moment that what I said was true.

"Sir, are you completely blind?" she finally responded.

"No, I believe I see quite well," I answered. "I have just come from walking among the people, and I have never seen such division and animosity between different people groups. It seems to me that the conflict between different people groups is worse than ever."

I could tell that my statements were like slaps in the face to this young lady. It was as if she just could not believe someone was even saying these things, much less believe that there was a chance there might be some truth to them. As I watched her, I could tell that she was so blind that she could barely see me. She was in such a high tower that there was no way that she could see the people below. She really did not know what was going on, but sincerely thought that she could see everything.

"We are changing the world," she said with obvious disdain. "We are changing people. If there are still people acting like beasts such as you described, we will change them, too. We will prevail. Mankind will prevail."

"That is quite a responsibility for someone so young," I remarked.

She bristled even more at that statement, but before she could respond, two women appeared and were walking toward the door of the guardhouse along the top of the wall. One was a black woman who appeared to be in her fifties, and the other was a very well-dressed white woman who was probably in her early thirties. They talked with each other as they walked, and both appeared confident and dignified. I could tell that they could see, which is obviously how they got to the top of the wall.

To my surprise, the young school teacher grabbed her gun and stepped outside of the guardhouse to meet them, obviously not wanting these women to get any closer. She greeted them with a very superficial cheerfulness and with an obvious air of superiority that she seemed to want to impress on them. To my surprise, the two women became timid and overly respectful of one who was so much younger.

"We've come to ask about something our children are being taught that we do not understand," the black woman stated, mustering some courage.

"Oh, I'm sure that a lot is now taught that you do not understand," the teacher replied, condescendingly.

The women kept looking at the teacher's gun which she kept handling in such a way so that they would constantly be aware of it. I was standing close by, amazed by this whole scene. The teacher turned and looked at me nervously. I could tell that she was afraid I might say something to the women. As she fingered the gun, she demanded that I leave. The women looked up to see who she was talking to, and I realized that they could not see me. Their fear had blinded them.

I called out to the women, entreating them to have courage and believe what they felt in their hearts. They looked in my direction as if they could only hear noise. They were losing their ability to hear as well. Seeing this, the young teacher smiled. She then aimed her gun at me and blew a whistle. I felt as if she perceived me to be the most dangerous person alive.

I knew that I could not wait for whomever she had called with her whistle. I also realized that if I just stepped back a little, I would be safe because this young teacher was so blind. I was right. I walked away with her screaming, blowing her whistle, and finally becoming so enraged that she began to shoot at the two women.

As I stood on top of the wall between two guard posts wondering about all of this, I felt the presence of Wisdom.

"You must return to the prison yard. I will be with you. Know that you have the vision to escape any trap or weapon. Only remember that fear can blind you. As you walk in the faith that I am with you, you will always see the way to go. You must also be careful to reveal your vision only to those to whom I lead you. Vision is what the guards fear the most. I know you want to ask Me a lot of questions, but they will be better answered by the experiences you will have there."

Chapter VII

The Young Apostle

I climbed down and began to walk through the yard. As I passed by the prisoners, they seemed almost completely disinterested in me and all of the commotion on the wall. I then remembered that they could not see that far. A young black man stepped onto my path and looked at me with bright, inquisitive eyes.

"Who are you?" we both said at the same time.

As we stood looking at each other, he finally said, "My name is Stephen. I can see. What else do you want to know about me that you do not already know?"

"How could I know anything else about you?" I inquired.

"The One who helped me to see said that one day others would come who were not prisoners. They would also be able to see, and they would tell us who we are and how we can escape from this prison."

I started to protest that I did not know who he was when I remembered what Wisdom had told me about those whom I would meet when I passed through the next door.

[229]

"I do know you, and I know some things about you," I acknowledged, "but I confess that this is the weirdest prison I have ever seen."

"But this is the only prison!" he protested.

"How do you know if you have been here all of your life?" I asked.

"The One who helped me to see told me that it was. He said that every soul who had ever been imprisoned was held captive here. He always told me the truth, so I believe this."

"Who is the One who helped you to see?" I asked, not only wanting to know who had helped him to see, but also interested in how this was the prison that held every soul captive.

"He never told me His real name but just called Himself 'Wisdom.'"

"Wisdom! What did He look like?" I questioned.

"He was a young, black athlete. He could see better than anyone and seemed to know everyone here. It is strange, though. I have met others here who said that they have also met Wisdom, but they all described Him differently. Some said that He was white, and others said that He was a woman. Unless there are many 'Wisdoms,' He is a master of disguise."

"Can you take me to Him?" I asked.

"I would, but I have not seen Him for a long time now. I am afraid that He has left or maybe even died. I have been very discouraged since He departed. My vision even started getting worse until I saw you. As soon as I saw you, I knew that everything He told me was true. He said that you knew Him, too, so why are you asking me so much about Him?"

"I do know Him! And be encouraged—your Friend is not dead. I will tell you His real name, too, but first I must ask you a few questions."

"I know you can be trusted, and I know that you and others like you who are coming will want to meet everyone who can see. I can take you to some of them. I also know that you and the others are coming to help a lot of these other prisoners to see. I am surprised by one thing though."

"What is that?"

"You're white. I never thought that the ones who came to help us see and be set free would be white."

"I am sure that there are many others coming who are not white," I responded. "I can tell that you already have considerable vision and intelligence, so I know you can understand what I am about to say."

THE VALUE OF VISION

As I looked at Stephen to be sure he was listening, I was moved by how open and teachable he was, in striking contrast to the teacher who had been about his same age. *This man will be a true teacher,* I thought as I continued.

"When we get to the place of ultimate vision, we will not judge people by the color of their skin, gender, or age. We will not judge others by appearances, but after the Spirit."

"That sounds like what our teachers used to tell us," Stephen responded, a little surprised.

"There is a difference though," I continued. "They tried to make you think that we are all alike, but we were

[231]

created different for a reason. True peace will only come when we respect the distinctions we have. When we really know who we are, we will never be threatened by those who are different. When we are free, we are free to show those who are different from us honor and respect, always seeking to learn from one another, just as you are now doing with me."

"I understand," Stephen replied. "I hope I didn't offend you by saying that I was surprised you were white."

"No, I was not offended. I understand. I am encouraged that you were able to recognize me in spite of the color of my skin. But remember, every time we open our hearts to learn from those who are different, our vision will increase. Your eyes are already brighter than when we first met."

"I was just thinking about how quickly my vision is being restored," Stephen remarked.

"I now know why I am here," I added. "You must keep in mind that your vision is your most valuable possession. Every day you must do that which will help to increase your vision. Stay away from the people and things that make you lose your vision."

"Yes, like getting discouraged."

"Exactly! Discouragement is usually the beginning of the loss of vision," I said. "To accomplish our purposes, we must resist discouragement in any form. Discouragement blinds."

"When I began to see, I started to feel that I had a purpose, maybe even an important one," Stephen continued. "Can you help me to know what my purpose is?"

"Yes, I think I can. To know our purpose is one of the greatest ways that our vision grows. It is also one of our greatest defenses against things like discouragement, which will destroy vision. I think my main purpose here is to help you and the others whose vision is being restored to know your purposes. But first we need to talk about something even more important."

BURIED TREASURE

When Stephen spoke, I could hear the voice of Wisdom, so I knew that he had been taught by the Lord. I also knew that he did not know the Lord's name and would have difficulty believing that Wisdom's name was Jesus. I knew that I would need wisdom just to share the name of Wisdom. I thought about the apostles, prophets, evangelists, pastors, and teachers whom Wisdom said I would meet when I went through that door. I never dreamed that I would meet them in a place like this. As I looked out over the great mass of people, I felt His presence. He was with me, and even in the gloom of this terrible prison, excitement was welling up in me. *This is what I have been prepared for,* I thought.

"Stephen, what do you see when you look at this great mass of people?" I asked.

"I see confusion, despair, bitterness, and hatred. I see darkness," he replied.

"That is certainly true, but look again with the eyes of your heart. Use your vision," I responded.

He looked for a long time and then said with some hesitation, "I now see a great field with buried treasure in it. The treasure is everywhere and in almost every form."

"That is right," I responded. "This is also a revelation of your purpose. You are a treasure hunter. Some of the

[233]

greatest souls who ever lived are trapped here, and you will help find them and set them free."

"But how will I find them, and how will I set them free when I am not even free?"

"You already know how to find them, but it is true that you will not be able to set them free until you are free. That is your next lesson. You must also remember that you will always know your purpose in a situation by seeing with the eyes of your heart. What you see from your innermost being will always reveal your purpose."

"Is that how you knew I am to be a treasure hunter?"

"Yes. But you must be free before you can become who you were created to be. Why haven't you escaped through those holes in the fence?" I asked.

"When I first began to see, I saw the fences and the wall. I also saw the holes in the fences and have gone through them. When I got to the wall, I tried several times to climb it, but fear would overcome me because I am afraid of heights. I also thought that if I got over the wall, I would be shot."

"Those guards cannot see nearly as well as you think," I replied. "They are almost as blind as the people here."

This seemed to really surprise Stephen, but I could also tell that it opened his eyes even more.

"Can you see the top of the wall?" I asked.

"Yes, I can see it from here."

"I want you to remember this," I continued. "I have now been in many places. Call them different worlds or realms if you will. There is one important principle that I have found to be true in every place, and you must remember it for the rest of your life."

[234]

"What is it?"

"You can always go as far as you can see. If you can see the top of the wall, you can get there. When you get to the top of the wall, you will be able to see farther than you have ever seen before. You must keep going for as far as you can see. Never stop as long as you can still see farther."

"I understand," he replied immediately. "But I'm still afraid to climb that wall. It's so high! Is it safe?"

"I will not lie to you and tell you it's safe, but I know that it is much more dangerous not to climb it. If you do not use your vision by walking in what you see, you will lose it. Then you will perish here."

"How will I seek out the treasure that is here if I leave?"

"That is a good question, but it is also one which keeps many from fulfilling their purposes. I can only tell you now that you have a great journey you must complete first. At the end of your journey, you will find a door leading you back to this prison, just as I found. When you return, your vision will be so great that they will never be able to trap you here again. Your vision will also be great enough to see the treasure that is here."

CHAPTER VIII

The Light

Stephen turned and looked again at the wall. "I still feel great fear," he lamented. "I don't know if I can do it."

"You have vision, but you lack faith. Vision and faith must work together," I said. "There is a reason why your faith is weak."

"Please tell me what it is! Is there something that will help my faith to grow as my vision increases?"

"Yes. Faith comes from knowing who Wisdom really is. You must know His true name. Just knowing His name will give you enough faith to get you over that wall to freedom. The better you get to know His name, the greater the obstacles and barriers you will be able to overcome on your journey. One day you will know His name well enough to move any mountain."

"What is His name?" Stephen almost begged.

"His name is Jesus."

Stephen looked at the ground and then up in the air as disbelief seemed to come over him. I watched as the struggle went on between his heart and his mind. Finally he looked at me again, and to my great relief, he still had hope in his eyes. I knew that he had listened to his heart.

"I suspected it," he said. "In fact, the whole time you were talking, I somehow knew you were going to say that. I also know you are telling me the truth. But I have some questions. May I ask them?"

"Of course."

"I have known many people who use the name of Jesus, but they're not free. In fact, they are some of the most bound people I know here. Why?"

"That is a good question, and I can only tell you what I have learned on my own journey. I think every case is different, but there are many who know His name but do not know *Him*. Instead of drawing closer to Him and being changed by seeing Him as He is, they try to make Him into their image. Knowing the name of Jesus is much more than just knowing how to spell it or say it. It is knowing who He really is. That is where true faith comes from."

I could still see doubt in Stephen's eyes, but it was the good kind of doubt—the kind that wanted to believe rather than the kind that wanted to disbelieve. I continued.

"There are others who really love Him and start to sincerely get to know Jesus, but they also remain prisoners. These are the ones who let the wounds or mistakes suffered on the journey turn them back. These have tasted freedom, but they returned to prison because of disappointments or failures. You can easily recognize them because they are always talking about the past instead of the future. If they were still walking by their vision, they would not always be looking backwards."

"I have met many of those," Stephen remarked.

"You need to understand something if you are ever going to have this question answered. If you are going to fulfill your destiny, you cannot be overly discouraged or encouraged by others who use the name of Jesus. We are not called to place our faith in His people, but in Him. Even the greatest souls will disappoint us at times because they are still human.

"Many who are like those I just described can also become great souls. Vision and faith can be restored, even in those who have become the most discouraged and disappointed. As a treasure hunter, this is your job. We cannot discard any human being—they are all treasures to Him. However, to really get to know Him and walk in true faith, you must not judge Him by His people, either the best or the worst."

"I always thought of Jesus as the white man's God. He never seemed to do much for our people."

"He is not a white man's God—He was not even white Himself! But neither is He a black man's God. He created all, and He is the Lord of all. When you start to see Him as the God of any one group, you have greatly reduced who He is, and you have greatly reduced your own vision."

FAITH AND OBEDIENCE

I watched silently as Stephen wrestled with many other things in his heart. I continued to feel the presence of Wisdom, and I knew that He would explain all things much better than I could. Finally, Stephen looked up at me with the light shining brighter than ever in his eyes.

"I know that all of the questions I have been wrestling with do not have anything to do with who Jesus really is, but who people have said He is. I know what you're saying is true. I know that Jesus is the One who gave me vision and that He is Wisdom, and I must find out for myself who He really is; I must seek Him, and I must serve Him. I also know that He has sent you here to help me get started. What do I do?"

"Wisdom is here now," I began. "You heard Him when I spoke, just as I heard Him speaking through you. You already know His voice. He is your Teacher. He will speak to you through many different people, sometimes even through those who do not know Him. Be quick to hear and obey what He says. Faith and obedience are the same. You do not have true faith if you do not obey, and if you have true faith, you will always obey.

"You said you will serve Him. This means that you will no longer live for yourself, but for Him. In the presence of Wisdom, you know the difference between what is right and what is wrong. When you come to know Wisdom, you also understand what is evil. You must renounce the evil that you have done in the past, as well as that which comes to tempt you in the future.

"You cannot live as others do. You are called to be a soldier of the cross. When you embraced His name, embracing the truth of who He is, when that great light came into your eyes and when the peace and satisfaction began to flood your soul just a few moments ago, you were born again and began a new life. Wisdom has been

[239]

speaking to you for some time, guiding you and teaching you, but now He lives *in* you. He will never leave you again. But He is not your servant; you are His."

"I do feel Him!" Stephen acknowledged. "But how I would love to see Him again!"

"You can see Him with the eyes of your heart at any time. This is also your call—to see Him more clearly and to follow Him more closely. That is what the journey is for. On your journey, you will learn about His name and the power of the cross. When you have been trained, you will return here in that power, and you will help to set many of these captives free."

"Will you still be here?"

"I do not know. Sometimes I will have work to do here, and sometimes I will have work to do helping others on their journeys. I might meet you again out there where you are going. I am also still on my own journey. This is part of it. On your journey, there will be many doors that you must go through. You never know where they are going to lead. Some may bring you back here. Some may take you into the wilderness, which all must go through. Some lead to glorious heavenly experiences, and it is tempting to always look for those doors, but they are not always the ones that we need to help us fulfill our destiny. Do not choose doors by their appearance, but always ask Wisdom to help you."

Stephen turned his gaze upon the wall. I watched a smile appear.

"I can climb that wall now," he said. "I even look forward to the challenge. I must admit that I still feel the fear, but it does not matter. I know I can climb it, and I cannot wait to see what is behind it. I know I'm free. I am no longer a prisoner!"

I walked with Stephen to the first fence. He was surprised to discover that there were not only holes in it, but that wherever he touched the fence, it would fall apart in his hand, making other holes.

"What are these fences made of?" he asked.

"Delusions," I explained. "Every time someone escapes through them, a hole is made for others to go through. You can go through the holes that are already here or make one yourself."

Stephen chose a place thick with barbed wire, stretched out his arms, and walked straight into it, opening a large hole as he went. I knew that he would one day return here and lead many others out through the hole he was now making. Watching him was sheer joy. I felt the presence of Wisdom so strongly that I knew I would see Him if I turned around. I did, and I was right. The great joy I was experiencing could be seen on His face as well.

Chapter IX

Freedom

A s I stood next to Wisdom, watching Stephen walk through the fences, Stephen called out, "What is the wall made of?"

"Fear."

I watched Stephen stop and look at the wall. It was huge. I knew that many never made it past the fences, and I knew that this was a crucial test for Stephen.

Without looking back, he called out again, "Will you help me climb it?"

"I can't help you," I responded. "If I try to help you, it will only take you twice as long and be even harder. To conquer your fears, you must face them alone."

"The more I look up at it, the worse it looks," I heard Stephen whisper to himself.

"Stephen, you have made your first mistake."

"What did I do?" he cried out dejectedly, already full of fear.

"You stopped."

"What do I do now? I feel like my feet are too heavy to move."

"Look at the hole you made in the fences," I said. "Now look at the top of that wall and start walking. When you get to the wall, keep going. Do not stop to rest. There is no rest to be found by hanging on the side of that wall, so just keep going until you get to the top."

To my great relief, he started moving forward again. He was going much slower, but he was moving. When he got to the wall, he began to climb, slowly but steadily. When I knew he was going to make it, I went to the wall and quickly climbed it so I could meet him on the other side.

I knew Stephen would be thirsty, so I waited for him by a stream. When he got there, he was a little surprised but very glad to see me. I was just as surprised to see the change in him. Not only were his eyes shining more brightly and clearly than ever, but he walked with a confidence and nobility which was stunning. I had seen him as a soldier of the cross, but I had not seen him as the great prince he obviously was called to be.

"Tell me about it," I said.

"It was so hard to start walking again and then to keep walking; I knew that if I ever stopped, it might be too hard to ever start again. I thought about the ones you told me about, the ones who knew the name of the Lord but had never climbed that wall to walk in faith in His name. I knew that I could become one of them. I decided that even if I fell, even if I died, I would rather die than stay in that prison. I would rather die than not see what is on this side and not make the journey that I am called to make. It was hard, even harder than I thought, but it is already worth it."

[243]

"Here, drink from this stream. You will find all of the water and food that you need on the journey. It will always be there when you really need it. Let the hunger and thirst keep you moving. When you find the refreshments, rest for as long as they last, and then keep going."

He drank quickly and then stood up, anxious to keep going.

"I will not see you again for a time, so there are a few things that I must tell you now that will help you on the journey."

Stephen looked at me with a focus and brightness that was marvelous. *Those who have known the greatest bondage will love liberty the most*, I thought. I directed him to look at the highest mountain we could see.

"You must now climb that mountain. When you get to the top, you must look as far as you can see. Mark well what you see and look for the path that will lead you there. Make a map of the way in your mind. That is where you are called to go."

"I understand," he replied. "But can it be seen from one of these lower mountains? I'm no longer afraid of climbing, but I am anxious to get on with the journey."

"You can see places from these lower mountains and get to those places much faster. You could choose to do that. It will take longer and be much harder to climb that high mountain, but from there you will be able to see much farther and see something much greater. The journey from the high mountain will also be more difficult and take longer. You are free, and you can choose either journey."

"You always take the highest mountain, don't you?" Stephen asked.

"I know now that it is always the best, but I cannot say that I have always chosen the highest mountain. I have often chosen the easiest, quickest way, and I was always sorry when I did. I now believe that it is wisdom to always choose the highest mountain to climb. I know that the greatest treasure is always at the end of the longest, most difficult journey. I think you, too, are that kind of treasure hunter. You have overcome great fear. Now is the time to walk in great faith."

"I know what you are saying is true, and I know in my heart that I must climb the highest mountain now, or I will always choose that which is less than I could have had. I am just so anxious to get going and arrive at my destination."

"Faith and patience go together," I responded. "Impatience is really a lack of faith. Impatience will never lead you to the highest purposes of God. Good can be the greatest enemy of best. Now is the time to establish a pattern in your life of always choosing the highest and best. This is the way to remain close to Wisdom."

"What else are you supposed to tell me before I go?" Stephen asked, sitting on a rock, wisely choosing to be patient and receive all he needed to know before he left. I thought that he might already know Wisdom better than I did.

A WARNING

"There is another wisdom that is not the wisdom of God, and there is another one who calls himself 'wisdom.' He is *not* wisdom; he is our enemy. He can be difficult to recognize because he tries to appear as Wisdom, and he

[245]

is very good at it. He comes as an angel of light, and he usually brings truth. He will have a form of truth, and he has wisdom, but it has taken me a long time to be able to distinguish him from *the* Truth and *the* Wisdom. I have learned that I can still be fooled by him if for one moment I start to think that I can't. Wisdom has told me that we can never outsmart the enemy—our defense is to learn to first recognize and then resist him."

Stephen's eyes were wide as that "knowing" look came over him. "I know who you're talking about!" he interjected. "I met a lot of people in the prison who followed that one. They were always talking about a higher wisdom, a higher knowledge. They always seemed like noble, fair people, but they felt foul. Whenever I told them about Wisdom, they said that they knew wisdom, too, and that he was their 'inner guide.' However, when I listened to them, I did not feel I was being led to freedom like they said, but rather to an even stronger bondage in that prison. I just felt darkness around them, not like the light I felt when I talked with Wisdom. I knew they were not the same."

"The true Wisdom is Jesus. You know this now. True wisdom is to seek Him. Any wisdom that does not lead you to Jesus is a false wisdom. Jesus will always set you free. The false 'wisdom' will always lead you to bondage. However, true freedom often looks like bondage at first, and bondage usually looks like freedom at first."

"It's not going to be easy, is it?" Stephen lamented.

"No. It is not going to be easy, and it is not supposed to be. Suspicion is not the same as true discernment, but if you are going to suspect anything, suspect anything that seems easy. I have not yet found 'easy' through any door or on any path that has been right. Taking the easy way may be the surest way to be misled. You have been called as a soldier, and you are going to have to fight. Right now the whole world is in the power of the false 'wisdom,' and you will have to overcome the world to fulfill your destiny."

"Already I have had to do things that were harder than anything I have ever done before," Stephen reflected. "You are right—it is hard, but it is worth it. I have never known such joy, such satisfaction, such hope. Freedom is hard. It is hard to have to choose which mountain I climb. Back there, I knew I could have chosen not to climb that wall. I felt like the fear of making that choice was the wall inside of me. But once I had made the choice, I knew I would make it over the top. But does it ever get easier?"

"I don't think so, but somehow 'hard' gets to be more fulfilling. There can be no victory without a battle, and the greater the battle, the greater the victory. The more victories you experience, the more you start to look forward to the battles, and you rise even higher to the bigger ones. What makes it easy is that the Lord always leads us to victory. If you stay close to Him, you will never fail. After every battle and every test, you will be much closer to Him and know Him much better."

"Will I always feel that darkness when the false 'wisdom' tries to mislead me?"

"I don't know. I do know the darkness comes when he deceives us into self-seeking. When he deceived the first man and woman into eating from the Tree of the Knowledge of Good and Evil, the first thing they did was to look at themselves. Once the false 'wisdom' can make us self-centered, our fall into bondage is sure. The deceiver always tries to get you to seek yourself. The call to fulfill our destinies is not for our sakes, but for the Lord's sake and for the sake of His people."

"Has anyone ever made it to his destiny without being tricked?"

"I don't think so. Even the great Apostle Paul admitted to having been foiled by Satan. Peter was tricked a few times, which were recorded in Scripture, and we do not know how many other times that were not recorded. But don't be overly concerned about being deceived. That is actually one of his biggest traps. He sidetracks many by having them fear his power to deceive rather than having faith in the power of the Holy Spirit to lead them into all truth. Those who have fallen into this trap not only fall into increasing bondage to fear, but will attack anyone who begins walking in the freedom that comes with faith. I am quite sure you will not make it far up that mountain before they ambush you."

"And they know the name of Jesus?" Stephen asked, a little confused. "They must have known His name to get over that wall and to have gone that far. I mean, didn't they really know His name once?"

"I'm sure they did. But stand and look throughout the valley ahead around every mountain. What do you see?"

"It looks like little prisons. It looks like there are many just like the one I came out of!"

"That's why I was surprised when you told me that Wisdom had said this was the only prison, but after I was there for just a little while, I understood what He meant. They are all the same. Look at the high walls. Look at the fences. They're all the same. If you get captured along the way, they will not bring you back here. They know you would choose death over that, but they will take you to one of the other prisons. When you get close to them, it is hard to see that they are prisons from the outside, but inside they are all the same, with people divided, imprisoned by their fears."

"I'm glad you showed them to me," Stephen offered. "I did not even see the prisons when I was looking this way from the top of the wall or when I was looking for the mountain I am to climb. And you think I will be ambushed many times by those who will try to capture me and put me in one of them? And these people will be using the name of Jesus?"

"The Lord Himself warns in Scripture that in the last days many will come in His name, claiming that He is indeed the Christ, and yet they will deceive many. Believe me, there are many like that, and I do not believe that most of them know they are deceivers. I can tell you a characteristic I have seen in all those whom I have met—they quit while on their journeys, stopping short of their destinies. It takes faith to keep going, and they chose to follow fear rather than faith. Then they begin to think that fear is faith and actually see the walls of fear around their prisons as strongholds of truth. Fear will do this to your vision, and you can start to see strongholds that way. Few of these people are really dishonest. They are sincere, but they are deceived by one of the most powerful deceptions of all, the fear of deception."

"Should I fight them?"

"I understand your question and have asked it many times myself. They destroy the faith of so many and do far more damage to the sojourners than all of the cults and sects combined. There will be a time when all such stumbling blocks will be removed, but for now they, too, are serving a purpose by making the way harder."

"Wisdom wants it to be harder? It is already so difficult just battling our own fears. Why does He want to make it harder by making us battle all of these fearful people as well?"

"The journey will be exactly as easy or hard as He wants it to be. This life is a temporary journey used to prepare those who will reign with Him over the age to be sons and daughters of the Most High forever. Every trial is for the purpose of changing us into His image. One of the first things we must learn on this journey is not to waste a single trial, but to seize them as the opportunities they are. If your path is more difficult, it is because of the high calling."

THE NECESSITY OF DISCIPLINE

"Many are called, but few are chosen. Many will come to the wedding feast, but few will be the bride."

We both turned to see Wisdom standing behind us. He appeared as the young athlete that Stephen had come to know.

"Run the race that is set before you, and the prize will be greater than you can understand at this time. You know the discipline that it takes to prepare for the race. Now discipline yourself for righteousness. I have called all to run, but few run so as to win. Discipline yourself to win."

Then He was gone.

"Why did He leave?" Stephen asked.

"He said all that needed to be said at this time. He spoke

to you of discipline. I would take this to be a most important word for you at this time."

"Discipline. I used to hate that word!"

"He spoke to you about the race. Were you once a runner?"

"Yes, I am very fast. I was always the fastest one in my school. I was even offered a scholarship to run for a major university."

"I take it that you did not accept it."

"No. I didn't."

"Was it because of a lack of discipline that you did not go to college?"

"No! It was...." There was a long silence as Stephen looked down at his feet. "Yes, I think it probably was."

"Don't worry about that now, but you must understand something. Most who are potentially the best in every field or occupation never become even high achievers for the lack of that one thing—discipline. What you are doing now is much more important than track or college. Obviously, the lack of discipline has been a weakness you have, and it has cost you much already, but in Christ all things become new. In Him the very things that have been your greatest weaknesses can become your greatest strengths. You are now His disciple. This means that you are 'a disciplined one.'"

"I know you are telling me the truth, and I know this is one race I do not want to lose."

"Do you see the path that leads up the mountain?"

"Yes."

"Its name is Discipline. Stay on it if you want to reach the top."

CHAPTER X

The Army

S uddenly I was on a high mountain overlooking a great plain. Before me, there was an army marching on a wide front. There were twelve divisions in the vanguard that stood out sharply from the great multitude of soldiers who followed behind them. These divisions were further divided up into what I assumed to be regiments, battalions, companies, and smaller squads. The divisions were distinguished by their banners, and the regiments were distinguished by their different colored uniforms.

Battalions, companies, and squads were distinguished by such things as sashes or epaulets that each different group wore. All wore armor that was polished silver, shields that appeared to be pure gold, and weapons that were both silver and gold. The banners were huge, thirty to forty feet long. As they marched, their armor and weapons flashed in the sun like lightning, and the flapping of the banners and the tread of their feet sounded like rolling thunder. I did not think the earth had ever witnessed anything like this before.

Then I was close enough to see their faces. There were male and female, old and young, and seemingly every race. There was a fierce resolution on their faces, and yet they did not seem tense. There was a sense of war in the air, but in the ranks I could feel such a profound peace that I knew not a single one was in fear of the battle they were marching to. The spiritual atmosphere I felt when close to them was as awesome as their appearance.

I then looked at their uniforms. Their colors were brilliant. Every soldier also wore rank insignias and medals. The generals and other higher ranking officers marched in the ranks with the others. They all seemed to be close friends from the highest ranking to the lowest. Though it was obvious that those with higher ranks were in charge, no one seemed overly sensitive to his rank. It was an army of what seemed to be unprecedented discipline, and yet it also seemed to be just one big family.

As I studied them they seemed selfless—not because they lacked identity, but because they were all so sure of who they were and what they were doing that they were not consumed with themselves and did not have to seek recognition. I could not detect ambition or pride anywhere in the ranks. It was stunning to see so many who were so unique, yet in such harmony, marching in perfect step. I was sure that there had never been an army on earth like this one.

Then I was behind these front divisions looking at a much larger group composed of hundreds of divisions. Each of these was a different size, with the smallest being about two thousand and the largest seeming to number in the hundreds of thousands. Although this group was not as sharp and colorful as the first one, this was also an awesome army, simply because of its size. This group also had banners, but they were not nearly as large and impressive as the first group's banners. They all had uniforms and ranks, but I was surprised that many of them did not even have a full set of armor on, and many did not have weapons. The armor and weapons that they did have were not nearly as polished and bright as those of the first group.

As I looked more closely at those in these ranks, I could see they were all determined and had purpose, but they did not have nearly the focus of the first group. These seemed much more aware of their own ranks and the ranks of those around them. I felt this was a distraction that was hindering their focus. I could also sense ambition and jealousy in the ranks, which was unquestionably a further distraction. Even so, I felt that these second divisions still had a higher level of devotion and purpose than any army on earth. This, too, was a very powerful force.

Behind this second army, there was a third one which marched so far behind the first two that I was not sure they could even see the groups ahead of them. This group was many times larger than the first and second combined, seemingly composed of millions and millions. As I watched from a distance, this army would move in different directions like a great flock of birds, sweeping one way and then the next, never moving straight in a direction for very long. Because of this erratic movement, it was drifting farther and farther from the first two groups.

As I came closer, I saw that these had tattered, dull, gray uniforms, which were neither pressed nor clean. Almost everyone was bloody and wounded. A few were attempting to march, but most just walked in the general direction in which the others were headed. Fights were constantly breaking out in the ranks, which was the cause of the wounds. There were frayed banners scattered throughout, which some were trying to stay close to. Even so, not even those near the banners had a clear identity because they were constantly drifting from one banner to another.

In this entire third army, I was surprised that there were only two ranks—generals and privates. Only a few had a piece of armor on, and I did not see any weapons except dummy weapons, which were being carried by the generals. The generals flaunted these dummy weapons as if having them made them special, but even those in the ranks could tell that they were not real. This was sad because it was obvious that those in the ranks wanted desperately to find someone who was real to follow.

There did not seem to be any ambition except among the generals. This was not because of selflessness as in the first army, but because there was so little caring. I thought that the ambition present in the second group would be much better than the confusion prevailing in this group. The generals here seemed to be more intent on talking about themselves and fighting with each other, which the little groups around the banners were constantly doing. I could then see that the battles within the ranks were the cause of the great sweeping, erratic changes of direction this group would make from time to time.

As I looked at these millions in the last group, I felt that even with their great numbers, they did not actually add strength to the army, but rather weakened it. In a real battle they would be much more of a liability than an asset. Just sustaining them with food and protection would cost more in resources than any value they could add to the army's ability to fight. I thought that a private in the first or second group would be worth more than many generals from the third. I could not understand why the first groups even allowed this group to tag along behind them. They obviously were not true soldiers.

THE WISDOM OF ZIPPORAH

I was suddenly on a mountain where I could see the entire army. As I watched, I noticed that the plain was dry and dusty before the army, but immediately after the first twelve divisions passed, the earth was dark green, with trees giving shade and bearing fruit and pure streams flowing throughout the land. They were restoring the earth. I thought of how different this was from what would happen when one of the world's armies would pass through a land. They would plunder and forage until the land was utterly stripped wherever they marched.

I watched as the second divisions passed over the same ground. They left bridges and many buildings, but the ground was not left in as good a shape as before they passed. The grass was not as green, the streams were somewhat muddied, and much of the fruit had been taken.

Then I saw what happened as the third group passed over the same ground. The grass was either gone or so trampled into the earth that it could not be seen. The few trees that remained were stripped. The streams were polluted. The bridges were broken down and impassable. The buildings were left in shambles. It seemed that this group had undone all of the good that the first two had done. As I watched them, anger welled up inside of me.

I felt Wisdom standing beside me. He did not say anything for a long time, but I could feel that He also was angry.

"Selfishness destroys," He finally said. *"I came to give life and to give it abundantly. Even when My army has matured, there will be many who call on My name and follow those who follow Me, but they do not know Me or walk in My ways. These destroy the fruit of those who follow Me. Because of this, the world does not know whether to consider My people a blessing or a curse."*

As Wisdom said this, I felt intense heat coming from Him, intensifying until it was so painful that it was hard for me to concentrate on what He was saying. Even so, I knew I was feeling what He was feeling and that it was an important part of the message He was conveying to me. The pain was a combination of compassion for the earth and anger at the selfishness in this army. Both feelings were so strong that I felt they were being branded into me.

As the anger of the Lord continued to rise, I felt that He might destroy the entire army. Then I remembered how the Lord had met Moses when he was on his way to Egypt in obedience to the Lord. The Lord sought to put him to death until his wife, Zipporah, circumcised their son. I had never understood this until now. Because circumcision speaks of the removal of the fleshly or carnal nature, the incident with Moses was like a prophetic foreshadowing of the sin of Eli the priest, who had brought a curse upon himself and defeat to Israel because he had failed to discipline his sons.

"Lord, raise up those with the wisdom of Zipporah," I cried out.

The burning continued, and a deep determination came over me to go to the leaders of this great army and tell them the story of Zipporah and that everyone in the Lord's army had to be circumcised in their hearts. The flesh, or carnal nature, had to be cut away. I knew if they marched any farther before this was done, the entire army was in danger of being destroyed by the Lord Himself, just as He had almost killed Moses when he was returning to Egypt.

Then I was standing in the Hall of Judgment before the Judgment Seat. The Lord still appeared as Wisdom, but I had never seen Him more fierce or His words come with more weight.

"You have already seen this army in your heart many times. The leaders I am commissioning now will lead this army. I am sending you to many of these leaders. What will you say to them?"

"Lord, this is a great army, but I am still grieved about the condition of the third group. I do not understand why they are even allowed to pretend to be a part of Your army. I would like to say that before they go any farther, the first and second armies should turn and drive away this third group. They were really very little more than a huge mob."

"What you saw today is still in the future. The ministries I am about to release will gather this army and equip them to be all that you saw. At this time, almost My entire army is in the condition of the third group. How can I let them be driven away?"

I was stunned by this, though I knew I had never seen any of the Lord's people who were in as good shape as even the second group of this army.

"Lord, I know I felt Your anger at this group. If almost Your entire army is now in that condition, I am just thankful that You have not destroyed all of us. When I was looking at this third group, I felt that their deplorable condition was due to a lack of training, equipping, and vision, as well as a failure to embrace the cross that circumcises the heart. I believe I must go to them with the message about Zipporah, but they also need drill sergeants and officers who will train them."

Wisdom continued, *"Remember the first army that you saw before the mountain? They, too, were unprepared for the battle, and when the battle began, those who were not prepared fled. However, many returned with their armor on, and their delusions were replaced with truth. The first two groups in this army were also changed by battles that woke them up to their true condition. Then they cried out to Me, and I sent them shepherds after My own heart.*

"All of My shepherds are like King David. They are not hirelings who are seeking their own places or positions, but they will lay down their lives for My people. They are also fearless in warfare against My enemies and pure in their worship of Me. I am about to send these shepherds forth. You must return with the message of Zipporah. The time is soon when I will not abide those who seek to be counted with My people who do not circumcise their hearts. You must warn them of My wrath.

"I am also sending you back to walk with the prophets I am sending forth as Samuels to pour oil upon My true shepherds. Many of these are now considered the least of their brethren, but you will find them being faithful shepherds of their little flocks, faithful laborers in whatever I have given them to do. These are My faithful ones who are called to be kings. These I will trust with My authority. They will prepare My people for the great battle at the end."

[259]

I then wondered in my heart that if we are now in the condition of the third group, what was to be done with the generals, who did not seem to be real generals at all?

"You are right; they are not real generals," the Lord answered. *"I did not appoint them, but they appointed themselves. Even so, some of them will be changed, and I will make them generals. Others will become useful officers. However, most will flee at the first sight of battle, and you will not see them again.*

"Remember this: At one time every one in the first two groups was a part of the last one. When you go with the message of Zipporah, declaring that I will no longer tolerate the carnality of My people, those whom I have truly called and are devoted to obeying Me will not run from My circumcision, but will stand against the carnality in the camp so that I will not have to bring judgment upon them. My shepherds are responsible for the condition of My sheep. My generals are responsible for the condition of My soldiers. Those whom I have called will take this responsibility because they love Me, they love My people, and they love righteousness."

CAPTAIN OF THE HOST

Then I was no longer before the Judgment Seat but on the mountain overlooking the army again. Wisdom was standing beside me. He was resolute, but I no longer felt the pain and anger that I did before.

"I have allowed you to see a little into the future," Wisdom began. *"I am sending you to those who are called to prepare My army and lead it. These are the ones who have been fighting the battle on the mountain. These are the*

ones who have met the army of the accuser and remained faithful. These are the ones who have watched over My people and protected them at the risk of their own lives. These are called to be leaders in My army who will fight in the great battle at the end. They will stand against all of the powers of darkness, and they will have no fear.

"As you see, this army is marching, but there will be times when it camps. The camping is as important as the marching. It is the time for planning, training, and sharpening skills and weapons. It is also time for those in the first group to walk among the second and for the leaders of the second group to walk among the third group, finding those who can be called to the next level. Do this while you can, for the time is near when Revelation 11:1-2 will be fulfilled, and those who want to be called by My name but do not walk in My ways will be trodden underfoot. Before the last great battle, My army will be holy, even as I am holy. I will remove those who are not circumcised of heart and the leaders who do not uphold My righteousness. When the last battle is fought, there will be no third group as you see here.

"Until now when My army has camped, most of the time has been wasted. Just as I only lead My people forward with a clear objective, when I call My army to camp, it is with purpose. The strength of the army that marches will be determined by the quality of its camp. When it is time to stop and camp, it is to teach My people My ways. An army is an army whether it is in battle or at peace. You must learn how to camp, how to march, and how to fight. You will not do any one of these well unless you do them all well.

"My army must be ready to do each of these in season and out of season. You may think that it is time to march, but I will direct you to camp because I see things that you can never see, even from this place of vision. If you follow

Me, you will always be doing the right thing at the right time, even though it may not seem right to you. Remember, I am the Captain of the host.

"An army's resolve will be determined by the nobility of their mission, how well they are prepared for their mission, and how well they are led. This army will march with the most noble mission that has ever been given to man. However, few of My people are being equipped for their mission, and those who are now leading My people follow their own desires. I will now raise up leaders who will train and equip My people. These will always follow Me because I am the Captain of this host.

"Many armies experience both victories and defeats. My army has been marching for many centuries. It, too, has had many victories and many defeats. My army has lost many battles because they have attacked the enemy when I did not command them. Others were defeated because they attacked the enemy with untrained people. Most of these leaders have done this because they were seeking their own glory. Paul wrote of those in his own time, **'They all seek after their own interests'** *(see Philippians 2:21).*

"Other leaders have had My interests at heart and sincerely sought a victory over evil for My name's sake, but they did not train their people well; they did not walk with Me as their Wisdom. That will now change. I will be the Captain of the host. Do not be discouraged by the way My people now appear, but remember what they will become. I will now raise up leaders who will only march when I give the orders. When My army follows Me, it will win every battle. When they camp, they will know My presence, and they will grow strong in My ways.

[262]

"You will come to a time in the future when you see My army exactly as it is now. At that time, you will feel My burning anger. Know that I will no longer abide those who remain in the condition of the third group. Then I will stop the march of the entire army until those in this group have been disciplined to become soldiers or dispersed. I will discipline those in the second group to cast off their evil ambitions and live for Me and for My Truth. Then My army will march forth, not to destroy, but to give life. I will be in their midst to tread My enemies under their feet. I am coming to be the Captain of this host!"

CHAPTER XI

The City

I then stood upon another mountain looking out over a city. The glory of this city was beyond anything I had seen or imagined before. While every building and home was unique and beautiful, each fit into breathtaking, overall symmetry with one another and the surrounding fields, mountains, and bodies of water. It was almost as if the city had grown like a plant instead of being built. I felt I was looking at something that had been built by a race who had not fallen, but had walked in the righteousness and purity of Adam and Eve in the beginning.

One feature that stood out was the large amount of glass windows in each structure or dwelling. This glass was so clear and clean and the windows and doors were so situated that I sensed I was not only welcome in each dwelling, but invited. It was also as if nothing was hidden, and there was no danger of anything being stolen.

Then I looked at the people in the city. They seemed familiar, but at the same time, I knew I had never met anyone like them. They were like I imagined Adam to have been before the Fall. The eyes of each one shone with what seemed to be almost total comprehension, an intellectual depth far beyond even the most brilliant person I had ever known. I knew this to be the result of an order and peace which was completely free of confusion or doubt, or maybe the confusion *of* doubt. There was no ambition because they were so confident and had so much joy in who they were and what they were doing. Because everyone here was free, they were also completely open. Poverty or sickness seemed incomprehensible.

I looked at the streets in this city. There were many major highways in the middle of the city that were all going in the same direction, and many smaller roads connected these great highways. As I looked at one of the largest of the highways, knowledge was imparted to me about the truth of holiness. I looked at another highway and knew the truth about healing. As I looked at another, I started understanding things about judgment. Looking at each street, I understood a different truth. I then realized that each one was a path to that truth. The people on each highway seemed to also reflect the truth of that highway.

My attention turned to the many streets connecting the highways. As I looked at each of these, I felt an impartation of a fruit of the Spirit, such as love, joy, peace, or patience. These came as feelings instead of the understanding when I looked at the highways.

I noticed that while some of these streets were connected to every highway, some of the highways only had one or two streets connected to them. For example, I could only get to the Highway of Holiness by walking on a street of Love. I could only get to the highway of Judgment by walking on the streets of Love or Joy.

However, the Highway of Grace was joined by all of the streets. To get on any of these Highways of Truth, I had to walk on a street named after a fruit of the Spirit.

People were walking on the highways and streets, while some were sitting on the edges of them. Some were in the houses on a street or highway, and others were building houses on them. Those who were living in each of the houses were constantly serving food and drink to those who were walking or sitting. I then noticed that there were no restaurants, hotels, or hospitals in the city. I quickly understood that none of these were needed because every home was a center of hospitality and healing.

Almost every home was open to the travelers. Those that were not open were used for special purposes, such as study or what appeared to be long-term healing. I wondered why anyone would even need healing here, but later I would be shown the reason. Even so, I could not imagine a more wonderful place for convalescence. I could tell that every home had been built for this great ministry of hospitality, helps, or healing, even those which were being built on the Highway of Judgment, which seemed to be the place of the most activity. Because of this, even the Highway of Judgment was appealing. It was apparent that every street was not only safe, but was more appealing than any road or highway I had ever seen, even in theme parks. This city was far more glorious than any utopia that philosophers had conceived.

My attention was then drawn back to the Highway of Judgment. It seemed to have been the least traveled highway, but now it was becoming much more active. I then saw that this was because the other streets and highways all flowed toward this one. Even though it was becoming the center of activity, it still seemed that people were hesitant to enter it.

As I looked toward the end of the highway, I could see that the road was on a steady incline, and there was a high mountain at the end which was enveloped in a subtle but profound glory. I knew that if people could see the end of this road, there would have been far more traveling on it. I then realized that I was drawn to this road because it had the same feeling to it as the Great Hall of Judgment. I knew this was the road which led to knowing the Lord as the Righteous Judge.

THE BOND OF PEACE

I wondered if this city was heaven or the New Jerusalem. Then I observed that even though these people were of stature far beyond any I had seen on earth, they did not have the glory or stature of those in even the lowest positions in the Hall of Judgment. I was wondering about this when I felt Wisdom standing next to me again.

"These are the same people who you saw in My army," He began. *"The city and the army are the same. My coming leaders have had visions of both My army and My city. I am building both, and I will use the leaders I am now preparing to complete what I began generations ago. My generals will become master-builders for My city, and My master-builders will also become generals. These are the same.*

"One day the army will no longer be needed, but this city will last forever. You must prepare the army for its present battles but build all that you build for the future.

"There is a future for the earth. After My judgments have come, it will be a glorious future. I am about to show My people the future so that the future will be in their hearts. Solomon wrote, 'Everything God does will remain forever' (see Ecclesiastes 3:14). As My people become like Me, they will build that which will last. They will do all that they do with a peace for the present time and a vision for the future. The city I am building to last forever is built on truth in the hearts of men. My truth will endure, and those who walk in truth will leave fruit that will remain.

"I am coming to earth in My people as Wisdom to build My city. The knowledge of truth will fill My city, but wisdom will build it. The wisdom that is coming upon My builders will cause the world to marvel at My city even more than they did before the city that Solomon built. Men have worshiped their own wisdom since they first ate of the Tree of Knowledge. The world's wisdom is about to pale before My wisdom, which I will reveal through My city. Then those who worship any other wisdom will be ashamed. All that Solomon did was a prophecy of what I am about to build.

"In all you have seen of the city I am building, I have only given you a superficial glimpse. From time to time you will be shown more, but for now you must see one thing. What did you notice the most about this city?"

"The one thing that stood out the most to me was the harmony. Everything in the city fit so perfectly together, and the whole city fit so perfectly in its environment," I responded.

"The perfect bond of peace is love," the Lord continued. *"In My city, there will be unity. In all that I created, there was harmony. All things fit together in Me. Everything I am doing in the earth is to restore the original harmony between*

My Father and His creation and between all creatures. When man lives in harmony with Me, the earth will be in harmony with him, and there will be no more earthquakes, floods, or storms. I came to bring peace on earth."

As He spoke I knew I was looking into the future, just as I had been when I viewed the army. I also knew that what He had said about building with peace in the present and a vision for the future was also essential for the harmony I saw. Time is also a part of His creation that we have to fit in with.

Wisdom then turned to me so that I looked directly into His eyes and said, *"I love My creation. I love the beasts and the fish of the sea. I will restore all things as they were intended to be, but I must first restore man. I did not come just to redeem, but to restore. To be a part of My ministry of restoration you must not just see men as they are, but as they are to become. Like Ezekiel, you must see in even the driest bones an exceedingly great army. You must prophesy life to the bones until they become the army that I have called them to be. Then My army will march. When My army marches it will restore, not destroy. It will fight evil, but it will also build the city of righteousness.*

"All of the treasures of the earth cannot weigh in the balance with the value of a single soul. I am building My city in the hearts of men, with the hearts of men. Those who keep the great wisdom, the knowledge of the eternal treasures, will be used to build My city. You will know My builders by this wisdom—they do not set their minds on earthly things, but on the treasures of heaven. Because of this the world will bring its wealth to My city just as they did in the time of Solomon.

"I am about to release My wise master-builders. You must walk with them, and they must all walk together. Each of the highways and streets that you saw in this city will begin as a fortress of truth in the earth. Each fortress will stand against the powers of darkness, and those powers will not be able to stand against them. Each will be like a mountain, with rivers flowing from it to water the earth. Each will be a city of refuge and a haven to all who seek Me. No weapon that is formed against them will prosper, and no weapon that I give to them will fail."

THE LORD'S BUILDERS

As Wisdom spoke, my eyes were opened to see the most beautiful valley I had ever seen. The mountains forming the valley and the valley itself were more green than any green I could remember having seen. The rocks were like fortresses made of silver; the trees were perfect and full. There was a river in the middle that was fed by streams from every mountain around it. The water sparkled with a blue tint that was the bluest tint I had ever seen and beautifully matched the sky. Every blade of grass was perfect. It was filled with many various kinds of animals which all seemed to be the very best of their breed, with no disease or even scars on any of them. They fit perfectly with the valley and each other. I had never seen such a desirable place on earth.

I wondered if I was seeing the Garden of Eden, and then I saw a few soldiers in full armor who were surveying the valley. Other soldiers were following each stream to the river and then following the river to the place where the first soldiers were surveying. At first I did not think that soldiers fit in this place at all, but for some reason I was quickly at ease with them because I somehow knew they were supposed to be there.

I looked at the soldiers. They were rough and battle hardened, yet kind and approachable. They were fierce and resolute, yet seemed to be at perfect peace. They were serious, yet full of joy and quick to laugh. I thought that even though war is always terrible, if I had to go to battle, there was no other group of soldiers that I would rather fight beside.

I noticed their armor, which seemed to have been custom-made just for them, fitting so perfectly that they moved with a grace as though they were not wearing any armor at all. I could tell that it was both lighter and stronger than any armor I had ever seen. The armor also seemed to be a perfect combination of the colors of the water, the mountains, and the blue sky, which I soon realized was the reflection of these colors in a purity I had never before seen in a reflection. The armor itself was of an "other-worldly" silver, deeper and purer than any silver I had ever seen. As I was wondering who these soldiers were, the Lord began to speak.

"In My Father's house are many dwelling places," He replied. *"These are My builders. Each of My houses will be a fortress from which I will send out My armies. Some will go forth as knights to fight for the poor and oppressed. Some will go forth as small companies who will raid the strongholds of the enemy and bring back the spoils. Others will send forth a host to conquer cities over which My truth and righteousness will reign. Some will join with armies from other fortresses to liberate whole nations with My truth, My love, and My power.*

"These fortresses are not just for the protection of My people, but for mobilizing, training, and sending forth My army through the earth. The darkest of times will soon come upon the earth, but My people will not be found hiding. They will go forth to conquer evil with good. They will conquer by not loving their lives even unto death and by loving others more than their own lives. These will be the fearless ones whom I will send forth before I return.

"Even the prophecies of their coming will strike terror into the hearts of My enemies. They will have no fear. They will love. Love is more powerful than fear, and their love will break the power of fear that has held men in bondage since the beginning. Because they have chosen to die daily, the fear of death has no power over them. This will give them power over every enemy, whose power is fear. I was once dead but am now alive forever, and those who know Me cannot fear death. Therefore, those who know Me will follow Me wherever I go.

"Each of My dwelling places will be in a valley like this. It is alive with the life that was in the earth before the Fall because here the power of My redemption has brought forth true life again. My dwelling places will only be found where all of My streams flow together into one. My builders will come from every stream, but they will work as one. Just as great houses need different craftsmen, so does My house. Only when they work together can they build My house.

"As you see in these, My builders will have the wisdom to complete the survey before they build. Each of My houses will fit perfectly into the land where it is located, not according to human measurements, but according to Mine. The first skill that My builders develop is the skill of surveying. They must know the land because I designed the land for My people. When you build with My wisdom, what you build will fit perfectly with the land."

Then I was standing by one of the streams in the valley. I started following it to the top of a mountain. As I got close to the top, I began to hear loud, terrible sounds. When I looked beyond the valley, I could see wars, great earthquakes tearing the earth, storms, and fires that seemed to completely encircle the valley. It was as if I was standing on the border between heaven and hell, looking into hell itself. I somehow knew that all of hell was powerless to encroach on the valley, but the sight was so terrible I started to turn and run back into the valley. I then felt Wisdom standing beside me.

"This is where you must live—between the dying and the living. Do not fear, but believe. You have been weak, but now I am with you, so be courageous and strong. Fear must not rule over you. Do nothing because of fear. Do what you do because of love, and you will always triumph. Love is the source of courage. Love will prevail in the end. Encourage My builders with these words."

CHAPTER XII

Words
of Life

When I was back at the Great Hall of Judgment, standing before the door again. I was a little stunned by what I had seen on the edge of the valley, but His words were still resounding in me. "Love, love," I repeated over and over. "I must not forget the power of love. There is perfect peace in love. There is courage in love. There is power in love."

I looked at the door. I knew this was the door to His church. I knew that the fortresses Wisdom talked about were churches and movements. I began to think of some congregations and movements which I knew were already preparing for what I had seen. I began thinking of spiritual surveyors whom I knew but had never thought of in this way before. Then again, it seemed like most of these were so battle-weary that they were just trying to survive, even fighting one another in their desperation.

I thought of the battle that had been fought on the mountain. The enemy had used Christians to attack other Christians who were trying to climb the mountain. Even though that battle was eventually won and most of the

Christians were freed from the accuser's power, I knew it would take a long time for the wounds from those battles to be healed. Many had been under the influence of the accuser for so long that it was still their nature to accuse, and it could be a while before their minds were renewed. I knew that the church was still a very long way from being united.

"Where do we begin?" I thought to myself. "What can I do if I go through that door?"

"You do not have to begin. It is already finished," Wisdom answered. *"I accomplished the unity of My people on the cross. Even though it looks like the enemy has prevailed since the cross, he has only worked into the plan which My Father and I had from the beginning. When you preach the cross and live by its power, you will do My will. Those who serve Me and not their own ambitions will soon recognize one another and be joined together. Those who have the true fear of God do not have to fear anything on the earth. Those who fear Me will not fear one another, but will love each other and sit together at My table.*

"I have called you to see, and you will see how My kingdom will come. The devil will be cast down to the earth, and he will come to the earth with great wrath. But do not fear his wrath, for I am also about to show My wrath against all iniquity. The evil one and all who follow evil will soon know My wrath. You must see these things, but you are not to fear them because I dwell in the midst of My people and I am greater than all. As you behold Me, you will not fear. If you fear, it is because you are not beholding Me.

"When the evil in mankind has become fully united with the evil one, the time of great trouble will come upon the earth. Then all of mankind and the whole creation will

understand the futility and tragedy of rebellion. At the same time, My people will become fully united with Me, and My great light will stand against the great darkness. Those who walk in lawlessness will fall into the deep darkness. Those who walk in obedience will shine forth as the stars of heaven.

"Humility and obedience will always lead to Me. As you come to Me, you will behold and manifest My glory. The heavens and the earth are about to behold the difference between the light and the darkness. You are called to live between the darkness and the light in order to call those who live in darkness to the light. Even now I do not desire for any to perish."

In the glory that surrounded us, it was even hard to imagine the darkness and terrible events that I had just witnessed. I thought of the difference between His glory and even the greatest pomp and splendor of man. "How pitifully insignificant we are!" I blurted out. "If men could just have a glimpse of Your Judgment Seat, they would all quickly repent. Lord, why do You not just show Yourself to the world so they will not have to endure this evil? People would not choose evil if they could see You as You are."

"I will reveal Myself. When evil has run its full course, then I will show Myself to the world. As the evil one is being revealed through fallen men, I will be revealed through restored men. Then the world will see Me, not just the glory that I have in heaven, but the glory stands against the darkness. My glory is more than what you see here; it is My nature. After I reveal My nature in My people, I will return in the glory that I have here. Until then I am seeking those who will follow Me because they love Me and love the truth, not just because they love this glory and power.

"*Those who choose to obey when the whole world is disobeying are worthy to be heirs with Me. These will be worthy to rule with Me, to see My glory, and to share it. These are the ones who do not live for themselves, but for Me. Some of the greatest of these brethren of mine are about to be revealed. They will stand for truth against the greatest darkness. They will remain steadfast through the greatest trials. I have brought you here, and I am sending you back to encourage them to stand and not faint, for the time of their salvation is near.*

"*I am also sending you back to warn these mighty ones. Satan saw the glory of My Father and beheld the myriads who serve Him, yet he still fell. He fell because he started to trust in the glory and power that the Father had shared with him instead of trusting the Father. Those who will be trusted with the power and glory that I share with them in these times must not put their trust in the power or glory, but in Me. True faith is never in yourself, your wisdom, or the power I have given to you. True faith is in Me.*

"*As you grow in the true faith that is in Me, you will grow in dependence on Me, and you will trust yourself less. Those who begin to trust in themselves will not be able to carry the weight of My power or glory; they can fall because of it, just as the evil one did. My strength is made perfect in weakness, but you must never forget that in yourself you are weak, and by yourself you are foolish.*

"*Those who are worthy to reign with Me in the age to come will prove this by living in the darkness and weakness of human flesh, yet they will serve and trust Me. Even the greatest angels will willingly bow before those who have been proven in this way. Even the angels marvel when suffering men and women, who have beheld so little of the glory here, remain steadfast for Me and My truth in times of darkness.*

These are worthy to be called My brethren and to be called the sons of My Father.

"On earth the truth often looks weak and easily defeated. Those who see from here know that My truth always prevails. The time when I stand up and bring My judgments to the earth has only been delayed so that My brethren could prove their love for Me by standing for truth at any cost. My truth and My goodness will prevail for all of eternity, and so will all who come to Me because they love the truth. These will shine forth as the stars which were made in honor of them."

As Wisdom continued to speak, it was like being washed in a shower of living water. At times I had been ashamed because even in the presence of His glory, I was as dull and easily distracted here as I was on earth. But now as He spoke to me, His words cleansed me so that a sharpness came to my mind beyond just mental exhilaration. The more I was cleansed, the more His words seemed to explode with cleansing brilliance. I not only saw His glory, but felt His glory inside of me. In His presence, I did not just hear the truth, I absorbed it.

HIS BELOVED BRIDE

This sensation of being cleansed by His words was more wonderful than can be described, but it was familiar. I knew I had felt this when listening to anointed preaching from one who had been in the presence of the Lord. It was not intoxicating, but the exact opposite. Instead of dulling the senses, it quickened them. In His presence, I felt that thousands of fragments of information that I had accumulated over the years were all tied together to give a deep and comprehensive meaning to everything He said. In this way, every concept became like a strong pillar of knowledge in my mind. Then it became a passion as I felt a deep love for each truth.

When He spoke, there was an energy released that enabled me to see each truth with a greater depth than I ever had before. His words did not just impart information, but life. This great illumination was similar to what I experienced when I decided not to try to hide anything when I was standing in front of the Judgment Seat. The more I opened my heart to His words to expose any darkness in me and to change me, the more power His words seemed to have in me.

The Lord did not just give information, but He was somehow rearranging my mind and heart so that these truths would be the foundation for understanding, and the understanding released a love for the truth. For example, I had what I thought was a sound understanding of the church as the bride of Christ. As He talked about the ministries being sent forth to prepare His bride, I saw in my heart what seemed to be every church I knew. They immediately became much more than just a group of people; they became *His Beloved*. I felt a burning passion to help them to get ready for Him. The repulsion of sin and harlotry with the world almost buckled my knees as I saw what it did to His people. I knew that I was feeling what He was feeling.

As He spoke, cleansing truth poured over me. The cleanness I felt was more wonderful than I had ever considered that it could feel. It was almost as if I had been living my life in a sewer and was now being given a hot shower. The power of cleansing truth gripped me so powerfully that I desperately wanted to carry this back to share with His people.

"I am about to release the power of anointed truth to cleanse My people," Wisdom continued. *"My bride will be cleansed of all of her defilements. I am sending forth My messengers who will be flames of fire, burning with zeal for My holiness and the holiness of My people."*

As He spoke, I felt the depth and power of the message of holiness. I then knew without question the power of truth to accomplish this. A vision of the glorious bride whom He so deserves was being burned into my heart. I wanted desperately to share this with His people so that they would become completely focused on getting ready for Him. I just could not comprehend doing anything again without this being the purpose.

He began to talk about the fortresses of truth and righteousness. While He talked, I began to see the congregations with whom I was familiar and how they were struggling. I became burdened as never before for them to be empowered with His truth. I knew they were weak because they were not walking in truth. The grief I began to feel for them became almost more than I could bear.

"Why do they not walk in truth?" I blurted out.

"You are beginning to feel the burden that Nehemiah felt when he heard that Jerusalem was in distress because her walls were broken down," Wisdom explained. *"I am imparting to My messengers the fire to see My bride cleansed, and I am also imparting to them the burden of Nehemiah to see the walls of salvation restored. Then My people will no longer be in distress.*

"You have seen My people as My bride, My city, and My army. Now you do not just see these, but you feel them. Only when My truth comes from the heart does it have the power to

change men. Living waters must come from the innermost being—the heart. Just as you felt My truth cleansing you, I am making My messengers flames of fire who will speak truth, not just to give understanding, but with the power to change men's hearts. The truth that I am sending will not just convict My people of their sin, but it will cleanse them from their sin."

Even as He was speaking, a great zeal rose up within me to do something. As He spoke, divine strategies began to come to me which I knew could help His people. I could not wait to begin. I could now believe that even the driest bones were going to become an exceedingly great army! In the presence of Wisdom, nothing seemed impossible. I had no trouble believing that His church would become a bride without spot or wrinkle or that His church would become a great city, standing as a fortress of truth for the whole world to behold. I had no doubt that His people, even as weak and defeated as they now seemed, were about to become an army of truth which no power of darkness could stand before. Feeling the power of truth as never before, I knew that His power was much greater than the darkness.

WORDS OF LIFE

In His presence, I felt as if I could speak forth the vision that I had received of His bride and whoever heard it would be changed. It seemed I could speak to the most defeated little congregation with such power that they would quickly become a mighty fortress of the truth. I also knew that on earth my words did not have this power.

"Your words will have this power when you abide in Me," Wisdom interjected. *"I did not call you to preach about Me; I called you to be a voice I could speak through. As you abide in Me and My words abide in you, you will bear fruit that will remain. By My word the creation was brought forth, and by My word the new creation will come forth, in you and in My people. My words are Spirit and Life. My words give Life. You are not called to just teach about Me, but to let Me teach through you. As you dwell in My presence, your words will be My words and they will have power."*

I began to think of something that Elizabeth Barrett Browning had once said, "Earth's crammed with heaven, and every common bush afire with God; and only he who sees takes off his shoes; the rest sit round it and pluck blackberries." (*Aurora Leigh*)

"Lord, I want to see You in everything," I said.

"I will give My messengers the vision to see My purpose in all things," He responded. *"I will make My messengers flames of fire, as I appeared at the burning bush. My fire will rest upon them, but they will not be consumed by it. Then men will marvel at this great sight and turn aside to see it. I will speak from the midst of My messengers to call My people to their destiny to rise up as the deliverers that I have called them to be."*

I then felt drawn to the door. I stepped closer to it and could see writing. I had never seen writing like this before. It was like the purest gold, and it was somehow alive. I began to read.

"For by Him all things were created, both in the heavens and on earth, visible and invisible, whether thrones or dominions

or rulers or authorities—all things have been created by Him and for Him.

And He is before all things, and in Him all things hold together.

He is also head of the body, the church; and He is the beginning, the first-born from the dead; so that He Himself might come to have first place in everything.

For it was the Father's good pleasure for all the fulness to dwell in Him,

and through Him to reconcile all things to Himself, having made peace through the blood of His cross; through Him, I say, whether things on earth or things in heaven.

And although you were formerly alienated and hostile in mind, engaged in evil deeds,

yet He has now reconciled you in His fleshly body through death, in order to present you before Him holy and blameless and beyond reproach—

if indeed you continue in the faith firmly established and steadfast, and not moved away from the hope of the gospel that you have heard, which was proclaimed in all creation under heaven, and of which I, Paul, was made a minister.

Now I rejoice in my sufferings for your sake, and in my flesh. I do my share on behalf of His body (which is the church) in filling up that which is lacking in Christ's afflictions.

Of this church I was made a minister according to the stewardship from God bestowed on me for your benefit, that I might fully carry out the preaching of the word of God,

that is, the mystery which has been hidden from the past ages and generations; but has now been manifested to His saints,

to whom God willed to make known what is the riches of the glory of this mystery among the Gentiles, which is Christ in you, the hope of glory.

And we proclaim Him, admonishing every man and teaching every man with all wisdom, that we may present every man complete in Christ.

And for this purpose also I labor, striving according to His power, which mightily works within me" (Colossians 1:16-29).

As I read these Words, they were like a transfusion of life. A single Word from God is worth more than all of the treasure on earth! I wondered how I could ever allow myself to be so carried away with the cares of the world when I have His Words. I began to think about how worthwhile it would be to cross the earth to hear just one anointed sermon, but I was sometimes so lazy I did not want to drive across town. I was appalled at my carelessness with His Word as I stood before the door. "Lord, I am so sorry," I blurted out.

As I said this, the door opened. As it did, I pondered how it had looked so dull and uninviting from a distance, but up close it was more intricate and beautiful than any door I had ever seen. "That is how people judge the church," I thought, "and how I have often judged it myself. I have loved God for a long time, but I have failed to love His people the way I should."

"Such repentance will open the door for you to go forth into the purpose for which I called you. You cannot fulfill your purpose apart from My people. I have called My people to be one, and now it will come to pass. Apart from them you cannot live what you have seen in your visions. Now you must go from seeing the way and knowing the truth to being a vessel for My life. This you cannot do apart from My people. The Father has given you His love for Me, that His love might be in you, just as I asked. Now I will give you My love for My people. My messengers must see them as I do and love them as I do. As you truly love My Word, the door to your destiny with My people will open for you."

His words touched not only my mind, but also my heart. I felt each one. Just hearing the love with which He spoke of His people imparted that love to me. This was a greater love than I had ever felt before, but it was also familiar, and I had experienced it to a degree when I had heard anointed preaching. I thought about how, in my foolishness, I had often said that there would be no preaching in heaven, but now I felt that it could not be heaven without preaching. I began to even crave the preaching of His Word.

"Yes there will be preaching and teaching in heaven. For all of eternity, My story will be told. That is why it is called 'the eternal gospel.' I am the Word and I am Truth, and words of truth will forever fill My creation. All of creation will delight in My Words of truth just as you are now. Even the angels love to listen to your testimonies of redemption,

and they will hear them. My redeemed ones will forever love to tell and listen to the stories of My redemption. But now you must tell them to those who dwell in darkness. The word of your testimony will liberate many. Those who love Me love My Word. They love to read it, and they love to hear it. You have been given the truth that will set men free, which is My Word in your heart. Go forth with My Word. Go forth and you will see the power of My Word."

CHAPTER XIII

The Manna

I stepped through the door. When I did, I was surprised that all of the glory I had been standing in before was gone. It was dark and musty, like an old cellar. It was disconcerting, but I still felt the power of the words that the Lord had spoken to me, and they steadied me.

"What you feel is the anointing of the Holy Spirit," a voice said from the darkness.

"Who are you?" I asked.

"Must you ask?" It did not quite sound like Wisdom, but some other familiar voice. Even so, I knew it was him. Gradually my eyes became adjusted to the darkness and I was surprised to see my old friend, the white eagle.

"He lives in you so you can abide in all that you just experienced here just as you did in His presence there. I know you have become addicted to His presence, and this is right, but here you must learn to recognize Him in many forms. First you must recognize His voice in your own heart and then as He speaks through others.

"This you have known before and have experienced from time to time, but not like you must know it now. He will never be far from you and will always be easily found. He will always lead you to the truth. Only by the Holy Spirit can you see and know anything or anyone the way that they really are. In the times that are before us, we will perish if we do not follow Him closely."

"I know this is true because I hear Wisdom speaking through you. Are you here to show me the way? I can hardly see here."

"I will come to you from time to time to tell you about the signposts that will let you know you are still on the right path, but the Holy Spirit must lead you. I will also help you to understand how He leads you in different places, but first I must tell you about the manna so that you can live."

"Manna! Do you mean like the manna that Israel ate in the wilderness? Is that what we eat here?"

"It is what all who have walked with God have lived on since the beginning. The manna that Israel ate while in the wilderness was a prophecy of this. The Lord will give you fresh manna every day. Just as He covered the earth with manna every day for Israel while they were in the wilderness, He covers the earth each day with truth for His people. Every way you turn you will see it. Even in the midst of the darkness and gloom, His word will surround you, and you can gather it. Those who are cast into the inner prisons will awake to find it every day. Those who live in great palaces can also find it every day. But His manna is as gentle and light as the dew and easily trampled. You must be gentle and light of heart to see it."

[288]

LIVING EPISTLES

"The Lord speaks every day to each one of His people. They cannot live by bread alone, but they must have the words that proceed from His mouth. These are not the words that He spoke in the past, but the words that He speaks to them each day," the eagle continued.

"Many are weak because they do not know how to gather the manna that the Lord gives to them each day. They go astray because they do not know His voice. His sheep know His voice, and they follow Him because they know His voice. The manna is the bread of life that each of His people are given each day. You must learn to recognize it and help His people to recognize this manna. When they taste it as you are tasting it now, they will diligently search for it each day. Do not be concerned about hoarding food or water, but learn to see and partake of the manna that He gives each day. This will preserve you when all else fails.

"The Scriptures are the meat that He gives to us, but His manna is found in His living epistles, His people. He will speak to you each day through His people. You must open your heart to the way that He is found in His people if you are to partake of the heavenly manna. Just as He said to Jerusalem, He is saying to us, **'You shall not see Me until you say, "Blessed is he who comes in the name of the Lord!"'** (see Matthew 23:39) This spoke of Him when He walked the earth then, and it speaks of the way that He walks the earth now through His people. As our love for manna grows, so will our love for each other. If you are growing in love, the manna that He serves will never taste old or stale to you, but it will be new each morning.

"His manna may come to you through the words of a close friend or one of His people who lived long before you as you ponder his writings. He will also speak through those who do not know Him, but you will know that He sent them to you. You will discern His manna when you go beyond just trying to hear His words and seek to hear the Word, Himself. It is not just hearing His words, but hearing His voice that will lead you in the way you are to go. Many repeat the words He has spoken, but His manna is the word that He is speaking now.

"We need the strong meat of the Scriptures to build ourselves up and to give us the container for gathering His manna. Grow strong on the meat of His written Word, but also develop a taste for His manna. The meat of His written Word will build us up and prepare us for what is to come, but manna will sustain us through what is to come.

"The words spoken to you through the saints in the Hall of Judgment were manna from Him. His people are also His manna to the world. The bread of life is the living words that He speaks to His people daily, and they are spoken through His people. The Scriptures are set and cannot be changed. They are the anchor for our souls. However, the Book of Life is still being written. He writes a new chapter in the Book of Life with each soul who comes to Him."

VICTORY OR DEFEAT

"The Scriptures are the blueprint for His dwelling place that He is building among men. They are the testimony of the way He has worked through men to bring about their redemption. His people are the vessels of His living Word and are a witness to the world that His Words are not just history, but they are still alive and still give life. If you are to know His Word, you must know both. The Scriptures are His eternal plans that will not change, which we must know to walk in His ways. His manna will give you the strength each day to walk. This is so that we might have fellowship. If we dwell in the light as He is in the light, we will have fellowship with one another.

"Many of His messengers do not even know they are being used in this way. They often do not know when He is speaking through them. Those to whom He is speaking seldom recognize His voice. This must change. His people are called to be in unity with Him in all that He does, but few even know His voice. Therefore, they seldom follow Him in the way He wants to lead them. He now wants all of His people to know when He is speaking through them or to them. Just as the sure communication between a general and his soldiers can determine the outcome of the battle, the strength of His communication with His people will determine their victory or defeat in the days to come.

"He is now preparing many messengers who will go forth with His messages. They will also teach His people to know His voice and to know His ways. These you must receive as if you are receiving the Lord Himself. You must help them along their way. The success of their ministry will determine the rise and fall of many."

For a moment I thought that if the Lord was sending them, surely they would not need my help. This brought a stern rebuke from the eagle, who could also discern my thoughts.

"Do not think that way! Many of His people fall because of that delusion! He could do all things without us, but He has chosen to do them through us. We are His provision for one another. He sent the Helper to live in His people; therefore, He intends for His people to receive their help through one another. Do not ever forget this. This is why He gives us our manna through one another. He has designed all things so that we must love Him above all things, but we must also love one another. We need Him above all things, but we also need each other. In this way we are also kept humble so that He might trust us with His grace and power."

"I'm sorry," I replied. "I know all of that very well, but I do tend to forget it at times."

"The times you have forgotten this have been more costly than you need to know at this time, but to forget this in the future will be more costly than you can bear. We need the Lord above all, but we also need all of His people. It is in His people that we will find the Helper, the One who leads us into all truth and the One who leads us to the Son.

"He is now sending forth His messengers. Some will be old and wise. Others will be young and have little experience, but they will know His voice. The enemy will also be sending his messengers to sow confusion. This, too, is a part of our training. Some will be deceived by the messengers of the enemy for a while, and some will suffer loss because of them, but those who love the Lord and His truth will not be deceived by them for long. Those who love Him and His truth will know the truth. Those who have been deceived for a time will learn from this, and they will be used to expose the deceivers in the days to come.

"Some who have been the most deceived in the past will become some of the strongest in the truth because of their wisdom. Wisdom is to know His voice and to follow Him. These will not be easily distracted from Him again. Do not judge men because of their past, but by who they have become. Those who have followed Wisdom will have their weaknesses turned into strengths. No one is stronger or more trustworthy than those who know His voice and follow Him.

"We must not stop encouraging His people to know His voice. We must charge His prophets to confront and expose the false prophets. This message we must carry to the end. We are being sent to help build His lines of communication with those who will be His soldiers in the great battle to come. *All* of His people must know His voice. The time will soon be upon us when all who do not know His voice will be deceived by the darkness. Those who know His voice because they know Him will not be deceived."

As the eagle spoke, his words continued to wash me just as they had when they came in the presence of Wisdom. Though I could not see Him, I knew He was just as present and that He was the One speaking to me. Though I could not see as much with my eyes in this place, I had a great clarity of mind which enabled me to understand. I had always felt that I had a very poor memory, but although He was now saying much more than He ever had before, it seemed like I could remember every word He said, even when it came through someone else. I knew then that this was the power of the Holy Spirit who brings all things to our remembrance. In Him, looking backwards or forwards was no different than looking at the present. As I was thinking about this, the eagle continued.

[293]

"This place seems musty and old because very little fresh air has been let in here for a long time. You have found the door and have entered. The same door that leads to this place also can now lead you back to the Hall of Judgment. What did you receive in the Hall of Judgment?"

"Wisdom and understanding," I replied.

"In a single word, you received grace," the eagle responded. "The Throne of Judgment is also the Throne of Grace. You can boldly go there at any time."

When he said this, I turned to see the door behind me. Now I could see beauty in it that was even greater than when I entered the Hall of Judgment. I opened it and stepped through.

CHAPTER XIV

The Call

I looked at Wisdom, who then turned me around so that I could behold the Great Hall again. I was startled to see, standing right behind me, everyone whom I had previously met there. I was even more surprised by how much more glorious they now seemed.

"They have not changed," Wisdom said. *"You have changed. Your eyes are opened to see more than you could before. The more clearly you are able to see Me, the more you will be able to see Me in others."*

I looked toward the Apostle Paul. He was regal beyond description. He had such great authority and dignity but was, at the same time, so graced with humility that I am sure the lowest peasant or sinner would have felt completely comfortable approaching him. The desire to be just like that flooded me.

I then looked at the others and felt as if they were all the closest family and friends that I had ever known. It is impossible to describe how I loved them and how I knew that they loved me. No fellowship on earth could compare to this, but the best on earth was somehow a foretaste of it. There was no pretension, posturing, or positioning. Everyone knew everyone else completely, and love was the source of every thought. Eternity with this family was going to be even better than I had ever imagined. I desperately wanted to take all of them with me, but I knew they could not leave their present domain.

Wisdom again answered my thoughts: *"They will be with you as I am with you. Remember, they are the great cloud of witnesses. Even when you do not see them, they are as close to you as they are now. All who have served Me from the beginning are one body, and they, too, will be with you in what is to come, but I will be in you."*

I wondered how anything that we experienced in eternity could be better than what was to be found right here in the Judgment Hall. The judgment came from every thought being made manifest. It was not a judgment of punishment, but liberation, if you did not try to hide anything. Freedom came with everything that was illuminated so that you desired for every flaw in your heart to be exposed. The love you felt was so great that you knew everything would be covered and made right.

"Everything you feel in My presence is true," Wisdom continued. *"This love and closeness that you feel with your brethren here is real. You are all one in Me. You will grow in this love as you grow in Me. As you do, this same love will help others to enter the freedom you have experienced here. When My people who now walk the earth embrace My true judgment, they will walk in a freedom that will enable Me to touch the world with My love.*

"It is not My desire that any should perish or suffer loss when they come here. I desire for all to judge themselves so that

I will not have to judge them. That is why My judgments are about to come to the earth. They are coming in ever-increasing waves so that the world may believe and repent. Each trumpet sound will be louder than the previous one. It is the job of My messengers to help the world understand the sound of the trumpets.

"Remember that those with whom you must walk on earth are also members of My body. They have not yet been glorified, but you must see them as they are called to be, not as they appear now. You must love them as you love these. You must see the authority and grace in them that you now see in these. Remember that those with whom you must walk upon the earth now see you as you do them. You must learn not to see them according to their appearances now but who they are to become.

"Only those who live by My judgments, who abide with Me as their wisdom, can see My authority in you or in others. Even so, do not strive to have men see My authority in you, but strive to see Me in them. Do not be concerned by whether others see you as you are; only be concerned about recognizing others as they are and seeing Me in them. When you become concerned about how others see you, you lose your authority. When authority becomes your goal, you will begin to lose true authority. You know the ministry and authority that I have given to you; do not ask men to call you by your position, but by your name. Then I will make your name greater than the position.

"In My kingdom, authority comes from who you are, not your title. Your ministry is your function, not your rank. Here rank is earned by humility, service, and love. The deacon who loves more is higher than the apostle who loves less. On earth, prophets may be used to shake the nations, but here they will be known by their love. This is also your call—to love with My love and to serve with My heart. Then we will be one."

[297]

CHAPTER XV

Worship
In Spirit

As I listened to Wisdom, it was hard to comprehend anyone, even this great cloud of witnesses, desiring authority or position in His presence. It seemed that in every moment I had spent here, He had become greater in glory and authority, and I knew my vision of Him was still limited. Just as the universe was obviously expanding at a great pace and the vastness of it was already incomprehensible, our revelation of Him would likewise be expanding for eternity. "How could mere men ever represent You?" I questioned.

"When My Father moves His little finger, the whole universe trembles. To shake the nations with your words does not impress anyone who dwells here. But when even the least of My brethren on earth shows love, it brings joy to My Father's heart. When even the most humble church sings to My Father with true love in their hearts, He silences all of heaven to listen to them. He knows that one cannot help but to worship when they are beholding His glory here, but when those who are living in such darkness and difficulty sing

with true hearts to Him, it touches Him more than all of the myriads of heaven can.

"Many times the broken notes from earth caused all of heaven to weep with joy as they beheld My Father being touched. A few holy ones struggling to express their adoration for Him have many times caused Him to weep. Every time I see My brethren touch Him with true worship, it makes the pain and grief I knew on the cross seem like a small price to pay. Nothing brings Me more joy than when you worship My Father. I went to the cross so you could worship Him through Me. It is in this worship that you, the Father, and I are all one."

Of all that I had yet experienced, the emotion I felt coming from the Lord as He told me this was greater than I had ever felt. He was not weeping or laughing. His voice was steady, but what He was telling me about worship came from such depths within Him that it was almost more than I could take. I knew I was hearing the deepest love of the Son of God—to see His Father's joy. True worship from the embattled, struggling believers on earth could do this, it seemed, like nothing else.

For the first time I now badly wanted to leave that place, even with all of its glory, just to get into even the most dreary little worship service on earth. I was overwhelmed by the fact that we could actually touch the Father. One person who worshiped Him from earth during these dark times meant more to the Father than the millions and millions who worshiped Him in heaven. From earth we could touch His heart like we might never be able to do again! I was so overtaken by this that I did not even realize I had fallen prostrate. I then fell into something like a deep sleep.

I saw the Father. Millions and millions were attending Him. His glory was so great and the power of His presence so awesome that I felt the whole earth would not have even measured as a grain of sand before Him. When I had once heard His audible voice, I felt like an atom standing before the sun, but when I saw Him, I knew that the sun was like an atom before Him. The galaxies were like curtains around Him. His robe was composed of millions and millions of stars which were alive. Everything in His presence was living—His throne, His crown, His scepter. I knew I could dwell before Him forever and never cease to marvel; there was no higher purpose in the universe than to worship Him.

Then the Father became intent on one thing. All of heaven seemed to stop and watch. He was beholding the cross. The Son's love for His Father, which He continued to express through all of the pain and darkness then coming upon Him, touched the Father so deeply that He began to quake. When He did, heaven and earth began to quake. When the Father closed His eyes, heaven became dark, and so did the earth. The emotion of the Father was so great that I did not think I could have survived if I had beheld this scene more than the brief moment I did.

Then I was in a different place, beholding a worship service in a little church building. As sometimes happens in a prophetic experience, I just seemed to know everything about everyone in the battered little room. All were experiencing severe trials in their lives, but they were not even thinking of them here. They were not praying about their needs. They were all trying to compose songs of thanksgiving to the Lord. They were happy, and their joy was sincere.

I saw heaven, and all of heaven was weeping. I then saw the Father again and knew why heaven was weeping. They were weeping because of the tears in the eyes of the Father. This little group of seemingly beaten down, struggling people had moved God so deeply that He wept. They were not tears of pain, but of joy. When I saw the love He felt for these few worshipers, I could not contain it either.

Nothing I had experienced gripped me more than this scene. Worshiping the Lord on earth was now more desirable to me than dwelling in all of the glory of heaven. I knew I had been given a message which could help prepare the saints for the battles that remained on earth, but now this did not mean nearly as much to me as trying to convey how we could touch the Father. Genuine adoration expressed by even the most humble believer on earth could cause all of heaven to rejoice, but even more than that, it could touch the Father. This is why the angels would rather be given charge over a single believer on the earth than to be given authority over many galaxies of stars.

Then I saw Jesus standing next to the Father. As He beheld the joy of the Father as He watched the little prayer meeting, He turned to me and said, *"This is why I went to the cross. To give My Father joy for just one moment would have been worth it all. Your worship can cause Him joy every day. Your worship when you are in the midst of difficulties touches Him even more than all of the worship of heaven. Here, where His glory is seen, the angels cannot help but to worship. When you worship without seeing His glory, in the midst of your trials, this is worship in Spirit and in truth. The Father seeks such to be His worshipers. Do not waste your trials. Worship the Father—not for what you*

[301]

will get, but to bring Him joy. You will never be stronger than when you bring Him joy, for the joy of the Lord is your strength."

Chapter XVI

The Sin

Then I was standing beside Wisdom again. He did not speak for a long time, but I did not need words. I needed to let what I had just seen saturate my soul. I strove to fathom the great business that we had been given just to be the Father's worshipers. To Him, the sun was like an atom and the galaxies like grains of sand. Yet He listened to our prayers, enjoying us continually as He beheld us and, I was sure, often grieving for us. He was much bigger than a human mind could ever conceive, but I knew that He was also the most emotional Being in the universe. We could touch God! Every human being had the power to cause Him joy or pain. I had known this theologically, but now I knew it in a way that shattered the seeming importance of anything else.

There was no way I would ever have words to convey this, but I knew I had to spend what time I was given on earth worshiping Him. It was like a new revelation: I could actually bring God joy! I could bring Jesus joy! I understood what the Lord had meant when He said that this was why He went to the cross. Any sacrifice would be worth it to just touch His heart for the briefest second! I did not want to waste another moment when I knew it could be spent worshiping Him. It was also obvious that the greater the trials or darkness from which the worship came, the more it touched Him. It made me want to receive trials so I could worship Him through them.

At the same time, I felt like Job when he said that although he previously had only known Him by the hearing of the ears, when he saw Him, he repented in dust and ashes. I was like Philip who had been with Jesus for so long and did not know that he was seeing the Father through Him. How astonishing our dullness must be to the angels! Then Wisdom spoke again.

"Remember the potential of even the least of My little ones to touch the heart of the Father. That alone makes their value greater than any price. I would have gone to the cross again for a single one of these. I also feel your pain. I know your trials because we share them. I feel the pain and the joy of every soul. That is why I still intercede continually for them. There will be a time when all tears are wiped away from every eye. There will be a time when only joy is known again. Until then pain can be used. Do not waste your trials. Your greatest worship and the greatest expression of your faith that pleases Us will come in the midst of your trials.

"You must see Me in your own heart, and you must see Me in others. You must see Me in the great and in the small. Just as I appeared differently in each of these who now stand before you, I will come to you in different people. I will come to you in different circumstances. Your highest purpose is to recognize Me, to hear My voice, and to follow Me."

As I turned to look at Wisdom, He was not there. I looked all around. I could feel Him everywhere, but I could not see Him. I then looked back at the group who stood before me. He was there. I could not see Him, but in a more profound way than I had known before, He was in each of them. As the Reformer began to speak, it was his own voice, but I could hear the voice of Wisdom in him just as when He spoke to me directly.

"He has always been in us. He is in you. He is in those to whom you must return. From time to time He will appear to you again, but you must know that when you do not see Him as He appears, you can better recognize Him where He dwells, *in* His people. He is Wisdom. He knows how, when, and through whom to speak to you. The ones whom He speaks to you through are a part of the message. Remember what He said when He wept over Jerusalem, **'from now on you shall not see Me until you say, "Blessed is He who comes in the name of the Lord"' (see Matthew 23:39).** You will not see Him unless you can see Him in those whom He sends to you."

"It is easy for me to see and hear Him in you," I replied, "but it is not nearly so easy with those on the earth who have not yet been glorified."

"It is not meant to be easy there," Angelo replied. "To search for Him is the call of the kings who will reign with Him. Those who love Him and who love the truth will search for Him more than they would for the greatest treasures or for the greatest conquests."

Conquered by Him

"The greatest calling of all is to be fully conquered by Him," a man whom I did not recognize offered, stepping toward the front. "I should know," he added, and then he told me his name. I was shocked that this man would be found in the company of the saints. He had been a great conqueror, but I had always felt that he had done more damage to the name of Christ than possibly anyone else.

"I, too, found the grace of the cross before the end of my time," he added. "You are not just going back to conquer for Him, but to be conquered by Him. If you will devote yourself to surrendering to Him, He will use you to conquer in His name. True conquest is to capture the hearts of men with the truth that sets them free. Those who follow Him more closely will be used to conquer the most and will be the greatest of kings. On the earth these will seldom realize they have conquered anything. They will not see what they have really accomplished until they get here. Those who lay up great treasures on earth, even spiritual treasures, will have little here."

"On earth you cannot measure eternal treasures," Paul said. "When I died, it looked like everything I had given my life to building on earth had already perished. The churches I had given my life to raising up were falling into apostasy, and even some of my closest friends were turning against me. During my last days, I felt that I had been a failure."

"Yes, but even I count Paul as a spiritual father," the great conqueror continued, "as do most of us who are here. Most who will come through the great battle of the end will be victorious because he was faithful to stand for truth. You will not measure true spiritual fruit rightly while you are on the earth. You can only measure your true success by how much more clearly you are able to behold the Lord, by how much better you know His voice, and by how much more you love the brethren."

Then Paul spoke again.

"For months before my execution, I did feel like a failure. However, on the day of my execution I was reminded of Stephen, who I had watched die at my own feet. The memory of the light that was on his face that day had carried me through many trials. I always felt he had somehow died for me so that I could see the true light. I knew if I died like Stephen, then even if everything else I had done had been futile, it would ensure that my life would not have been in vain. I was so thankful that I really was dying for the sake of the gospel, even if it did not look then like my ministry had accomplished very much.

"As the revelation of this came upon me, so did the grace, and my last day on earth was the most wonderful of all. I then realized that as I had lived and sincerely tried to die daily to my own desires in order to serve the gospel, every time I denied myself, there were eternal seeds being planted even though I could not yet see them in the temporary realm. Being here, I can now see that this was certainly true. You must not try to judge by the fruit that you see on earth, but do what you must do because it is right.

"Even so, more than bearing fruit, your call must be to know the Lord. If you seek Him you will always find Him. He is always near to those who draw near. Many want His presence, but they do not draw near. You must do more than want Him—you must seek Him. This is part of your call. There is no higher purpose. Your victory will be measured by your seeking. You will always be as close to Him as you want to be. Your victory in life will be according to your desire for Him."

Then Paul lifted his hand and pointed to me. "You have been given much, and much will be required of you. Even if you bury many of the talents entrusted to you, you can accomplish far more than others, but you will have failed in your commission. You must never measure yourself by others, but keep pressing forward, seeking more of Him. And yet, with all of the glory which will be revealed to you, never take off that cloak!"

SOWING AND REAPING

I looked down at the cloak of humility to which he was pointing. In all of the glory I was now seeing, its drabness seemed multiplied. I was appalled that I looked so bad while standing in their presence. I drew it back to see the armor under it, which was now more brilliant than I had seen it before. It was so brilliant that the more I uncovered it, the more the group in front of me faded because of its brightness. However, I was feeling far less embarrassed with the brightness of my armor shining out. I then decided to take the cloak all of the way off while I was there so I would at least not feel as repulsive in the presence of so much glory.

To my shock, when I spoke no one answered. I stood quietly for a few moments. I could not see anything because of the brightness of my own armor. I did not understand why I could not hear anything either. I then called out for Wisdom.

"Put your cloak back on," I heard Him reply. I did as He said and began to dimly see the outline of the Great Hall again.

"Lord, what happened to everyone? Why is everything so dim again?"

[308]

"You can see nothing here without wearing that cloak."

"But I have it on now, and I still cannot see very well," I protested, feeling a terrible desperation.

"Every time you take off humility, you will be blinded to the true light, and it will take time for you to be able to see it again."

Even though I was beginning to see the glory again, it was nothing like before. My vision was coming back, but very, very slowly. I was grieved beyond words.

"Where is Paul?" I asked. "I know he was about to tell me something very important."

"When you took off your cloak, all of those who were here departed."

"Why? Why would they depart just because I took off the cloak? I was just embarrassed by my appearance. Did that offend them?"

"No, they were not offended. They knew you could not see or hear Me through them without the cloak, so they returned to their places."

I was more grieved than ever at this statement. "Lord, I know what they were about to say to me was very important. Will they return?"

"It is true that you missed an important revelation by taking off your cloak. It would have helped you, but if you learn the lesson not to ever take off the cloak again, especially for the reason that you just did, you will have learned another important lesson."

"Lord, I think I have learned that lesson. I do not remember ever feeling this bad. Can they not come back and share what they had for me now?" I begged.

"All truth and all wisdom come from Me. I speak through people because the people I speak through are a part of the message. While you remained humble enough to keep your cloak on, I could speak to you in glory. Whenever you take off that cloak, you become spiritually blind and deaf. I will always speak to you if you call on Me, but I must change the way I speak to you.

"I do not do this to punish you, but to help you get your vision back more quickly. I will give you the message that I was going to give you through these witnesses, but it must now be given through your enemies. It will come with trials, and you will have to bow very low to receive it. This is the only way that you will get your vision back as quickly as you will need it. For what is coming, you must be able to see."

BROKENNESS

The grief I felt was almost unbearable. I knew that what I could have received in such a glorious way was now going to come through great trials, but even worse than this was the fact that the great glory which I had beheld just a few minutes before was now so dim.

"Lord, I am sorry for what I did. I now know how wrong it was. The pain of this mistake is almost too much to bear. Is there no way I can just be forgiven and receive my vision back? It does not seem right that one brief moment of pride should be this devastating," I pleaded.

"You are forgiven. Nothing is being done to you for punishment. I paid the price for this sin and all others. You live by My grace. This is not because of the Law of righteousness. It is because of My grace that there are consequences for sin. You must reap what you sow, or I could not trust you with

My authority. When Satan took his first step into self-seeking and pride, multitudes of My angels whom I had trusted into his authority followed him. When Adam fell, multitudes suffered. For those to whom I give such authority, there is a corresponding responsibility. There can be no true authority without responsibility. Responsibility does mean that others will suffer if you go astray. Mistakes have consequences.

"The more authority you are given, the more you can either help or hurt others by your actions. To remove the consequences of your actions would be to remove true authority. You are a part of the new creation that is much higher than the first creation. Those who are called to rule with Me are given the greatest responsibility of all. They are called to a position higher than Satan held. He was a great angel, but he was not a son. You are called to be a joint heir with Me. Your whole life, both the trials and the revelations, are all for the purpose of teaching you the responsibility of authority.

"For every lesson that you must learn, there is an easy way and a more difficult way. You can humble yourself, fall on the rock, and be broken, or the rock will fall on you and crush you into powder. Either way, the final result will be brokenness, which is humility. Pride caused the first fall from grace, and it has caused most of the falls since. Pride always results in tragedy, darkness, and suffering. It is for your sake, and those you are called to serve by having authority over, that I will not compromise the discipline you must learn by reaping what you sow.

"Adonijah boasted that his father, King David, did not discipline him. Solomon complained that he could not get away with anything without his father disciplining him. Solomon thought that he was not being treated fairly. David was not being unfair. He knew that Solomon was

called to be a king. Those who receive the most discipline are those who are called to walk in greater authority.

"You were blinded because you stepped out of humility and began to move in pride. The humble cannot be embarrassed. When you start to feel embarrassed, it is because you are beginning to move in pride. Let the embarrassment be a warning that you have departed from wisdom. Never let embarrassment control your actions. If it does, you will fall even further. Learn to embrace every opportunity to be humbled, knowing that I will then be able to trust you with more authority.

"Do not boast in your strengths, but in your weaknesses. If you will openly talk more about your failures in order to help others, I will be able to more openly display your victories, 'for everyone who exalts himself shall be humbled, and he who humbles himself shall be exalted' (Luke 14:11)."

I knew that everything He was saying was true. I had preached the same message many times. I thought of how Paul had warned Timothy to pay attention to his own teachings and realized that I needed my messages more than those to whom I preached. Now I was more ashamed of the shining armor I wore than of the humble cloak. I pulled the cloak even tighter. When I did this, my eyes brightened and my vision got strikingly better, even though it was still far from what it had been.

I turned to see the door. I was afraid to go back through it, at least until I had received more of my vision back.

"You must go now," Wisdom said.

"What is on the other side?" I asked.

"Your destiny," He replied.

[312]

I knew that I must go. I was still very sorry that I could not enter the door again with the vision that I had previously because I already knew how dark it was on the other side. I will be even more dependent on others for a time, I thought, and committed myself to trusting the Lord and not my own vision. Immediately, my eyes grew brighter again. I started to look back once more at the Great Hall to see if they were as bright as they had been, but I decided not to. I just determined that it was better now not to look back. Then Wisdom appeared beside me, almost as brilliant as before. My eyes had adjusted to the light so fast that I could now look at Him. He said nothing, but just looking at Him gave me great courage. Even so, I still felt remorse that I had not received the message that I was about to receive from the witnesses.

"If you turn that remorse into resolve, then the trial will be much easier. Then when your enemies appear to exalt themselves over you, you will grow even more in the authority to prevail over My enemies."

When I looked back at the door, I was amazed. I saw so much more on it now than I had seen before that for a moment I thought I was at a different door. It seemed to have grown still more beautiful and was not like any door I had ever seen, even in this realm. There were exalted titles written in a most beautiful script, all in gold and silver. There were beautiful jewels that I did not recognize, but they were so compelling that it was hard to turn my gaze from them. They were all alive. I then realized that the entire door was alive.

As I gazed at the door, Wisdom laid His hand on my shoulder. *"This is the door to My house."* When He said this, I immediately understood that the attraction I now felt for this door was the same that I felt when I looked

[313]

at Him. It *was* Him somehow. I wondered how anything this beautiful could have looked so plain and uninviting before. The Lord answered.

"You cannot see My house as it is until you see Me in My people. As you began to really hear Me through My people just before you took off your cloak, your eyes were opened to begin seeing My house as it is. There is much more glory to be seen in it than you can now behold. This is the door, but there is much more. When you return to the realm of your own time, this is what you must seek. This is what you must lead My people to. This is what you must fight for, and this is what you must help to build—My house."

With Wisdom's hand upon me, I walked toward the door. It did not open, but I passed right through the midst of it. I do not believe that there is a human language which could describe what I felt as I passed through it. I saw the glory of all ages in a single moment. I saw the earth and the heavens as one. I saw myriads of people who were more glorious than any angel I had yet seen. I also saw myriads of angels. These were all serving in His house.

Now I knew the call. Even though I had already been through so much, I knew the quest was just beginning.

THE TORCH
AND THE SWORD

INTRODUCTION

This book is a compilation of fourteen years of prophetic visions, dreams, and experiences that began in 1988 and continued through 2002. It was not until 2002 that I saw how these fit together, forming an important part of the message that was first published in *The Final Quest* and continued in *The Call*. This book includes experiences that came both before and after those written in the previous two volumes.

You may wonder why the Lord would give prophetic revelation in such a jumbled timeline. I often wonder the same thing. However, a message in these visions helped me to understand the reason. Also, if you become a student of biblical prophecy, you will quickly learn that the events foretold in a single chapter of Scripture can jump back and forth thousands of years. It is my opinion that the Lord does this kind of thing to keep us dependent on His Holy Spirit, not only for the revelation, but for the interpretation and application as well.

Understanding prophecy has obviously been intentionally placed beyond the realm of human science or wisdom. To those who are inclined to depend on their own abilities in their search for understanding, this can often be disconcerting and discouraging. To the true God-seeker, the mysteries are a part of the glorious, ultimate quest—the great adventure that seeking God is supposed to be.

The quest to know God and His ways is full of mystery. There are keys to unlocking these mysteries, such as faith, devotion to truth, integrity, and sanctification. However, these are not to earn gifts and revelation from Him, but to separate those who are true worshipers of a holy God from those who are just seeking knowledge.

Even so, we are completely dependent on the Lord's willingness to show us something before we can understand it the way it is intended. Thankfully, one of the greatest of His promises is that if we will seek Him, we will find Him (see Proverbs 8:17). It is my hope as you read this compilation of experiences that you will gain understanding of His ways. Even more, I hope you are drawn to experience Him for yourself, with the end result that you love Him more and are closer to Him than before.

THE PROPHETIC PACKAGE

It has always been interesting to me that more people ask how I receive the things I write about than about the issues which they address. This is not wrong. In fact, there is merit to understanding the package in which revelation comes. This is because often the package is a part of the message. For this reason, I included in this introduction, and occasionally in the text of the book, the way in which they came to me.

Very often I am also asked for more personal information about myself. This, too, is a fair request, as we are exhorted **"to know them which labor among you" (see I Thessalonians 5:12 KJV).** I think some issues and events in my personal life can help give more understanding to the prophetic experiences, so I have included those in this introduction, also. However, if you are not interested in this kind of information, I encourage you to go straight to Chapter One where the vision begins.

A PERSONAL JOURNEY

Most of the dreams, visions, and prophetic experiences included in this volume were personal messages to me, so I have written them in first person just the way they came. Therefore, understanding some of the parts of my personal journey at the time they came may be helpful to understanding the message. However, I have not included anything that I believe was intended to be just a personal message for me.

As I was repeatedly told in these experiences, I am but one of many who are called to the things addressed in them. In this same way, the events throughout Scripture, which happened to individuals and were personal messages for them or personal letters to specific groups, also speak to all Christians. If these apply to you or your situation, you should freely take them personally.

To lay a brief foundation for the messages contained in this book, in 1980 I left full-time ministry because I felt my personal relationship to the Lord had become shallow. I felt too superficial in my faith and experience to be leading others. I was deeply convicted by Galatians 1:15-16:

"But when He who had set me apart, even from my mother's womb, and called me through His grace, was pleased to reveal His Son in me, that I might preach Him."

I was beginning to understand that even though God had called me to the ministry I was attempting, I had confused His calling with His commissioning. Because of this, I began the ministry prematurely. The Lord had been revealed "to me," but not "in me," which Paul explained had to happen before he went forth to preach.

Paul was also preaching **"Him,"** Jesus. My ministry had been mostly devoted to principles and formulas for success—spiritual and Christian success, but still my message was more about us than Him. I felt like the men of Athens, worshiping an **"unknown God" (see Acts 17:23)**. Most of my knowledge of God had come from other people rather than revealed to me by the Spirit, which Paul acknowledged as being crucial for his own ministry.

All of this combined to make me a very shallow and ineffective minister of the gospel, compelling me to resign from the ministry and seek secular employment until I felt the Lord had truly been revealed **"in me."**

As a licensed Airline Transport Pilot, I took a flying job. This usually required me to fly a couple of hours a day and then spend many hours sitting in airports and hotel rooms, so I had plenty of time for studying and seeking the Lord. I was often able to spend as much as forty hours a week in study and prayer.

Then, the corporation I was working for moved its plane, and suddenly my job ended. As I began to search for another job, I was surprised when I received a word from the Lord that I needed to return to the ministry full-time. In fact, I was shown that even though I was as superficial and inadequate as I had seen myself, I had overreacted and the Lord had not intended for me to leave the ministry. This word came in 1982.

Still, by no means did I feel ready to go back into "ministry" then, but rather felt it would probably take me many more years to be adequate. When I shared the word with my wife and best friend, they, too, felt this was not the course I should take at that time. I was easily persuaded to reject the call because of my feelings of inadequacy, so when an opportunity came for me to start an air charter business, I took it.

I consider starting that business to have been the biggest mistake of my life, though I did learn a lot through it which has helped me greatly since. The Lord is in the redemption business, and He will use even our mistakes for our good. However, it is always better not to make the mistakes, and I am in no way implying that we should make mistakes so that good can come. As the Apostle Paul said—that kind of thinking is foolishness which brings judgment. Even so, we can be thankful that He will use even our mistakes for our good if we really love Him and are called according to His purpose. So good came of it, but it would have been even better had I obeyed His call instead of taking a seven-year detour.

FLYING HIGH, THEN CRASHING

The air charter business became successful very quickly. Soon the business included a flight school, aircraft sales, maintenance, insurance, and overseeing the busiest airport in the state we were living in at the time. This all left me with little time for study and seeking the Lord. Though I learned a great deal about business and management, these were mostly wasted years spiritually.

The more successful I became, the emptier I felt inside. Even so, I was very close to having a net worth which would enable me to retire completely and devote myself to the ministry again without needing any outside support. This is how I justified being so driven to keep building the business and making more money.

While on a hunting trip in 1986, I was sitting in a field alone. Suddenly, I felt the presence of the Lord, and He began to speak to me, asking me to lay my business "on the altar." I noted that He said this was *my* business instead of His, as I had always claimed.

To my surprise, the Lord was also offended by my vision of being able to make enough money to support myself in ministry so I would never have to take up an offering. He was offended because it implied that He was not capable of taking care of those who were in His service. He showed me that this was rooted more in my pride than in a noble devotion. I "gave" the Lord my business and asked Him to do with it whatever pleased Him.

Immediately, the business that I had worked so hard to build began to collapse. Soon I was in bankruptcy court, having lost a small fortune. I was able to sell our assets, including our dream home and property, to pay our debts. When it was all over, I owned a car and had a couple of thousand dollars. I felt I had been a failure in ministry and now a failure in business.

Some who were the closest to me were faithful to remind me that I was a failure, but I hardly needed reminders. It was the low point of my life.

I knew I was called to a ministry and wanted one day to be devoted to it full-time, but I did not want to enter the ministry as a failure, but as a success. I was ashamed that I felt I had nothing to offer the Lord, but this, too, was pride. I had proven in all ways to be both weak and foolish. I know the Scripture that says this is usually the kind of person He calls, but there is a big difference in being a failure in business (financially) and being a failure spiritually, where people could be hurt. I was still reticent to return to the ministry where others might be hurt by another failure.

Then one week in early 1987, two people from different parts of the country, whom I knew did not know each other, came to me and gave me the same word from the Lord—if I did not return to the ministry immediately, He would give my commission to someone else. I did not know what my commission was, but it shook me enough to enable me to lay everything aside and return to the ministry. My apparent weakness and foolishness would just require me to trust the Lord more, which is of course exactly what He wanted.

I had self-published my first book, *There Were Two Trees in the Garden*, in 1985 while still in business. The only advertising for this book had been by word of mouth, but by 1987, distribution was growing rapidly. This was bringing in quite a few invitations to speak in churches and at conferences. After the word to return to ministry came, I decided to take some of these offers. I especially wanted to get a sense for what was happening in the body of Christ at that time, as I had been out of circulation for seven years.

After only a couple of trips, I came home quite discouraged by the seemingly overwhelming lack of purpose and direction of the church. This lack of direction of the church did not help me to understand my own purpose and direction for ministry either. As I was praying about this situation, I had a two-and a-half-day prophetic experience in which I was shown a panorama of coming events (which I published in my book titled, *The Harvest*). That vision imparted to me a great hope for the future and the church, which has given considerable purpose and direction to my ministry since.

A New Level of Prophetic Encounters

During the two-and-a-half-days in which I was given this extensive vision of the coming harvest, I felt I had received more prophetic revelation than I had in any other seven-year period of my life. In those two-and a-half-days, I felt the time I had missed in the seven years that I had been

[323]

distracted from my ministry was made up. In a very real way, the Lord made up for me **"the years the locust have eaten" (see Joel 2:25 NIV)**. It also made me appreciate the value of prophetic experiences like I never had before.

Within months of having this vision, I started meeting other people who had some of the most remarkable prophetic gifts of which I had ever seen or heard, except in Scripture. Many of these people would become my lifelong friends. One of these was Bob Jones.

When I met Bob, he shared a couple of dreams that he had had about me which described my plight. He then gave me some answers to where I was headed, all with amazing clarity. There were even details in these dreams about my family of which I was not aware, but later they were confirmed to be true.

In the coming months, Bob called and gave me words or shared dreams which were incredibly specific and detailed and they would come to pass in the most amazing ways. This was more wonderful than can be described, imparting to me a sense of being in the will of the Lord like I never felt before in my life. Every day became an amazing and wonderful adventure. I was convinced this was the way the Christian life was supposed to be!

Then Bob gave me a word that I was to have a visitation from the Lord in October of 1988. He said that in this visitation I would receive a commission which would establish me on my course. I naturally waited with great anticipation, but October passed with no visitation. I assumed that Bob had missed something and just continued my increasingly busy schedule.

THE GREAT REBUKE

In March, I was scheduled to meet Bob in Louisiana to visit a few churches. Before leaving I received a word from the Lord that I had become too busy, and I was already five months behind in what He had given me to do that year. I determined that after this next trip I would slow down.

Before meeting Bob, I went to Texas to do some television programs with James Robison. After taping the programs, James and I were sitting in his office talking. Suddenly, James started chastising me for being too busy. Having just heard the same rebuke myself, I took his counsel even more seriously.

After leaving James' office, I asked for the Lord's forgiveness. He spoke, reminding me that I was five months behind in finishing a project that He had given me to do. He also reminded me that it was five months since the promised visitation, and this was the reason I had not received the commission yet. He said that if I would repent and go home, He would visit me.

I called and left a message for Bob that I was not going to meet him in Louisiana. I called my wife and told her the same thing, as she was visiting her parents in Slidell, Louisiana and was planning to come over with the kids for the meetings. I then left for my home in Charlotte, North Carolina.

A VISITATION

When I arrived at our empty house, I began praying and seeking the Lord. I wanted more clarity about how I had gone so far off track in such a short period of time. All He said was for me to go to bed because He was going to visit me that night. I assumed He meant in a dream, but I was so

[325]

excited that I did not think sleep would be possible. Even so, I turned off all of the lights in the house and determined to go to bed.

The Lord must have put me to sleep because I do not even remember lying down. In the middle of the night, I suddenly awoke feeling a Presence in the house. I was surprised since it seemed like all of the lights were on, and yet I remembered turning them all off. I wondered if one of my neighbors had come in, not knowing I was home. Suddenly, the Lord walked into my room. There were no lights on in the house—the light was coming from Him.

I was terrified. I was grasping my pillow and wanted to get up, but I was not able to. He walked over to me and placed His hands on my shoulders. I felt power building up within me like electricity. It was not painful as much as it was uncomfortable because a great pressure was building up inside. Soon the pressure became so great that I was afraid I was going to explode. When I did not think I could take it any longer, He took His hands off, and the power receded. He did this over and over, each time taking His hands off right when I thought I was about to die.

Then He turned and started to walk out of the room. I was concerned that He had not said anything to me, and I did not know what this experience had meant. He turned just before going through the door and said, "Bob Jones will explain this to you." I could not help but wonder why He did not just explain it to me Himself. The next thing I remember was waking up in the morning.

I lay in bed for a while remembering everything that had happened. I started to wonder if He had really come or if it had just been a dream. When I sat up and reached for my clothes, I felt a surge of power go through me just like when He had laid His hands on my shoulders. Electricity arced from my hands to the post of the metal bed. I knew then that it had been real and not just a dream.

For a few minutes I was afraid to touch anything for fear I might electrocute myself! I felt so much power inside that it was scary. When the power finally receded, I got up and dressed.

During the morning, the surges of power would go through me every hour or so. I did not know if I wanted them to stop or continue because I did not really understand what it was. I could hardly do anything but sit in awe. Finally, I went next door to visit my neighbors, Harry and Louise Bizzell. As soon as I walked through the door, Harry looked at me and said, "You had a visitation!"

I don't know if I just looked that scary or if Harry discerned it, but he knew. This made me feel free enough to tell him about it. I told him the one thing that bothered me was that I could not remember how many times the Lord had laid hands on me, and I knew this was important. Harry suggested that I call Bob Jones since the Lord had said he would explain it to me.

I had been hesitant to call Bob because I wanted him to hear from the Lord and call me. However, at Harry's suggestion I decided to call him just to ask how things were going in Louisiana but was determined not to give him a hint about the visitation. I wanted to be sure that anything he received was from the Lord.

When I talked to Bob on the phone he said that everything was going fine. However, when he had tried to pray that morning, he was amazed by "how the heavenlies were stirred up." He said the only time he had ever seen them that stirred up "was when Jesus passed through to visit someone."

[327]

I still did not tell Bob anything but was greatly encouraged by the way the heavens were stirred up. It was just another confirmation to me that the visit was real and not just a dream. It should not have mattered because a visit from the Lord in a dream is real, but for some reason it was important to me then.

The next day Bob called me. He had received a visit from an angel who had told him about my visitation from the Lord and my commission. He told me why the Lord had laid hands on me five times, and other details, giving me Scriptures which further explained it, as well as some things about my future.

I acknowledged everything and thanked him. I was surprised when he rebuked me for having such a lack of faith, which required him to have to confirm things like this. I did not know if Bob was joking or not, but when I laughed at his rebuke, I noticed he did not.

THE MESSAGE

What the Lord had imparted to me was a commission to help release the five equipping ministries listed in Ephesians 4 to the church, which are essential for her to fulfill her last-day ministry. This is central to my purpose and is therefore a part of every message I give, every book I write, and nearly every thought I think. Few things are more fulfilling to me than seeing someone begin walking in one of these ministries, truly becoming one who **"equips the saints to do the work of the ministry" (see Ephesians 4:12).**

Another part of the message had to do with walking in His power and calling, and commissioning those who are called "the messengers of power." These are also the ones which Enoch prophesied about, and they are soon going to be released upon the earth. When this happens, the works of the Lord will be seen throughout the earth in a way which they never have been before.

I have seen some extraordinary works of power from time to time, but I am just now starting to move toward walking in this commission. Also, the Lord never showed me that I would be one of these messengers of power. I would surely like to be, but I was simply given the commission to awaken and help prepare those who would walk in this. I was also told that I am only one of many who are called to do this.

What the Lord had given me to do, which was already five months behind schedule, was to finish the book *The Harvest*. This was the message He had given to me the year before in the two-and-a-half-day experience, which I described previously. I resolved to finish it as quickly as possible.

This book went on to surpass *There Were Two Trees in the Garden* in distribution, but over the next couple of years the Lord showed me how it would have reached far more people had it been released on time. Being on time with messages was a basic mandate the Lord gave me for starting MorningStar Publications and Ministries, which came from Matthew 24:45-47:

"Who then is the faithful and sensible slave whom his master put in charge of his household to give them their food at the proper time?

"Blessed is that slave whom his master finds so doing when he comes.

"Truly I say to you, that he will put him in charge of all his possessions."

The Lord wants His household to get their food **"at the proper time,"** and already timing was one of my great weaknesses—I think it still is. I tend to get so busy, mostly in ministry, that I miss important directives, messages, meetings, and getting the food out on time, which He has given to us for His household.

I should have returned to the ministry when He first called me rather than starting the air charter service. I had almost lost my commission to someone else because of my reticence and feelings of inadequacy. Then I had overreacted and become so busy that I almost missed my commission because I was doing too much. There is a ditch on either side of the path of life, and I had fallen into it on each side!

The reason I am sharing some of these personal things is because they are common mistakes for Christians, especially those in positions of leadership in the church. It is also something that must be corrected, or the consequences will be more costly as we approach the end of this age. These are primary reasons most Christians are not walking in their calling and not fulfilling their destinies and purposes. They are missing in both of the same ways that I almost did.

Many miss because they are too hesitant to start. Others get into ministry and quickly become so busy doing things for the Lord that they fail to draw close to Him. A successful Christian life will not be based so much on how much work we have done, but rather on how close to the Lord we have become and how obedient we have been.

It is not possible to walk as we are called without a personal encounter with the Lord every day. We need a holy addiction to His Presence so that He becomes more important to us than oxygen. I do not consider to have attained this yet myself, but it is my greatest pursuit.

THE COMMISSION

When I told Jack Deere about the visitation I had in early 1989, he remarked that he could not wait to see me praying for the sick. He felt that the power imparted to me from this visit was going to release many miracles. I, too, couldn't wait. However, the results were not very impressive. In fact, I felt so unanointed praying for the sick, I was afraid if I prayed for someone who was crippled that they might leave both crippled and blind!

I then rationalized that the prophetic gifts in me would go to another level. They didn't. In fact, I could not tell that I had any more anointing to do anything. Even so, it was during this same year that revelations did come which would lead our ministry toward some of its ultimate purposes. Without realizing it until recently, it was during that year that I was given the foundational understanding of my life's message.

Not long after this, Bob Jones told me I was going to receive another visitation from the Lord and another commission. It would come to me on the first of spring when I was in London. Much of what you are going to read in this book came during that experience.

A CALLING TO PREPARE THE WAY

In late 1989, we were able to lease an estate in Charlotte, North Carolina, as a base for MorningStar Publications and Ministries. We moved there in early 1990. Roger Hedgspeth and Steve and Angie Thompson became our first staff members. Shortly after them, Leonard Jones joined us as a worship leader, even though we did not have any meetings yet that required one and we did not have any planned.

As typical of where the ministry was at the time, we found a little shack in the woods, fixed it up for Leonard, and just told him to do what he does before the Lord. Leonard was a faithful, hard worker, showing up every day and staying long hours. What he did was worship. As he worshiped, he also did some composing. When he first played what he was writing, I was stunned. I had never heard music like it before. I was also impressed that Leonard was finding others who needed such an opportunity. I knew if we could find them, greater things than we ever expected would be released from them.

I determined to continue reducing my travel schedule so I could devote myself to establishing the ministry in North Carolina. Steve Thompson, Robin McMillan, Leonard Jones, and I began what we called School of the Spirit (which was quickly dubbed "SOS") meetings. Amazing things started happening from the first meeting.

These meetings were stirring up gifts in many people, so Steve Thompson asked if he could hold some training meetings for people who felt called to the prophetic ministry. I agreed and was amazed at how quickly extraordinary gifts were being released in numerous people, many of whom had never been used in that way previously. Soon, all of the believers around us began to be confident that they could personally know the voice of the Lord and be used by Him to do exploits. It started to feel like New Testament church life.

THE VISION

When the Lord called me to return to the ministry in 1982, He had shown me a teaching center and prophetic community. He said that when the prophets and teachers learned to worship Him together as they had at Antioch, we would again be able to release apostolic authority on the earth.

In the succeeding years, I was shown many things about the coming last-day ministry and the last-day church, that it would truly be an apostolic church. I was shown how the Lord would be revealed through His people before He returned to rule the earth. I saw a church on earth which was without spot—pure, holy, and full of such grace and power that the nations would all be in awe of her. Her message of the coming kingdom would shake every kingdom on the earth.

My ultimate part in helping to prepare the church for her calling revolved around the teaching center and prophetic community. It would be a place from which prophetic words and teachings would be distributed around the world. To see this come to pass soon became my primary devotion. Even so, I knew the timing for this had to be right and that the most important things usually take the longest time to unfold. I knew I would have to stay focused as well as patient.

This community is still in the formative stages. I expect it to take a few more years before even the foundation is completed. In fact, I think my primary job is to lay a foundation for some things that others are called to build upon. This is important to understand if you are to grasp the message of this book.

It is my calling to summon those who will live to do the will of God. They will live in a way which will forever be a testimony that truth is greater than any lie, and that love is stronger than death. At the same time, mankind is learning for certain that anything done without the Lord will ultimately lead to a most terrible disaster. They will also see the most wonderful consequences from things that are done in obedience to Him.

I have been promised that I will see at least the beginning of the most extraordinary move of God since God Himself walked the earth. And this move will be in preparation for

Him to walk the earth once again. If you are a Christian, it is your calling and destiny to be a part of this.

A SECOND VISITATION

The second visitation was in 1995 after Bob Jones visited our base in Charlotte. After we had finished one of our SOS meetings and were sitting in our kitchen, Bob was looking around as if there was something specific he wanted to find. He then asked me where the building was with the loading docks and the sign that said, "No empty boxes." I told him our warehouse had a loading dock, and I would show it to him the next day. He said he had seen it in a vision and that it was important.

Later, Bob asked me if I had planned my trip to London yet. I had in fact just accepted an invitation to go to London to speak at a conference. I was surprised that Bob knew about this. He then said that I needed to be there on the first day of spring. I thought about my schedule and realized that I was in fact going to be in London on the first day of spring. I asked Bob why I needed to be there at that time, and he reminded me of the word he had given me years before, which I had forgotten. A little perturbed at my forgetfulness, he started asking me a series of questions.

First, he asked me how long we had lived on that property. I answered that it had been five years. Then he asked me how long it had been since he had given me the word about London. It turned out to have been five years. He asked me how long we had been publishing *The Morning Star Journal*. It had been five years. He asked me how many children I had. Our fifth child had just been born.

He then asked me Amber's age. (She was our third child and Bob had prophesied her birth two years before she was born, having given us the date on which she would be born, August 8, 1990, and her weight, which was exactly 8 pounds). Amber was then five years old. All of these dates related to her birth because she was a sign of a new beginning coming to the church.

He then asked how long we had been holding the School of the Spirit meetings. It had been five years. Finally he said that I was going to London to receive a commission from the Lord in which I would receive five things.

"No Empty Boxes"

The next day I took Bob to our warehouse, loading dock, and offices. He said he had seen our place in a vision, but this was not it. He kept looking for a sign which said, "No empty boxes," but we had no such sign.

Since we had been looking for a larger building for our meetings, we decided to take Bob by one which we were close to leasing. As soon as we were near, Bob perked up. When we walked inside, he was sure it was the building he had seen in his vision. He wanted to see the loading dock. As we were looking around, we went through a door that had on the other side a sign that read, "No empty boxes." Not far away was the loading dock, just as Bob had seen it in the vision. So we signed the lease right away, and this became the home of MorningStar Fellowship Church in Charlotte.

Remembering the time the Lord had laid hands on me five times, I left on this trip to London with great anticipation. As I sat in my hotel room in London on the first of spring, it was a dreary, rainy day. I was a bit depressed because of some things I had seen in the ministry that had hosted our meetings. Then suddenly I was caught up into another realm.

It was in this experience that the Lord gave me the five things that are written about in this book. Over the next eight years He added to my understanding of each one. Recently, in a series of prophetic experiences, I was taken back to revisit the same places. The second visit was, in some ways, even more powerful than the first. When the Lord speaks two times like this, it often speaks of the level of importance. That is when I also determined that these experiences needed to be written. This message was not just for me, but for the many who are about to be awakened to an awesome destiny. These things will soon begin to unfold.

SUMMARY

Again, I have written these visions in first person because that is the way they came. I was in these experiences. I have been told by some that the message would be more palatable if I had written them in third person or as an allegory. This may be true, but I did not feel this would be honest or accurate. I tried to write them just as I experienced them.

I have also seen many change their minds who had a hard time believing that the Lord still speaks to people in this way, mostly because they started having the same kind of experiences. We can expect much more of this as we proceed toward the end of this age, and this is clearly stated in Acts 2:17-18:

"In the last days," God says, "I will pour out my Spirit on all people. Your sons and daughters will prophesy, your young men will see visions, your old men will dream dreams.

"Even on my servants, both men and women, I

will pour out my Spirit in those days, and they will prophesy" (NIV).

You simply cannot believe we are coming to the last days without understanding that there will be a dramatic increase of prophetic revelations and experiences. In fact, every time the Holy Spirit is poured out, there are accompanying dreams, visions, and prophecies.

The text in Acts 2, which is taken from Joel 2, emphasizes this release of prophetic revelation because in the last days it obviously happens on a much more expansive scale. I have watched with great interest, and sometimes amusement, as many who do not believe that these experiences are for today start having them! Like it or not, they are coming. As this Scripture states, it is one of the signs that we are truly coming to the last days.

Even so, one of the reasons these experiences will become so common as we proceed toward the end of this age is because we are going to need them. They are not for our entertainment or just to make our services better. They are crucial for our guidance, and we are going to need more specific guidance in the times ahead. It is this conviction which has compelled me to be far more open in writing about the experiences that have come to me.

I have two personal goals which compel me in almost all I do. One is to become so obedient to Christ that literally all of my thoughts are obedient to Him. The second is that I want to be more at home in the heavenly realm than the earthly, just as the Apostle Paul said about himself.

I live for the day when Christians can sit on the side of a mountain with an entire army seeking them and have perfect peace because they can see that those who are with them are more than those who are with their enemies. I want to see prophetic ministry restored to the body of

Christ so that even our enemies will say of us what they did of Israel, "There are prophets there who know what the kings of this world say in our innermost chambers!" I believe this is the heritage of the body of Christ. This is supposed to be normal Christianity.

Paul wrote in II Corinthians 3:7-8, **"But if the ministry of death, in letters engraved on stones, came with glory, so that the sons of Israel could not look intently at the face of Moses because of the glory of his face, fading as it was, how shall the ministry of the Spirit fail to be even more with glory?"**

This states that the glory we are supposed to be experiencing in the New Covenant is greater than what Moses experienced! Moses met with the Lord face to face and even had to put a veil over his own face because of the glory that reflected from him. We are supposed to be experiencing something greater than that!

One of the ultimate questions should be this: "Where is the glory?" One thing we can count on before the end of this age is that the glory of the Lord will be manifested on His people, just as we are promised in Isaiah 60:1-3:

"Arise, shine; for your light has come, and the glory of the Lord has risen upon you.

"For behold, darkness will cover the earth, and deep darkness the peoples; but the Lord will rise upon you, and His glory will appear upon you.

"And nations will come to your light, and kings to the brightness of your rising."

At the very time darkness is covering the earth, and deep darkness the peoples, the glory of the Lord is rising on His people and appearing on them. These are the times to which we are coming. This is what I have seen in almost every vision, dream, or prophetic experience that I have written about—darkness and conflict, glory and magnificence. I would prefer to see only the glory, but the two are coming together, and we must see and understand them both.

Accordingly, the body of Christ is about to go through a metamorphosis. It has been like a caterpillar crawling along the ground, but it is about to emerge into a glorious butterfly which soars above the earth. The church that is about to arise will be more at home in the heavenly realm than the earthly.

The kinds of experiences I am writing about will not seem strange to that church, and those who are going to the end of this age is that the glory of the Lord will be manifested on His people, just as we are promised in Isaiah 60:1-3:

"Arise, shine; for your light has come, and the glory of the Lord has risen upon you.

"For behold, darkness will cover the earth, and deep darkness the peoples; but the Lord will rise upon you, and His glory will appear upon you.

"And nations will come to your light, and kings to the brightness of your rising."

At the very time darkness is covering the earth, and deep darkness the peoples, the glory of the Lord is rising on His people and appearing on them. These are the times to which we are coming. This is what I have seen in almost every vision, dream, or prophetic experience that I have written about—darkness and conflict, glory and magnificence. I would prefer to see only the glory, but the two are coming together, and we must see and understand them both.

Accordingly, the body of Christ is about to go through a metamorphosis. It has been like a caterpillar crawling along the ground, but it is about to emerge into a glorious butterfly which soars above the earth. The church that is about to arise will be more at home in the heavenly realm than the earthly.

The kinds of experiences I am writing about will not seem strange to that church, and those who are going to be a part of it will soon hear a clear trumpet call, which is revealed in Revelation 4:1-2:

"After these things I looked, and behold, a door standing open in heaven, and the first voice which I had heard, like the sound of a trumpet speaking with me, said, 'Come up here, and I will show you what must take place after these things.'

Immediately I was in the Spirit; and behold, a throne was standing in heaven, and One sitting on the throne."

A door is standing open in heaven with an invitation for us to go through it. Those who answer this call will be caught up into the Spirit, with the result that they will always be seeing the One who sits on the throne. This is the ultimate purpose of all true, prophetic revelation— seeing the glorious, risen Christ and the authority that He now has over all.

There is a difference between believing in our minds and believing in our hearts. We may well know and believe the doctrine that Jesus is now above all rule, authority, and dominion, but if we really believed this in our hearts, our lives would be radically different. Romans 10:10 states, **"for with the heart man believes, resulting in righteousness."**

One of the primary results of any experience is to change concepts into heart beliefs. This is going to be the result of the prophetic revelation which will be poured out "in the last days." This will bring about a transformation of the church that is as radical as a caterpillar becoming a butterfly. For this reason, I pray that you are not satisfied with just reading about my dreams and visions, but that you will have your own.

This vision is not complete and is still unfolding. I ended this book at a place that seems like the middle of the story, because it is. There is much more to come. However, the rest is so extensive that it will require another book. Even so, the message contained in this book is enough for us to deal with for some time to come.

This is not a fantasy. True Christianity is the greatest adventure that anyone can ever have on this earth. True church life, the way it was intended to be, is a supernatural experience. It is life from another realm beyond this earth that brings true life to the earth. My prayer is that the message of this book will open, to those who read it, life in a greater reality—a life which testifies that heaven is real and that our King is seated on the throne which is above all others.

Rick Joyner
2003

CHAPTER I

The Torch

As I sat in my hotel room in London, I felt restless and thought about walking to Buckingham Palace, which was just a few blocks away. Even though I knew I was in the right place at the right time, it was one of my most difficult ministry trips ever.

I began thinking about the prophecy which had foretold this trip, so I laid my head back in the chair to rest for a moment. Suddenly, I was in another world.

I was standing on a beach, and water was gently lapping at my feet. I thought I must be dreaming, but I knew I was not asleep. I looked at the sky which was brilliant with color. It was like no sunset or sunrise that I had ever seen. I pondered why I could not tell if it was a sunrise or a sunset.

Then I noticed the air. It was more than just clear and fresh. With each breath I felt I was being rejuvenated, my mind was being quickened, and my thoughts were becoming increasingly more sharp and clear.

I looked at the mountains in the distance and began to study them. They seemed to be at least fifty miles away but maybe much farther. The air was so clear that it was hard to tell. I love mountains and have seen some of the world's most majestic, but these were more wonderful than any I had ever seen. They were like great fortress walls which exuded strength and purpose, yet they were also hospitable and inviting.

Next, I looked down at the water between the mountains and me, wondering if there was a way around it so that I could go to the mountains. As far away as they were, I was drawn to them like a magnet and wanted to go to them immediately.

I felt compelled to look more closely at the water. It too was crystal clear with just a hint of blue—a stunning contrast to the sky. I wondered if there could possibly be a more perfect place. In a strange way it seemed like home, like the place I belonged. I was coming alive in a way that was more than wonderful. It was like waking up from a dream into reality, but a much more wonderful one.

Suddenly, I noticed a figure walking toward me on the beach. I could see from the distance that He was carrying a torch. It gave off light which was the same color as the sky. I knew immediately that it was the Lord—I could tell by the way He walked, with purpose but not in a hurry. He is never in a hurry because time submits to Him. As He walked closer, I could see that He wore a white robe with a golden sash tied in the front. The hem at the base of His garment had a pattern of gold, as did the end of His sleeves.

"It is sunset and sunrise," He said. *"A sunrise in one place is a sunset in another. You live in the sunset of one*

[343]

age and the dawning of another. That is why you are here, to learn about the end of the age in which you are, and the beginning of the one which is dawning."

As He drew close, He extended the torch to me indicating that I should take it.

"This is yours," He said. *"I started this fire, but you must keep it going."*

As I took the torch, I was surprised it was so light, which made me think it must also be fragile.

"It is neither light nor fragile," the Lord said, answering my thoughts. *"It has more substance and more weight than the earth itself. This is the light of My presence. If I was not close to you, you could not hold it. If you drift from My presence, it will become heavy. If you drift very far from Me, you will have to lay it down. Then someone else will pick it up and carry it. It is yours to carry for as long as you stay close to Me."*

As I continued to study the torch, the Lord continued,

"This torch breathes the air of heaven, not earth. No power on earth can put it out if the torchbearer walks with Me in this realm. Its brightness and power depend on the life of the torchbearer and on how close he stays to Me."

I was still looking at the torch when the Lord began walking down the beach. He had only taken a couple of steps when I noticed the torch was getting heavy. I quickly caught up to Him. Then another voice behind us started speaking.

"Even the torch itself can distract you from following Him."

I turned to see a middle-aged man dressed in a simple monk's garb. He had a serious but cheerful face. He continued talking as we all walked.

"In your times there will be as many who carry this torch as in all of the times before you. You will know these torchbearers when you meet them. You must encourage and help one another. Because none of you can stand alone, you must join with other torchbearers. When you do, you will be able to overcome the power of the evil that will confront you. You can set people, cities, and even nations free with the light of this torch."

I then noticed the torch was breathing—it was alive! I grabbed it with both hands, and a surge of power flowed through me as if I had completed some kind of electric circuit. My vision increased, my mind became even sharper, and I felt my strength growing. I could not comprehend how anyone could lay aside such a treasure.

"You have not yet felt the pain of it," the Lord interjected. *"I uphold the universe with My Word. It is My Word that enables you to hold this torch. This torch is the light of My presence, and it is also what you call 'a movement.' I Am the Living Truth, and truth which is living is always moving. In the beginning the Holy Spirit moved, and He has not stopped moving. Life moves."*

The monk who was walking with us added, "In Him we live and move. The Holy Spirit is always moving.

When He moved upon the formless void, the chaos, He brought forth life. That is His purpose—to turn the chaos that evil has made in the world into the life of a new creation. When you move with the Spirit-life, creativity will be the air your spirit breathes."

"Who are you?" I asked.

"I am the one you call 'Thomas à Kempis.'"

"I am honored," I said. "I know your writings well. They sustained me through some dark times. In

[345]

fact, overall I think your writings are some of the most powerful I have ever found written outside of Scripture."

Thomas continued as if he had not even heard my remarks. "The times of great darkness will soon come upon the earth. There was darkness on the earth in my time, but not such as you are about to see. Remember, you will never be in the dark if you stay close to the Lord. The torch you carry has been the source of every true movement of the Spirit. The leaders of these movements were all torchbearers. The movements that stopped moving, and therefore stopped living, did so because the torch was laid aside. If you are going to endure to the end, you must stay close to the Source of this light and fire. He is moving, and you must not stop moving."

The Lord motioned for Thomas to come beside Him. As He put His hand on Thomas' shoulder, His affection for him was obvious.

"Men thought of Thomas as a humble laborer, one to cook, wash dishes, and weed the gardens, but he, too, carried this torch. From his post of washing dishes, he became more powerful than kings or emperors. He prophesied to millions over generations. Even today My message goes forth from his writings to help prepare the coming ones. You can be more powerful washing dishes and staying close to Me than you would be leading armies or nations but drifting from Me."

As we continued to walk, Thomas began to speak again.

"This torch is offered to all of His messengers. Only a few have carried it, and fewer still have carried it for very long. Not many have learned to abide in His presence. If you will stay close to Him, you will take what you see and feel here with you and impart it to many others. Many will be drawn to Him by this. If you take this torch and then lay it down, you can also be used to do much evil."

[346]

"How could anyone who has seen the Lord and carried this torch of His presence be used to do evil?" I protested.

"This torch will give its bearer great influence. Those who have carried it and then laid it down often did so because they began to esteem the influence of the torch more than His presence. As they drifted from Him, the torch became too heavy for them, they laid it aside, and began to substitute their own words for His Words. This is how the doctrines and traditions of men began to eclipse the influence of His Spirit over men. This has happened to every movement until now. Do you think you can do better than all of the other torchbearers?"

I felt the seriousness of this warning. I knew very well my tendencies to drift from seeking the Lord and staying close to Him. I also knew my pride and presumption at times to think that my thoughts were His thoughts and my words were His Words.

Even in the glory of His presence, as we walked, a chill came over me. Once I was given this torch, my failures would be compounded, with many more people affected. I thought about my previous failures in ministry and then my failure in business. Each one had been a little more devastating. Now my ministry was growing again. Could I carry the weight of this responsibility? In almost every way that counted, everything which I had started in the past had ended as a failure. "Would it be any different this time?" I thought.

The Lord looked at me in a way that conveyed both kindness and forgiveness, but at the same time, I felt the severity of the warning I was there to receive.

"My Spirit will go with you, and will convict you of your tendency to drift from Me. Even so, you must follow

My Spirit. Even the torchbearers will not be forced to follow Me. All will fall who do not love Me more than sin and wickedness. All will fall who do not love the truth more than they love the praises of men. If you love Me and My truth more than the idols that the world now worships, you will not fall. This will be your daily choice—to follow Me or serve idols which can easily eclipse your affection for Me."

I gripped the torch much tighter. As I did, I felt so much energy flowing through me that it was as if every cell in my body was awakened and ready to spring forward. I thought about Romans 8:11: **"But if the Spirit of Him who raised Jesus from the dead dwells in you, He who raised Christ Jesus from the dead will also give life to your mortal bodies through His Spirit who indwells you."** Being close to Him was causing my mortal body to come alive like I had never felt it before.

Being awakened in this way, I began to realize everything in this place was alive—the trees and grass, but also in a strange way it seemed that the mountains themselves were alive. Even the clouds were somehow trying to speak. In a profound way it felt natural. It was right. I began to have a kind of fellowship with everything I could see. As I drank this all in, the Lord continued.

"It is now time to show the earth that heaven exists. Lower the torch to the sea."

I lowered it to the water until it touched. Then I lowered it farther until it was completely submerged. The fire of the torch continued to burn brightly and even more beautifully under the water. Then the water caught on fire. Flames spread out from the torch and began to sweep toward the horizon. It proceeded slowly and steadily, reminding me of the way the Lord walked. I wondered if the sea was actually composed of some kind of fuel. As I looked at it more closely, I could tell that it, too, was alive!

I watched as the fire burned. There was no smoke and no fumes. There was some heat, but it was gentle, a kind of penetrating warmth which seemed to release even greater energy inside me. As I stood by, it continued to increase. Soon I felt I could leap over a house, or maybe even lift one. It was an extraordinary, wonderful feeling. As I became alive, I was joining a life force that gave me the strength of the whole. It was like experiencing a spiritual critical mass.

Thomas was watching me closely and soberly. He then added: "As you abide in Him and do His will, you will begin to flow with His life force, which is in all of the living. In this way, as we help others to come alive, the life grows in us too. Do not fall to worshiping this life force; you will only stay on the path of life if you seek the Source of life."

I knew this was another important warning—a trap which many cults and new age movements had fallen into. Even so, I wanted to remember the feeling. I knew that everyone who ever tasted of this life force would be forever addicted to it, perpetually seeking it like a junky seeks his next fix.

Thomas, also obviously reading my thoughts, continued. "There is no intoxication like life itself, but remember that it is still intoxication. Many fall under even the slightest touch of His Spirit and can become drunk in the Spirit by just a taste of this. However, the priests had to learn to stand and minister even in the presence of His glory. If you yield your body to this life, you will be drunken. If you yield your spirit, you will be quickened, strengthened, and see even more clearly. You must train the coming ones not to seek to feel good and not to become intoxicated by this power, but rather to be sobered, able to see clearly and function in their duty. You will have forever to feel good after you have accomplished your purpose."

The Lord turned and looked directly at me.

"You can set nations on fire with this torch. This is the same fire Moses saw in the bush. This is the fire I sent with him to set My people free. It is what I am about to send with My messengers to again set My people free."

I looked at the fire on the water, and I saw that the water was composed of multitudes of beings—people! They were on fire, but they were not being consumed. They were coming alive. This was a fire that would one day cover the earth. It would consume the wood, hay, and stubble, but it would purify the gold, silver, and precious stones in every life. I thought about what the Lord said in Luke 12:49:

"I have come to cast fire upon the earth; and how I wish it were already kindled!"

I looked over at Thomas. He knew what I was thinking.

"Yes, the time has come. The fire is now kindled!"

CHAPTER II

The Messenger

W e remained by the burning sea for a long time. The life, energy, and peace I felt continued to grow. It was like a rush of joy that did not pass away, but rather increased toward a certain fullness of joy. I knew there was nothing on earth that could compare to this, yet it seemed vaguely familiar.

"You are experiencing the joy and strength that man knew before the Fall," the Lord explained. *"You are only beginning to experience what is actually a normal life for man, the way I created him to live."*

As the flames of the sea swept over me gently, I began to recognize the feeling. It was what I had started to call "the Emmaus Road burning heart." It is the way our hearts burn when we walk close to the Lord and He personally teaches us. I began to think of Adam, who had walked with God in the Garden, and Enoch, who had walked with God so closely that he was translated straight into heaven.

The Lord again answered my thoughts. *"When I walked with Adam, I taught him about the creation and his purpose for cultivating and maintaining it. I also gave him the freedom to be creative as he cultivated it. He was created to bear My image. To bear the image of the Creator, one has to be creative. In this we had great fellowship.*

"True creativity can only be found by those who walk close to Me. It is a relationship with Me which few have experienced, but one I cherish very much. Some walk very close to Me, even though they do not know My name. They do not know that I was made flesh and walked on the earth. The time has come for all who seek Me and My ways to know My name and to know My ways, which were revealed when I walked the earth.

"When Adam walked with Me, he was in harmony with the creation and felt the energy and strength you now feel. He was so full of life that he lived almost a thousand years after sin entered him and the discord of sin entered his soul. Great power is in life, but all life will lose its power if it does not stay close to Me.

"Enoch yearned for what Adam had lost. He walked with Me, and I began to teach him like I did Adam. He discovered the source of life, walking with Me. The life became so great in him that he would have still remained on the earth if I had not brought him up to dwell with Me here. He was too full of life to die, so I had to take him up."

"I am still learning about life," another voice behind me said.

I turned and saw a man standing far away in a beautiful green meadow. His voice seemed to be much closer than he actually was. He began to walk toward us in a way similar to the Lord's walk—resolute but unhurried. As he approached I noticed that his face was the same color

[352]

as the sky, the torch, and the Lord's face. He also wore a garment similar to the Lord's. He walked up and took the torch out of my hand.

"I must bless you before you go—I must bless the torchbearers. The purpose of every movement on the earth is to compel men to do what I did—to walk with God until they are more at home in the heavenly realm than on earth. Man was created to dwell on the earth with his body while his spirit soars into the heavens."

"Are you Enoch?" I asked.

"I am," he said as he reached over and touched my heart.

"The fire burns, but what you lack is discipline and endurance. You walk adequately for short periods. Now you must learn to walk with endurance. You must resolve to walk each day in the domain over which the Lord has given you to rule. He has given you authority, but you must walk with Him in your domain. Only then will you be fruitful and multiply as you are called. Your domain is your garden. The path of life always leads to unity and harmony—with God first, and then with all that is His. This takes strength and endurance because the whole creation is now in discord and opposes unity."

Enoch then took the torch and touched it to my heart. It caused a great rush of energy and power and then a joy that almost could not be contained. When he pulled it away, the fire continued to burn inside of me, and the energy continued to surge in waves throughout my body. I knew I had felt this before.

"The Lord makes His messengers flames of fire. You cannot walk with God, or fulfill His purpose for you on the earth, unless you keep this fire burning in your heart. Lukewarmness is your deadly enemy. You must not let the fire wane by drifting from His presence. This fire which now burns in your heart must be given fuel each day. Its fuel is the atmosphere of heaven, which is the breath of God. What He breathes upon lives, and what He does not breathe upon dies. Seek this life and pursue it. If you do, you will leave a trail of life where the River of Life will break out and flow. If you walk as you are called, you will help restore true life to the earth."

Enoch then took my face in his hands and looked into my eyes. He was the very definition of graciousness. He seemed to be so saturated with joy and love that I felt he was the most like the Lord of anyone I had ever met. I felt that anyone who saw him would spend his life trying to be like him. I then realized the main reason he was looking into me was so I would look into him. I did. Then he released me and walked back in the direction from which he had come.

"Enoch has a special investment in you," the Lord said, as we both watched him go. *"He prophesied the coming of the mighty ones who are soon to be released on the earth. From the time he was allowed to see them, he has waited for this time. You are called to help awaken these mighty ones to their destiny. When they are awakened, they will have the heart of Enoch. Their might and strength comes from this torch which Enoch first picked up and other faithful ones have kept alive on the earth.*

"From among those coming, there will arise many like Abraham, Moses, Elijah, John the Baptist, Peter, Paul, and John. There will be as many as a thousand like each of the great messengers in the age that is now ending.

"After each of the torchbearers departed the earth, they left their mantles of authority to be picked up by others. These have been divided just as Mine were at the cross. When one

has a part of a mantle and comes together with one who has another part, their authority will be magnified. Many of these mantles were hidden and kept for this time. These have been reserved for those who will be My messengers in the last days.

"It is true that spiritual authority multiplies with unity. One can put a thousand to flight, but two can chase ten thousand. The unity that these last-day messengers of power walk in will multiply the authority of the mantles they carry. The earth has never seen anything like what I am about to release through these messengers. They will walk in the fire of all who went before them. So now you must help them find their way and their mantles."

"Lord, here I feel I can do anything. Will I still feel this way when I return to the realm of earth?" I asked.

"No. When you return, this will all seem like a dream to you. The earth is under a shroud of fear and doubt which is growing thicker and darker. Even so, this realm is more real than the earth. But those in your time who break through the fear and doubt to walk in the power of life here will exhibit the greatest faith, and they will be trusted with the greatest authority.

"You may only vaguely remember what you see and feel here. Even so, the yearning for what you are now experiencing has been imparted to you, and this yearning will not go away. It is real and will lead you to reality.

"You can have all that you experience here again, but you, too, must grow up into it as you walk with Me on the earth. Only by this will you be wise and humble enough to be trusted on earth with the authority and power that you feel here. Wisdom and humility are more important than the power. Without them the power will corrupt you, and you will be used for evil. It is by your wisdom *and humility that you will be able to help My messengers along their way."*

I turned to see Enoch again and was surprised that he had gone only a few paces back. He was watching me with a very keen interest. He had a look of resolution which bordered on ruthlessness but was also combined with affection. Together this made him seem to be the very definition of rock-solid stability. I thought of how wonderful it would be to have had a mentor like him on the earth. The Lord once again answered my thoughts:

"You are called to be like him, as are all those I am sending to prepare My messengers of power. As you see My glory in Enoch, you will be changed by it. This is what you are called to be for other torchbearers, and they will be for you. You are not alone. Many others are called to this just as you are. However, you cannot be like him until you have walked with Me as he has. That is your whole purpose now— to walk closer to Me each day."

I then looked up at the clouds. They were as regal as the mountains. Each one seemed precisely in its place like those an artist would use to perfectly grace a painting. In no way did they hinder or block the light or the sky, but they framed it in a way which accentuated it. There was one directly above us which formed a perfect canopy. The clouds were so alive that personality exuded from them. They had purpose. I knew they were devoted to accenting the glory of everything that was around them as perfectly as they could, and they were doing this for us. The clouds were so wonderfully loveable that I wished there was some way to show them to every child on the earth.

The Lord let me drink this in and then continued.

"I created man to be the torchbearer for all of creation.

All men have this calling and were created to walk with Me and carry the light of life. Many are called, but few are chosen. You must now go and find those who have persevered to become My chosen ones. They will keep the fire and ignite in all men the fire that man was created to have.

"You will know these chosen ones by the fire that already burns in them. They will never be content with religious practices, for they yearn for Me and the reality of this realm. Because they seek Me, I will be found by them. I will give them their heart's desire—My fellowship. I will be their inheritance.

"I will also give them greater authority than I have yet entrusted to men on the earth. They will receive this because they will have the wisdom and humility to use it. When the Day of Judgment comes, their testimony will be that they walked with Me and their fire did not dim. These are My messengers that the whole creation has been waiting and travailing for. It is time for them to awaken."

The Lord then stepped out on the water, into the midst of the flames. I watched as He began walking toward the mountains. I knew I had to follow. As He walked out onto the burning sea, the torch became heavier. If I was going to continue holding the torch I would have to follow Him, but I was hesitant about trying to walk on the water. Finally I determined to step out without thinking anymore about it. When I did, I was able to walk on the sea as if it were a paved road.

The fire on the sea was hot, but it did not burn me. Instead, like the torch, it seemed to be imparting energy to me. As we walked, He turned and said: *"You are here because you have learned to see. To see is to evaluate and to seek understanding. This is the eye of the child. As long as you keep it, I can teach you and I can lead you.*

[357]

"Those who walk with Me grow in the strength which is in Me. I gave all men the capacity for this, to grow in both natural and supernatural strength. Those who do not walk with Me have a void in their souls for this supernatural strength. Those who do not walk with Me turn to the evil one for power to fill the voids in their hearts.

"I give My power to those who are wise and mature enough to use it. The evil one gives his power to those who are foolish and immature enough to be used by it. The time is coming upon the earth when all must choose to walk with Me or be taken over by the power of an evil greater than has yet to be known on the earth."

As we walked, waves of fire spread out from us on the sea as if we were a wind blowing. When the Lord pointed in a direction, the flames intensified in the direction He was pointing. I tried pointing, and it did the same. Then the Lord stopped and turned to look at me.

"I have a fire to cast upon the earth that has now been kindled. Pray for My fire to come. It will purify the earth. Pray for it to consume the chaff and to purify My chosen ones. I gave authority over the earth to man, and therefore I must be asked before I will move on the earth. This is the great purpose of those who walk on the earth, to know Me and My will. Then they can ask for My will to be done on earth just as it is done here in heaven, and it will be done. What you will now see here is so you will know My will on the earth for your time."

Suddenly, I was standing in a valley.

CHAPTER III

The Horse and the Girl

As I surveyed the valley, the first thing that caught my attention was a beautiful stream flowing through the middle. It was a natural setting, yet in some way it seemed wonderfully manicured. It was so seemingly perfect that I could not tell if I was still in the realm of heaven or back on the earth.

Then I heard a noise above me and on both sides. It sounded like many thousands of stomping feet. It was an alarming sound, especially in such a peaceful setting. I knew right away that something was not right. A great multitude appeared all around at the top of the mountain. It was an army of some type. As I watched, they began to descend from the top, moving slowly, even tentatively, but relentlessly.

I began to feel very strongly that this was an evil army with evil intent. Then thousands of vultures appeared like a cloud above them, circling as if waiting for a slaughter. I was appalled by what they would do to this beautiful place, not to mention afraid for myself since I was obviously hemmed in by this evil horde.

"What are you going to do about it?" a voice behind me asked.

I turned to see who was speaking and saw a large, white stallion. It was beautiful, with muscles rippling even as it stood still. I had never seen such intelligence in an animal's eyes before, so I wondered if it had spoken.

"What can I do about it?" I asked.

"I see you are a torchbearer. This horse is for you," the voice continued. "You must learn to ride it if you are going to help stop the evil horde that is coming."

"Is there time to learn to ride a horse?" I asked, looking around for the owner of the voice, since it was now clear that the horse was not speaking.

"There is still time."

Then a young girl, who seemed to be ten to twelve years old, stepped from behind the horse. She was dressed in what appeared to be a school uniform, but it was covered with silver and gold armor which was worn and battered. A sword was strapped to her belt. She was thin with a beautiful face and brilliant blue eyes which were set in a fierce, penetrating focus. She exuded a boldness and confidence with a childlike purity that was stunning in its nobility.

"I am here to teach you how to ride," the girl said. "We have time," she repeated as if trying to calm me.

I was captivated by this little girl but still agitated by the huge, dark force that was descending on us. I marveled at how calm she was. I wondered if she was just too young to understand what such a horde from hell would do to her and this place. However, as I looked at her it was obvious that she had both experience and intelligence beyond her years.

"I understand much more than you think," she replied as if my thoughts had been spoken out loud. "I am here to fight with you, but first you must learn to ride this horse. We do have time, but not time to waste. We must get started."

"Let's get started then," I said, not wanting to waste a second. "I know how to ride a horse. Is there anything special I need to know to ride this one?" I asked.

"I don't know," she answered. "I have never ridden a horse."

"But I thought you just said you were here to teach me how to ride. How are you going to teach me if you have never ridden a horse yourself?"

"You will learn by teaching me. You will not be fully trusted with this horse until I have my own and can ride it as well as you do. You also must understand that this is not like any horse you have ridden before."

"Tell me all that you know," I replied. "Can we drink from this stream?" I asked, feeling thirsty and weak.

"Of course. That is why it is here."

I reached up and touched the reins on the horse. I gently pulled, and it followed me without a hint resistance. When we reached the bank of the stream, I reached down and brought a sip of water to my lips. Immediately, my eyes brightened and my mind became clear.

As I continued to drink, I felt stronger. I gently nudged the horse forward, and it knelt down on its knees and drank. I had never seen a horse do that. The little girl did the same, getting down on her knees to drink. I decided to do the same and drank my fill.

"Fear makes you weak," the girl said when she had finished.

[361]

"You're a very wise little girl," I responded, thinking how truly extraordinary this child was. "How do you know so much, and how do you know about this torch?"

Before she could answer, the increased noise from above caused us both to look up. There was obvious confusion in the ranks of the evil host. My eyes were so sharp now from the water that I could make out some of the banners over the different divisions.

The banners I could see were named after different philosophies, religions, and strange mystical teachings, some of which I had heard about but were not very familiar with. There were other banners, but they were too small or far off for me to read.

As we continued to watch, the confusion increased until some of the divisions started fighting with each other. A huge cloud of dust was rising, and battles were breaking out in all directions. Soon the entire horde was disappearing back over the tops of the mountains. However, they did not go far because I could still hear them and see the dust rising from the great commotion which was obviously going on among them. So it seemed we were safe for a while.

"That is why we still have time," the little girl explained. "Demons hate each other as much as they hate us. They can't march together for very long before they start fighting each other. The only thing that can keep them unified is a battle with us. Their fear of us is stronger than their jealousy of each other. That is why we must be ready to defeat them when we fight. When we fight we must destroy them completely."

"You talk as if you are a seasoned warrior," I said, examining her armor. "Please tell me more."

"I have already watched well-meaning but foolish people try to fight the evil ones before they were strong enough to defeat them. This only made the enemy stronger and more unified. Battles that are not fought through until there is a complete victory always result in our losing more ground to the enemy.

"Even though it was before my time, I was told that we once had control over much of this country. Now we are surrounded in this little valley. The next time we fight we must win or all will be lost."

Then she looked at me with her penetrating blue eyes. They were like the blue of the hottest part of a fire. "Retreat is not an option! We have nowhere left to go!" she declared with more seriousness than I had ever seen in such a young child.

This startled me as I had been looking around to see if there was any way of escape.

"How old are you?" I inquired. "How do you know so much?"

"I am twelve, but I have been fighting since I was five. I have learned much in the battles, but my wisdom comes from this River. This is the River of Life. It gives the life which transforms experience into wisdom, the vision that is true."

"This is a beautiful stream, but hardly a river! This can't be the River of Life!" I protested.

"It is. Here it is small because it is always as large or small as its demand. Not many will come here to drink anymore because they would have to get past the evil ones who have seized the high places. Most would rather drink from the polluted streams which are not under attack than from the true living waters which are now always under attack. Few are thirsty enough to fight for this, but there is nothing more worth fighting for that I know of."

"Did you have to fight your way here?" I asked.

"I did. I came right down that path," she said, pointing to a place at the far end of the valley behind me.

"How did you get past the evil army?" I inquired. "Are there still gaps that you can get through?"

"No. They have us completely surrounded now. But anyone with the courage to keep moving even when they are attacked can make it through their ranks. I chose the weakest part of their army and walked right through the middle of it."

"What was the weakest part? And how did you know it was weak?"

"There was a large division called 'Ridicule.' I chose to walk through it because I knew they could not really hurt me. I was told that when they saw my resolve they would give way before me, and they did. They raved and screamed insults and obscenities, but they parted and let me pass. I blocked all of their shots with my shield and was not even wounded."

"Who told you that you could do that?" "My mother."

"Is she here, too?" I asked. "No."

"Where is she?"

"She didn't make it through. When we were passing through the ridicule, she stopped and said she was going back to get more people and lead them through. She said she would join me later. I don't think she will though."

"Why not?"

"She taught me very well, but she could not do what she taught me to do. I saw her waver from the insults and ridicule. She went back to get more people because she needs the approval of people. No one can make it through who cares too much about what others think of him."

"Can she make it in some other way?"

"It is possible, but going through the ridicule is by far the easiest way. In fact, when she hesitated and started to retreat, she was quickly overcome. She then began ridiculing me with the rest of them. Once you begin to retreat before the evil ones, you are easy prey for them. She is now one of their prisoners."

"I'm sorry. I know you must miss her. She was at least a great teacher. She did a great job teaching you."

"Thank you. I do miss her. It has been very lonely here, but it is still better than being out there, under the influence of that evil horde."

I watched the little girl drift far off in her thoughts, then quickly she snapped back to the conversation.

"I knew when we started, it would be hard for her and that she probably could not make it. I also knew I could not let that stop me. The only hope for her to ever get free and be able to drink from this stream is for me to not stop until I have fulfilled my destiny."

After a pause, she continued, "I have not given up on her, but myself and others like me are the only hope for people like her. We are here to defeat that evil horde and set its prisoners free. I do believe the time will come when she will drink with me at this stream—she and many others until this is a great river again. It will then flow to the sea and bring life to all."

"If there are many others like you, then I have no trouble believing that you will win the victory. Have you met others like yourself who have this vision and resolve to do this?" I asked.

"I think I have met some, but we keep getting separated. I know from my dreams that there are many more, and I will meet them soon. That's why you are here. I have seen you in my dreams, too."

"Tell me, what did you see about me?"

"Well, I did not see you specifically, but I saw the coming of the torchbearers. At first there were just a few and then more and more kept coming. I, too, will one day be given a torch to carry. In fact, many of the torchbearers are quite young."

As she was speaking, a large division of the evil army crested the top of the mountain and started down much more rapidly and in relatively good order. We watched transfixed as it advanced almost a third of the way down the mountain. Then it was attacked from the rear by another one of the evil divisions. Soon it sounded like several more joined in the assault on it.

The advance was stopped at that point while most of the column turned around to fight. However, a large part of this group remained at the point of its farthest advance and started setting up defenses, which quickly began to appear like a fortress.

As I looked at the little girl, I saw her nervous for the first time. I then noticed that the horse was also agitated.

"What do we do now?" I asked, surprised that I was asking a little girl for instructions.

Without answering, the girl knelt down at the stream again and drank with purpose. Soon she regained her composure, but her attention was still fixed on the fortress that was quickly being built. The horse had become so agitated that I was afraid it was going to run.

I walked over to take its reins and was surprised by how it looked me straight in the eyes. I tried to stay as calm as I could because I felt if he sensed fear in me, he

THE HORSE AND THE GIRL

would certainly bolt. He let me take the reins and lead him back to the stream. It was not as easy as before to get him to drink, but he did. Then he calmed down. I also drank, and the peace and joy again filled my being, while my vision grew stronger.

"What do we do now?" I asked again. "Have you seen anything in your dreams about this?"

"I did not see this in a dream, but I have seen this happen before. If we do not act soon, we will lose this valley."

Then she looked straight at me to be sure I would hear what she was about to say.

"Whenever I am asked what to do, I always turn to the river first and drink. Then I pray, as we must do now. I have been in two other places where this river ran, and both were taken over by the enemy. We must not let this happen here. We must fight this time," she said, looking at me kind of skeptically. "I will fight even if I have to do it alone. I don't think there is anywhere else left to go where this river flows."

"It is very noble to want to fight and to even be willing to fight alone," I replied, "but how can just the two of us stand against so many?"

She did not answer me, but started praying. I listened for just a few minutes. Her requests were concise and to the point. She did not try to explain anything to God. She mostly asked for the Holy Spirit, courage, wisdom, and power to defeat the enemy.

She then prayed for her mother and other loved ones who were captives of the evil horde. She asked for specific places to be retaken from the enemy. It was the prayer of a seasoned warrior who had seen many battles and did not want to waste time or words. It was also like a conversation with her friend. It was so moving that I did not believe the Lord could possibly reject her requests. When she ended, she looked up at me. All I could say was "Amen."

"You asked how we could defeat such a huge army. Why couldn't we? We have the Lord on our side."

"I understand, but how were the others lost that you fought for? What can we do differently this time? And are you sure there are no other streams like this one?"

"The way they have all been lost is by retreating. I will not retreat again. I will not listen to those who speak of 'strategic retreats' or any other kind. I am going to stand even if I have to do it alone. I also think that we lost them because there were too many of us."

"How could there have been too many when you are fighting against so many?" I asked, not doubting her as much as feeling that the answer to this was important.

"It is better to have a few who are in unity than many who are divided, who do not have a single, focused vision. Many of those who were with us before seldom drank from the stream, and I hardly ever heard them pray. I felt they would not last long, and I was right. Such people are more of a detriment when the battle begins. Our leaders had to spend more time trying to encourage them than fighting.

"Many of the weak ones even turned on us. I determined before the next battle that I would not encourage anyone too much, trying to get them to stay and fight. If they want to leave, then they should because we would be better off. There is also something else very important we have never had before that we must have to win."

"What is that?"

"The torch. This water is the truth, and we must have and love it enough to be willing to die for it. But the torch is like the presence of the Lord here with us. When I am close to you and the torch, I feel Him!

"There is no greater encouragement than feeling His presence with us. If we had carried the torch before,

I don't think our leaders would have had to spend so much time encouraging the people, and I don't think they would have been so weak.

"And yes, there are other streams like this one, but there is only one River. It rises out of the earth in different places like this. I have been told that they used to be very common. Now there are not many streams because so few have been willing to fight for them. I am not even sure there are any more like this one.

"Right now we need more true warriors, not more streams. I have heard that every time new streams break out, they are quickly lost because so few are willing to fight for them. This is why we need torchbearers."

"I know what you are saying is true, but I still don't know why more people won't fight to defend them. Are they always as hopelessly outnumbered as we are at this time?"

"I do not believe in the word hopeless, but I think those who seek this River are always outnumbered. Like I said, I don't think the numbers are that important. We need more warriors, but we need more who are true warriors.

"I've heard some say that digging hidden wells is better than seeking the River because they are not as big a target for the enemy. Too many who seem to love this water also seem to have an already defeated attitude.

[369]

"This is hard to understand because if they would drink the water they could not help but to believe and be strong. I am afraid that they have only occasionally tasted it but have not really drunk from it. Their love is more for the idea of it than the reality. It is almost as if it is some kind of romantic fantasy to them, not reality."

"Do you know of any of the wells nearby?" I asked. "At the wells we must find some who are really drinking and who may be willing to join us in this fight for the River."

"I know of a couple of wells not far from this valley. The water there is good, but not as good as this. Most of the wells have been too shallow to last for very long. They also get muddy quickly. The wells do help some people, but it is only when the water flows like this in the open that it can turn a valley into a paradise like you see here. And this water must flow to stay alive and pure."

I then heard footsteps behind me. I turned to see a man approaching.

Chapter IV

The Plan

As I watched the man approach, it seemed that he was dressed in the style of Colonial American times. His hair was long and gray, and I suspected it was a Colonial wig. He walked with purpose and was a little bowlegged as if he had spent much of his life on a horse.

"She is right. Wells can help a few people, but they are mostly temporary. They often become polluted or dry up. You certainly have a treasure here," he remarked.

"Yes, I have never tasted anything so wonderful," I replied.

"I was talking about the girl," he said.

"Yes, she is truly remarkable for one so young. I have never met anyone like her," I responded.

"You are about to meet many more like her, both boys and girls. They will be better fighters than most men in your times. You must be prepared for them."

"How do I prepare for them?" I asked. "You must

learn to ride this horse." "Who are you?" I inquired.

"I am John Wesley. I am speaking to you as a torchbearer who was also given a horse like this one. You are here to help prepare the coming ones. In my time there were but a handful of torchbearers and only a couple who rode the white horses. In your time there will be thousands of torchbearers and hundreds of these great stallions.

"You are here to learn about your purpose. You are called as one of those who will help awaken the coming great host. Then you must help to train them, preparing them for the last battle."

"I hardly feel that I can train anyone here. I am learning more from this little girl than I am teaching her," I responded sincerely.

"It is because you are willing to learn from her that you will become a trusted teacher. Keep drinking and keep listening. I will help you, as will all of the torchbearers who have gone before you. I can teach you in a few hours what it took me a lifetime to learn. What we cannot give you, the children will. They are wise because they are teachable.

"If you remain teachable, you will be wise beyond your years, regardless of how old you get to be. You can receive the wisdom of the ages. Remember that your primary purpose is to learn, not teach. The primary teaching that you have for the coming ones is to teach them how to learn. This is what it means to be a disciple— you are forever a student. Each one that you meet will teach you more about how to learn, and you will teach them the same."

"We are certainly in a situation that is beyond my present knowledge or wisdom to know how to handle," I responded. "It seems that this horse and learning how to ride it are the keys to us defending this stream. If you are

[372]

here to help me, I am ready."

"One thing that you must know and not forget," Wesley said sternly, "Is she was right when she said you cannot retreat. You are now surrounded, and there is nowhere to run. A few wells are left in this region, but they are drying up fast. You must defend this River and gather your army here."

"How do I gather an army if there are just a few wells in this region? Are there enough faithful ones to build an army?"

"No, there are not. You may gather a few from them, but your army is the very one that is descending on you here. Your victory over this evil horde is to convert its soldiers. Then you must teach them to drink from this stream. You must add others to them, and they must go forth to conquer. I can also assure you that if you will fight and not give up, you cannot lose."

Then the little girl spoke up. "I knew it! Many of my friends and relatives are in that evil army. I knew they would one day be soldiers of the King."

"You are right," Wesley continued. "You must do more than just set them free from their bondage. You must train, equip, and release them to go and recover the wells the enemy has stopped up and heal the streams of the river which have been polluted and buried."

As I looked up and thought about the huge horde above us, I remembered what a great general once said when told that he was surrounded: "Great! Now we have them where we want them—they can't get away this time! Attack in every direction!"

As I was thinking about this, I noticed Wesley looking at me. He asked, "Can you be so bold?"

"It doesn't seem that we have a choice," I replied. "It is a remarkable thing. They are so numerous and have us surrounded, and we are so few, but they are in our trap! Certainly, only the Lord could ever pull off such a victory."

"And certainly it will be the Lord who gets the credit for it," Wesley and the girl both said.

I looked at the fortress that the evil horde was building in the valley. Already it would be hard to conquer with many soldiers. I listened to the commotion of the horde at the top of the mountains all around. It was massive, multitudes and multitudes. What could a girl, a horse, even John Wesley and I do against such a force?

"I can no longer fight the battles which are on the earth. I am now a part of the great company of witnesses. Through my life I can still speak and teach, but you must do the fighting. I can encourage you that several times in my life I was surrounded like this, with very few with me. Each time I saw the victory of the Lord. Do not become discouraged by how dark it becomes or how many rise up against you. You cannot lose if you do not retreat."

Then the little girl chimed in, "I know my mother is a captive in the division called 'Ridicule.' She is there because she needs the approval of others. I also know she has never known true love in her life. I know that if I can love her faithfully she will be freed.

"I believe all who are in that division are like her. We can free the captives with the truth of God's love. If we can do this with them, then there must be other keys which will set the captives in the other divisions free."

Wesley did not say anything but just looked at me to be sure I understood how true this was. It was obvious that this simple truth was the key to our victory. The truth of who God is can break any bond.

I then had to ask, "Please tell me, why are some given a torch but not a horse? How can we use them together, other than just being able to cover more ground?"

"Many have the honor of carrying a manifestation of the Lord's presence, but few are called to start a movement. The torches are all given to start movements, but not many carry them forward in such a way to start an advance of the truth. The horse represents the movement which you have been called to start.

"Movements have the purpose of taking ground back from the enemy. They are for establishing strongholds of truth, which the enemy cannot prevail against. These become safe places for the captives who are released from their bondage to be healed, restored, and armed to go back out into the battle. Many will draw close to those who have the torch, but they will only follow into battle those who have the horse as well.

"Your first mission is to defend this place. Then mobilize those who are true seekers of the Water of Life. They must be trained and equipped to go and retake what the evil horde has fouled and trampled under its feet.

"Every captive who is freed from that horde can heal and restore more than they once destroyed. Life is stronger than death. Remember that you are not called to just take back the earth, but to restore those who are called to rule over the earth.

"As your armorbearer here has told you, the more who drink from this stream, the larger it will grow. In this way you can turn this little stream into a river that overflows until it reaches many other places. As it begins to grow here, when it breaks out in other valleys and deserts, it will be much stronger and deeper."

[375]

"How do I draw others here?" I asked. "It is obvious that we need a lot of help if we are to convert this army that surrounds us."

"You will draw others by drinking from the River yourself. Remember, the River grows as you and others begin to drink from it. The blind will follow anyone who can see, and the better you can see, the more who will be drawn to you. When they come, many will still be blind, and most will be wounded.

"You must teach them to drink until they are healed and can see. Regardless of what they look like at first, many who come to you will be the mighty ones that Enoch prophesied would come in your times."

Then he looked at me with a penetrating stare as if looking to see if I could understand something very important.

"The torch that you carry will also draw many to it, but the presence of the Lord is not enough."

"How could the presence of the Lord not be enough?" I asked. "There is nothing greater than that! It is even more wonderful and invigorating than this water," I protested.

"You are right about that, but many who love His presence still remain weak and immature because they only want to experience the joy of the Lord. Such are seldom willing to face the conflict of the times. His presence will always be the best and the most wonderful gift. Even so, for eternity we will have this. Right now there is a battle to be fought."

Wesley walked over to the little girl and laid his hands on her shoulders. Then he looked up at me and continued.

"You need worshipers who are also warriors. All who are not trained and equipped for the battle will be overcome by it. Even if they do love His presence, they must also be taught to love truth and to love it enough to resist the evil one. This is a strength that I developed—to train and equip people to stand for truth and fight for it. That is why there are things you must learn from me.

"Few have been able to build the people into a force which conquers. I did this by building small groups of people into small fortresses of truth. Some of these rose up to take their neighbors for the gospel. Others grew into mighty fortresses that took villages. A few took cities. Together we shaped the destiny of nations—even your nation."

I felt when he said the words "your nation" that it was, in some strange way, the valley where we were standing. As I pondered this and looked back at him, he had that unmistakable knowing look. Then he continued.

"Your nation still honors Paul Revere for waking up the people and calling them to the battle, but even more than that, heaven will honor those who wake up the people and call them to the battle, which must soon be fought.

"Just as the great messengers of the church age were all only seeds of the mighty ones of valor who are about to be released on the earth, the enemy has been sowing his seeds, too. You will have to fight every evil that has been released on the earth, and fight it in its full maturity.

"With this horse you must ride and warn the people about the invasion of their land. You can mobilize them to fight the good fight. You cannot retreat any farther. There is nowhere else to go, but if you resist the enemy he will eventually flee. If you do not resist, you are doomed."

The little girl was watching me intently. She stood erect, vigilant, and ready. Both Wesley and I were looking at her. I thought she must be like a Joan of Arc. If there are

[377]

even a few more like her, I knew that these would certainly be marvelous times. Wesley continued.

"The Lord called a dozen men. He changed them, and then they changed the world. In your time He is going to do the same with children. It is also the time of the lioness. Great are the company of women who will preach the gospel. There will be many great men of God in your time—but the great marvel and great honor will be for the women and children who walk in the ways of the Lord.

"Remember, it was the woman who was deceived and had enmity with the serpent, but it will be her seed that crushes its head. Women have a special place in this fight."

He looked into the eyes of the little girl. "It is your time as a woman. It is your time as a child, for the children will be for signs and wonders. They will turn the tide of the last battle. Gather the children and help their mothers. Great is the Lord in you for all you need."

My attention was then caught by something flickering out of the corner of my eye. The fortress that the evil ones had built was being used to hurl fiery arrows in all directions. It was apparent that they were trying to scorch the beautiful valley we were in.

Wesley turned and put both hands on my shoulders just as the Lord had done, saying, "You can't put out every little fire. You must destroy that fortress."

Then I was suddenly alone, sitting in my room.

CHAPTER V

The Sword

As I sat in my hotel room, I wondered if it had all been a dream, a vision, or if it had really happened.

I wanted to quickly write everything down so I would not forget it, but I was exhausted. I decided to lie down on the bed for a few minutes to rest.

Immediately, I was suspended in a brilliant blue sky. As a pilot I used to say that my office was the sky and had always deeply cherished the time that I spent there, but I had never seen a sky as beautiful as this. I felt more at home than I ever had before.

Then I felt earth under my feet. I was again on a seashore. I knew I was in the heavenly realm again by the air that I was breathing and the breathtaking beauty of all that I saw.

As I looked, I felt that this was the earth as it was meant to be. The desire grew within me to take this beauty and this air to the earth somehow. As much as I loved just standing in that place, I knew I had to leave soon, that I had to go back. There was a deep compulsion growing within me to make the earth right again.

Then I felt the presence of the Lord behind me, but when I turned to see Him, He was not there. I closed my eyes to just focus on breathing the air. When I opened my eyes, I was standing in yet another place.

I was in the middle of a street, alone. I did not recognize it, but I knew it was a street in London. The peace I had felt in the heavenly place was still with me but fading fast as I looked at my surroundings.

The torch was in my hand, but as my peace faded, the torch became heavier. I knew that I had to focus on the Lord and sense His presence again. As I did, the peace returned somewhat, and the torch became a little lighter. I began to feel great danger. I determined to keep my peace, and even though I was not afraid, I was more vigilant.

I determined to keep my main attention on the torch while glancing periodically at my surroundings. I saw no threat but continued to feel danger. Down the middle of the street there was a grass strip that was about fifteen meters wide. It had trees down the center that were surrounded by little protective metal fences.

I began to walk down the street. Then I noticed one little fence that did not have a tree near it. I just assumed the tree that had been there had died. This did not seem like a big deal at first, but I began to feel grief for the missing tree that I could not shake. I stopped beside the empty fence to ponder what I was feeling. When I did this, I felt the Lord standing behind me.

"Put the torch there," He said.

I walked over and placed the torch in the middle of the little fence, gently pushing it into the ground so that it stood up straight. It was quickly planted firmly as if it had sunk deep roots into the ground. I reached out to see if I could pick it up, and I could very easily, even though there were already long roots attached to it. I put it back and watched it. It was strongly rooted again, and the fire did not dim.

"You were able to pick it up easily because you have the authority," a voice behind me said.

I turned around to see who had spoken and saw a man who appeared to be a street person or homeless man. He was standing beside a stairway to a house.

"Pardon me," I said. "How do you know about this torch?"

He did not answer my question but just continued his statement, "Each of these trees was once a torch and carried by someone like you. This is a city where movements become monuments."

I did not like the sound of that at all. My torch was still alive, and I did not want it to just become a tree lining an obscure street. I wanted to pick it up and take it with me, but then, the Lord had told me to place it there. I did not know what to do. Obviously seeing my dilemma, the man continued.

"Before the end comes, there will be movements that do not stop moving. Maybe you are one of those who can carry such a movement. Even so, for now you must do as the Lord told you and leave the torch where it is. I perceive that you are not yet ready to carry it very far, much less carry it to the end."

"Who are you?" I asked.

[381]

"I am a watcher," he said, and with that he vanished.

I then looked at the street again to try to recognize it. I wanted to know the name of the street and where it was located in the city. I knew I was in a vision, but I felt like this was a real street in London as well. I wanted to find it when I came out of the vision. I felt that it was an avenue of monuments though I could not see any monuments from where I was standing.

I turned around to touch the torch so that its fire could surge through me. I needed more clarity. As I did, I was suddenly in yet another place, standing in front of the Lord. He was holding a large sword. The blade was brilliant, made of something that looked like silver, but it was almost transparent. It flashed with brilliant colors like a diamond. The thought came to me that silver would not make a very strong blade, and as the Lord often did, He answered my thoughts.

"This is silver, but it is stronger than any metal. This sword is a divinely powerful weapon. It is the power of My redemption. The one who carries it must be in unity with My redemptive purposes. You must have a heart to redeem or it will become too heavy for you to carry. You must be able to carry this too if you are to carry the torch very far."

I continued to look at the sword. It was a plain design, and it did not just reflect light—it emitted light. The light coming from it was of many different colors, like light that has passed through a prism. The glory of the light that came from it made it the most beautiful sword I had ever seen, even though it was a plain design. It was as captivating as the torch.

The Lord took the sword by the blade and extended the handle to me so I could take it. I thought it would be very heavy because of its size, but it seemed to not weigh more than an ounce or two.

"It will only become heavy if you try to wield it in your own strength. This is My Word of redemption. It cannot be destroyed but will stand forever. This is from My armory. This is the weapon that will be carried by My prophets in the last days.

"No power on the earth is stronger than My redemption. However, if you use it wrongly, it can bring great troubles to the earth. With this sword those whom you bless will be blessed. If you bless a devil, it will be blessed and will prosper. You must be careful not to try to redeem that which My Father did not plant, but you must go forth to redeem."

As I looked at the handle, I noticed five brilliant gems. One was blue, one green, another one was clear like a diamond, one was red, and one was amber. The handle itself was plain, but the beauty of the seemingly transparent gold was stunning. It was the most beautiful sword I had ever seen, not because of its design, but because of what it was made of. Even so, it was obviously not made for show. I knew even the gems were there for a functional purpose, but I was not sure yet what it was.

I raised the sword and waved it in the air. My arm did not get tired at all, but rather the opposite—the waving of it gave me strength. As strength came into my arm, it continued through my whole body. When I felt it reach my eyes, everything became brighter, more clear. As I continued to wave the sword, I could see farther.

I then looked at the sword again. As I looked, my eyes began to magnify it like a powerful magnifying glass. I could see that the sword was also alive. Even the gems were alive!

"The Spirit moved in the beginning," the Lord continued. *"The Spirit never stops moving. This is the sword of the Spirit. As it is moving, strength is released to the one who bears it. It will quicken your mortal body.*

"Remember that My Word is never still, but living, sharp, and active. Life always moves. This is why My work on the earth is often called 'a movement.' Just as I created the universe to ever expand, My Word will be forever moving and expanding. Those who know the life that is in Me will also forever be expanding in knowledge, wisdom, and power. They will never stop growing.

"As long as you abide in Me, you will forever be growing in both knowledge and power. I now give you the command to move and grow. In due time I will give you the command to multiply and conquer, not by taking lives, but by saving them."

As always when the Lord spoke, I wanted to memorize every word. I felt the life coming through them was like that which came by waving the sword. As I considered what He had said, my love for the sword grew.

I could not believe such a gift was possible. I wanted to hold it forever. What it imparted to me was different from the torch but was just as wonderful. It strengthened me and gave me courage. I knew that together the sword and the torch would give me a clarity of perception that was greater than anything I had yet experienced. Even as I was thinking this, I could tell that I was not only getting stronger but healthier. I felt toxins in me being washed away.

Then I began to feel a deep passion in my heart for this sword. I wanted it to touch everyone whom I loved. I knew if it touched those I did not love, I would begin to love them.

"What you are feeling is the passion for My Word. You are holding My living Word. This is what the true love of My Word does. Those who have the true love of My truth love those for whom I gave it. The Spirit is again going to breathe on the Scriptures, and this love for My Word will come upon My messengers in your time," the Lord said very soberly.

"What a treasure," I continued to think. "How could anyone not love this?" I wondered. I badly wanted to start using the sword. Then I felt a strong compulsion to use it on myself—to plunge it deep into my own heart.

"Do it," the Lord said.

I pointed its blade at my heart and thrust it into my chest. As I did, it disappeared as if it had been absorbed into me. There was just a slight tinge of pain, but when I looked there was no wound. Then the sense of strength that I had felt it imparting to me grew much faster.

In just a few moments, I felt as if I could fly, lift buildings, and even walk through walls. I began to feel that I could do anything because the power within me was so great that I did not have to obey the physical laws. I also felt there was no limit to how far I could see or how much I could magnify anything that I looked upon to see it in more detail.

My mind then began to awaken. Understanding began to grow within me until I felt like the universe was opened before me, perceiving and understanding its secrets. This was another kind of incredibly wonderful feeling.

I was seeing everything by the Spirit, not just through my own eyes and mind. I felt at one with everything that I looked upon. I also felt great love for everything that I looked upon. There was no earthly feeling that could compare to this, and it was growing.

[385]

"That is the power of My Word for those who will receive it into their hearts," the Lord explained. *"To receive My Word into your heart must be your quest every day. Then you will begin to see. Then you will have understanding.*

"It was by My Word that the universe was created, and it is by My Word that it is held together. My Word is the answer to every human problem. If you will receive My Word into your heart, it will grow within you, and you will never stop growing.

"Your mind will continue to open, and your knowledge will forever grow. I created the mind of man to ever expand so that you could know Me, My ways, and My works.

"You must receive My Word into your heart first, then it will open your mind. If you only receive it into your mind, it will not live. My living Word must be received into the heart first, and then your mind will open."

I could not help but to think of the ancient controversy: "Does one need to understand in order to believe, or must we believe in order to understand?" I knew the answer.

"You are right," He said. *"Only when you believe can you understand. Even so, it is right to seek understanding. When your understanding ceases to grow, you have departed from the path of life. As long as you are on that path, you will grow. Your understanding will grow as well."*

As the Lord spoke, I turned to look at Him. I began to see glory that was beyond any human language to describe. I physically felt the glory that I was seeing. I knew it was because He and the sword that I had plunged into my heart were one. When His Word was in my heart, I was able to see His glory as never before.

As I looked at Him, my vision continued to grow. As it grew, I saw more and more of His glory. I knew this could be never ending, and I never wanted it to end. I understood how the cherubim and angelic majesties who had worshiped before Him for ages and ages were in a continual state of such awe and wonder that they never wanted to do anything else. I wanted to stand there forever and join them.

"This is a taste of the joy that is in true life," the Lord continued. *"True life is only found in Me. This joy is your strength. For those who follow Me, this joy will not only be theirs forever—it will grow forever.*

"Now you must remember this. The joy of My presence can alone sustain you through what is coming upon the earth. You will know My joy, and it will increase in you, but to do My work on the earth you must also know My sorrow."

Then He turned around and I saw His back. He was still wounded, and the wounds were terrible. As I looked at them, they were magnified. I began to see darkness, disease, despair, and death. I felt grief and mourning that were worse than anything I had ever felt before. The grief grew to be as strong as the joy had been. I felt that I was gazing into hell itself.

As I continued looking, I saw anger cascading into rage and murder until blood flowed like a river. I saw lust grow into a raging, hot disease that was erupting like a volcano, destroying everything in its path.

Over everything I felt a gripping selfishness, which was the exact opposite of the oneness with everything that I had felt before, and it released a choking darkness that burned my lungs. It, too, was growing and expanding. When I felt I could not live much longer in the terror and despair that I was feeling, I cried out for the Lord to save me or kill me.

The Lord turned around. My strength had left me. I collapsed to the ground and still wanted to die. Lying there I could hear Him, but He seemed to be very far away. I had seemingly lost all comprehension of the glory that I had seen just moments before. "Could the darkness be that much stronger than the glory?" I wondered.

"That was a taste of the power that you are facing in your times. If you had not first tasted of My glory, you would not have lived. I have overcome all evil, and you will come to know the power of My glory over all evil, but you must know the power of the evil that men on the earth are about to face. You must learn to walk in My presence in the midst of evil and prevail. If you do not abide in Me, you will be overcome."

I heard everything the Lord said, though He still seemed far away. I then felt something in my hand. It was the sword. It was moving back and forth on its own. It gripped my hand rather than me gripping it. Soon strength began to return to me.

Slowly I got up. I felt filthier than I could ever remember feeling. Gradually, the feeling began to fade as if I was being washed by the gentle breeze, which the waving sword was creating. Soon I was able to stand. Then I could see the Lord and His glory again.

"What you saw is the burden that I carry," the Lord said. *"You saw what is now happening on the earth. The darkness is growing too. The earth itself will not be able to bear the evil of man much longer and will rebel against man. Terror will increase as the earth begins to rage and travail.*

"Man is about to know fear such as has not been known since the beginning. Those who abide in Me will likewise rise in faith as has never been demonstrated on the earth before. Because of the fear which is now being released, I have reserved the greatest demonstrations of faith for this time."

[388]

"Lord, how can anyone survive?" I begged, still feeling a little shaken from what I had seen. "The darkness even seemed to overcome the glory and beauty that I was beholding."

"The time is approaching when no man can survive what they have released upon themselves, and they would all perish if I did not put an end to it. I will redeem the earth. In the greatest darkness, I will release an even greater light. The greater light is My love for the world and My redemption.

"You must learn to carry the torch and the sword into the darkness. You must learn to carry My love and My redemption at all times. When you learn to love the most wretched and most worthless, even those who are in the grips of the deep darkness, then My Word of redemption is truly established in your heart. The power of My redemption will then flow through you.

"When Moses asked to see My glory, I showed him My back. He saw the stripes that I was to take for the sins of the world, and he saw what you saw, which is what I bore at the cross, the sin that I have already paid for. That is My glory too.

"It is right for you to want to see My face, to know the beauty and the life that is in Me. It is right for you to want to carry that to the world, but there is another glory which you must know and carry. This is the pain that I bore for you.

"The world's greatest heroes are those who overcome the greatest enemies. The greatest saints are those who overcome the greatest darkness. You are being sent to call those who will serve Me in the darkest of times. Therefore, you must know the depths of My redemption.

"You must know in the depths of your heart My love for those who are in the grip of the greatest evil. You must also know that the power of My redemption is great enough even for them. The sword that is being given to My messengers in

the last days can break any yoke and cut through any chain. My light is stronger than any darkness."

His words washed over me so that I continued to feel a deep cleansing from all I had seen of the darkness. As I listened, I continued to wave the sword until I felt my vision and strength completely return. I knew that I could not forget the power of the Word of redemption to cleanse my soul and restore my vision and strength.

My heart was warming, and I knew that it was the life of the sword which had been thrust into it, as well as its power in my hand. I knew this connection between the Word in my heart and my hand was the connection between faith and works. It took both to cleanse and restore me just as it does everyone. This was the understanding that I could never forget. After a time the Lord continued:

"You must have the sword and the torch. You must live in My manifest presence, and you must have My Word in your heart and your hand. You must teach this to My messengers. No one will make it through the times ahead without both. You must grow in the light faster than the darkness is growing. My light is stronger, but to remain light it must be growing."

As I listened, I instinctively continued waving the sword, and the strength continued to increase. Again I began to feel that I could fly—that I could overcome any earthly power. As I continued looking at the Lord, His glory was growing and expanding.

I then grasped the sword with both hands as tightly as I could. I knew what was coming, and I knew what I had to do. The Lord turned around again so that I could see His back. When He did, I stepped into the darkness.

CHAPTER VI

The Power

I was once again on the avenue where I had placed the torch. I realized then that I had entered into the darkness without taking the torch with me, but I had somehow returned to the street where I had left it. I could not see the torch from where I was, so I began to walk, waving the sword as I did. I knew I had to find the torch.

As I walked, I started to feel increasing darkness and oppression. It was indeed an avenue of monuments. As I waved the sword and my vision grew, I became alarmed that there did not seem to be life anywhere. The trees and grass in the middle of the street were green, but I did not feel life in them. I suspected that they were artificial, but when I looked more closely they had all of the functions of life, but were dead somehow.

I continued to walk. It was a cold, damp, and dreary place. Finally, I came to a monument, which was green and brown tarnished bronze and seemed to increase the dreariness of this place. The statue was fastened to a marble foundation, but it all felt cold and meaningless. Even so, I felt that it was the statue of a great person, though I did not recognize who it was.

I continued on, gently swinging the sword, not knowing what else to do. Then I saw a golden glow in the distance. It appeared to be life. As I approached it, I saw that it was a tree. It was still rather small, hardly taller than I was, but I was astonished by what I saw as I stepped up to it.

The tree was the torch that I had left. It had grown and now had branches. It was full of life. It stood out in this place like an oasis in a desert. I reached out to grasp the branch closest to me. Immediately it fell into my hand. It was a torch just like the first one, which was now a tree.

"Take it back to the monument," a voice behind me said.

I turned to see the white eagle. He was whiter than I had remembered him, having seen him before, but I thought it must be because of the darkness of the place we were in. I also knew that he had become even wiser. His talons stood out, sharper and more powerful, and his eyes were more piercing.

"You were right to plant the torch. If you had held onto it, you would have had one good torch, but now you will have many."

"How is that?" I asked. "And where are we?"

"You are in the heart of a great city that has died but is about to live again."

"Is this where you're from?" I asked, knowing that it

wasn't, but I wanted to keep the conversation going until I thought of something better to say.

"I have friends here and a few disciples. They will help you with what you are here to do."

"What is that?"

"You have the torch and the sword, and you are here, so you are going to use them here."

"I hardly know how to use them. They were just given to me." Sensing a bit of impatience rise in the eagle, I continued, "But I will do the best I can. Tell me what you know about my purpose here."

"That's my job, and I will tell you all that I can. I'm also glad to hear that you do not know too much. You're safer that way. You will know what to do when it is time to do it. My young friends will help you."

"Where will you be?"

"I will be watching, just as I was when you touched the sea with the torch a few years ago."

"A few years ago—it could not have been more than a couple of hours ago!" I protested.

"No, it was over five years ago. Remember, time in the heavenly realm does not seem the same as on the earth. I saw you when you did it. From the time the Lord gave you the torch until you touched the water with it was three years, so He gave it to you eight years ago."

"I don't remember you being there. Where were you?"

"Remember, I don't have to be there to see. I also saw the other gifts you received and those that you will soon be given. It is time for them, but there are still many things for you to learn. Your training is not over, but the time on earth is short. You must learn fast, and you must learn to teach others faster."

I looked down at the sword and torch that were in my hands. I looked around and wanted to use them both but did not know what to do with them. So I just held on to the torch and waved the sword.

"I am here to help you get started," the old eagle said, "Others will help you along the way. Now, go back to the monument you passed. Touch it with the torch and watch."

The old eagle spread his wings and he lifted high on a wind that I could not feel into the dark sky. Even though he soon disappeared, I could feel him and knew that he was watching. I then began to feel many others watching me as well.

I started to walk, holding the torch out in front, waving the sword as I went. I felt increasing strength, and my vision grew. As this happened I wanted to attack the darkness. "I was born for this," I thought to myself.

"Yes you were," an unfamiliar voice answered. "You and many others, too. This is your time."

Turning, I saw another eagle, much younger than the first. Even so, this young one seemed even more regal than the older one. It was the way he thrust his chest out a little more, and his wings were slightly open as if ready to soar at any moment. It was obvious that he had explosive energy but contained it with great grace. As if he heard every thought, he responded.

"I am of another generation. I am not greater than my father, but I have been given more authority. I am here to awaken and guide the great champions who are now maturing on the earth. I will help you and the others who are to prepare them for what is to come."

"How will I prepare them?"

"First you will learn to use the sword and the torch for more than just edifying yourself. That is important to know, but it is just the beginning. When you have used what is in your hand, you will begin to understand the rest of what you are to be given. Then you will know what you are to do with all of your gifts."

We began to walk. My eyes turned toward the trees that we were passing. I then noticed the fruit. It was beautiful, compelling, and I felt a tinge of hunger.

"Don't even look at it," the young eagle stated as if he had to repeat this often.

"Why?" I asked. "It looks like very good fruit, and I am very hungry." Then I sensed why I could not eat from them. "These are all trees of the knowledge of good and evil, aren't they?"

"They are. How did you know?"

"They seem to be alive, but they're dead, and the fruit looks delicious. Why is it they are on this avenue of monuments? And why is it full of these trees?"

"The monuments are to people who were alive but are now dead. These monuments are to people who were given life to give to the earth, but after beginning in the Spirit, they tried to complete the work by their own wisdom and ways. By that they began to cultivate these trees. That is why they exist together on this road.

"This is one of the main avenues that the people of this city come to. They do not love these monuments, but the monuments make them feel secure and significant, as if they were the heirs of the greatness of those represented. They also love the fruit from these trees, even though it is poison to them and it kills them just as it killed their empire."

As we walked, my vision continued to increase. I began to see that the street was very wide, well manicured, and would have been very beautiful in sunlight. It still felt dead. The young eagle soared above me, and I knew he was watching me closely and discerning my thoughts.

"What am I going to do here with the sword and torch?" I asked him.

"First, understand these monuments. Even the smallest touch of life from God has the power to grow into that which would have restored the earth and made it a garden again. These monuments are to people who had life. They froze into dead monuments because they started thinking about how to build monuments to their own lives. There is no purpose in building monuments on the earth! They will all perish!

"What you are to build is part of the heavenly city. You will fail in your purpose if you care what men think of your work. You must only care what the Lord thinks of it. You are not here to build monuments, but a movement that will not stop moving. The River of Life never stops moving. The Spirit never stops moving. If you stop, you will have departed from the way of the Spirit and the way of life."

As we approached the monument that I had passed earlier, the young eagle stopped and said, "You must bring this monument to life again."

"Why would we want to do that?" I protested. "And how?"

[396]

"The Father loves redemption. The King loves redemption. He also honors the fathers who walked in His ways upon the earth, even if they only walked in them for a little while. These monuments were not His will, but He is going to redeem them and use them for the sake of the fathers and for the sake of their children who now live in this city.

"Remember, Ishmael was not His will either. Even so, He blessed Ishmael and made him a great nation. You will be surprised by how the sons of Ishmael will glorify the Lord at the end, and you will be surprised by how these monuments will also.

"If you want to stay on the path of life, you must love redemption the way He does. It is a part of your purpose to help redeem monuments. That is why you are here with the sword and the torch."

"But I thought they fell by building these to themselves," I protested again. "How am I going to help redeem them? What will either the sword or torch do for these dead monuments?"

"You will continue to walk in darkness if your understanding of redemption does not grow. You must honor these fathers and mothers. You must touch them with the word and with the fire. When you do, the life that was in them which is eternal, will flow from them again. You cannot attain to your own destiny without the life that they had.

"The Lord is going to make these monuments live, and living water will flow from them again. This will be a token of His redemption power and His resurrection. These trees look alive but are dead, and their fruit is death. These monuments look dead, but they still have life in them. The life that they carried is eternal. Put the torch to that statue."

I lifted the torch and put it under the face of what was a great English poet's statue. Quickly it renewed the bronze so that it began to shine. Soon the whole face was glowing.

"That is enough," the eagle said.

I backed up and watched. The statue was still a statue, but there was life in the face just as there was life in the torch and sword that I held. I then took the sword and plunged it into the heart of the statue. It went in easily all the way to the hilt.

As I drew it out, the breast of the statue began to burn with the glow of sunset/sunrise colors and of the torch. As this happened, there was also a slight glow on the horizon. I was again astonished by the wonders of the torch and sword—how they did not take life but gave it.

"They can kill, too," said the eagle who was now soaring above me. "They bring life back to that which had life, but the great danger is they can also give life to that which was dead."

"What do you mean?" I asked.

"You have the power of blessing in your hands. What you bless will be blessed, even if it is not what the Lord wants to be blessed. If you bless the work of the enemy, it will prosper. You must only bless by the command of the Lord.

"The enemy only receives his authority on earth from man. The greater the authority you have been entrusted with, the greater the harm you can do when you use it wrongly and the greater the enemy is empowered when you give it to him.

"You have great blessing or great destruction in your hands. You must only build what the Lord wants built and tear down that which the Lord wants you to tear down. You have been given both tools and weapons. The more powerful they become in your hands, the more careful you must be."

"Well, I think I should begin to kill those trees," I replied.

"Yes, that you will do at the proper time, but now is not the time. For now we will concentrate on giving life. These trees are still useful to the Lord."

"How is that?"

"The Lord put The Tree of the Knowledge of Good and Evil in the center of the Garden of Eden for a crucial reason. There can be no obedience from the heart unless there is the freedom to disobey. These trees attract people to this place, and some who come because of the trees will notice that there is life again in our friend here.

"When anyone touches him, that life will grow. Life grows with interaction. We do not know if his message will be completely restored, but it is possible. His teaching could begin to flow through the earth again. But that is not in our hands. You have done your part, so now we must move on."

"Where are we going?"

"There are other monuments in this city that you must touch and help to bring back to life. If the people respond to them, streams of living water will begin to flow throughout this city. Then they will join to form a great river. If enough are awakened to those who lived in their past, there will be life in the present, and they will flow together down the great river that will carry them to a glorious future."

"If you are an eagle here, you must have seen into the future of this city. Will that happen here again?" I asked, not wanting to waste time with monuments if it did not produce results.

"It is not our place to be concerned with results. The Lord gives everyone a chance, even when He knows they will reject it. However, when I fly high enough I can see into the future, but only a narrow part of it. I know that life will flow through this city again, and I know that so many of my kind would not be here if the potential of this city were not great.

"It is our place to use the gifts that we have been given and to trust the Lord with the results. You must learn well the lessons of this city. You will then be sent to many cities and nations to do it again. You are called to give life to cities and nations by giving life to their past, their monuments. Others are doing the same, and others are also preparing for the harvest in additional ways, but this is your part."

As I walked and the eagle continued to soar above me, I felt an urge to strike one of the trees of knowledge with my sword just to see what would happen.

"Go ahead," the faint voice above me encouraged.

I struck the tree just above the little fence at its base. The sword easily passed through it. I watched to see if it would fall over, but it did not. Then the fruit began to fall from it. Soon it gave off a terrible stench. I looked at the fruit still on the tree, and it was rotting right before my eyes. I backed far enough away so that none of it would fall on me.

"That's how the Lord cursed the fig tree," I heard the eagle say from above, also marveling at the sight. "That sword is His Word. It can give life, or it can take it."

I then stepped close enough to put the torch to the side of the tree. The fire took to the tree as if it was dry paper, consuming it quickly. There was nothing but ashes. A breeze came that blew the ashes away. Soon there was no evidence that the tree had even been there.

"Those are divinely powerful weapons!" the eagle remarked. "That tree has deceived many people."

"That was fast," I responded. "I can't believe it happened so fast."

"I wouldn't call seventeen years fast," the old eagle retorted, having appeared seemingly out of nowhere. He was obviously irritated.

"You have both been very foolish! Remember, time is not the same here. That is why on the earth patience must be joined to your faith, or you will miss the timing of the Lord. We will have to return to clean up this mess," he said, departing as fast as he had come. He seemed to be in a terrible hurry.

I still did not know why the old eagle had been so irritated. I could also tell that my young eagle friend was likewise confused. I was sorry that he had not explained it to us. I began to walk again and touch more monuments. Soon I could tell that the day was dawning. It was not as dreary either. I knew the sun would soon break through the fog.

"Many thought that this city had no future, that its night had come for good, but its greatest day may just be starting," I said to the young eagle who was still with me.

I could feel a great hope rising in me for the city. I then noticed that he did not seem to hear. He was trying to look far away into the future.

I, too, became lost in my own thoughts. I began to think of the valley, the horse, and the little girl. I wondered if Rivers of Life were about to begin in this city again. I wondered if there was a connection so that they could flow into that valley also.

I became deeply concerned for that brave little girl. Her grace, wisdom, and maturity so far beyond her years made her one of the greatest treasures I had ever found. I wanted to get back, but I knew that what I was being given here, and what I was learning, was part of the plan for her and the valley she was trying to defend.

I looked up again at the eagle. He had obviously seen something, but I could not tell if he was rejoicing or alarmed. As I looked up at him, I soon began to feel what he felt. I knew that my training was almost over. The alarm was about to be sounded. A great battle was about to begin.

Chapter VII

The Queen

The young eagle landed beside me.

"I know what you are about to tell me," I said.

The young eagle looked at me with raised eyebrows and then continued with what he had started to say.

"Things are happening faster than I thought. For the first time I did not want to fly higher so I could see farther. I was not ready to see what I did. I must gather the other eagles and find our father. The future is very dark. Keep going and I will see you again soon."

He was off before I could protest. I was sorry I had been so quick to speak, implying I already knew what he was about to say. I knew his news was bad, but I did not know the details.

My stupid pride, I thought. I resolved never to try to do that again. It always seemed to cost me knowledge. I walked on, waving the sword and holding the torch as close as I could, wondering what the young eagle had seen.

I then came upon the statue of a lady. She was astonishingly beautiful, and I presumed that she had been an English queen. As I looked at her closely, my heart almost stopped. Not only did I know her face very well, but she was alive and pointing her scepter straight at me.

Eagles sat on her and were all around her base like pigeons usually are around statues. They, too, were all looking at me. When she spoke, it was with a dignity I knew very well, and she had an authority which made me tremble.

"You're the little girl I left in the valley! How did you get here, and how is it that you are a monument?" I stammered. She did not answer, but she looked at me curiously. One of the eagles then spoke.

"You forget that time here is not the same as in the earthly realm. However, this is not the girl you have seen, but she is a descendant of our lady."

I turned to the lady. "I'm sorry. I was just shocked when I saw you since you look so much alike."

The great lady seemed to disregard what I said and continued to hold her scepter out toward me as she began to speak.

"Will you awaken mothers to the glory of their calling? Will you give my daughters swords and torches? They are the ones who keep the torches alive, and they will wield the sword wisely. My daughters will stop the death and bring back the life!"

I stood in speechless awe. Her words came with authority and nobility, which were as beautiful as she was. I did not want her to stop speaking because her words were so exhilarating.

"Are you Elizabeth?" I asked.

"No."

"Are you Mary, the mother of Jesus?"

Gazing at me with eyes that were warm, yet firm, it seemed that the faintest smile crossed her lips as she answered.

"You know me. Elizabeth knew me. Abraham searched for me. I am not Mary, but I, too, am a mother to Jesus. I am Jerusalem above. I am your mother too, because I am the mother of all who worship in Spirit and truth."

As I looked at her, I thought how she seemed to be motherhood in all of its glory. Her words did not just impart truth, but life, hope, courage, and strength. It was impossible to consider that a woman could be more attractive, and yet there was not a hint of seduction or sexual attraction.

I just wanted to get as close to her as I could. Her presence was so warm and inviting that I began to move closer. I could not help but marvel at how anyone who was such a light could be on this avenue of monuments and not wake up the entire city.

"Why are you here? Why are you in this city?" I asked. "How could anyone with such grace and life be on this avenue? Why are there not multitudes sitting at your feet?"

"Men have made many monuments to me, but I have never died. Many have tried to bring me down to earth. They have mostly been those who have sat at my feet trying to use me. They try to bring me to earth through their own works rather than faith, which alone can establish me on the earth.

"You can see me as you do now because of the vision that you have. If your vision was greater, I would be even more to you. You are actually only seeing a little more of me than those who only see a bronze statue.

"I do have some in this city who have begun to see me as more than just a statue. That is why I am alive here. As their vision grows, I will be revealed more and more to this city.

"When they start to believe their vision in their hearts and not just their minds, I will be free from this avenue of monuments and will be raised above the palaces and castles of men. When that happens, the King will come to this city."

Then she looked at my hands and another faint smile creased her lips.

"You have the torch and sword. It is time for them here. No one can see me who does not honor the fathers and mothers. If you honor the fathers and mothers, you will give swords to the sons and the daughters."

Her words were like fire and honey together. They burned, but they also sweetened and soothed. I could not imagine anyone not wanting to stay as close to her as possible. She, too, could obviously hear my thoughts, and she answered them.

"As I said, most only see me as a monument, cold and tarnished. When people begin to see me as I am, they are drawn to me like a nursing child to its mother. I, too, have been made to be a desire of every searching heart. The King and I are one.

"You must remember this. It takes the light from both the fathers and mothers, sons and daughters, to reveal me as I am. I am much more than you are seeing now, and I am also as the child you met in the valley.

"No one can see me as I am if they do not see the glory of spiritual motherhood, as well as fatherhood. Because many honored only the fathers and not the mothers, they and their fruit did not remain long on the earth. You must honor the fathers and mothers to bring forth the sons and daughters.

"No one can see me as I am who does not see the glory in the children. I have the wisdom of the ages and the wisdom of the new birth. It is the wisdom of the fathers and mothers, old and young, which the path of life follows."

As I listened, I was drawn to the trees which lined the avenue. It did not escape her notice, and she again answered my thoughts.

"Yes, the woman was deceived and ate the forbidden fruit first. However, the man ate it even though he knew what he was doing. And does the prophecy not say that the seed of the woman will crush the head of the serpent?"

"I'm sorry," I responded. "It's just that I have had so much teaching on how women are so easily deceived that I was actually wondering if anyone could think that way in your presence."

"I understand why many think this way, but you must now understand this—those who are redeemed are a new creation and are higher than the former creation. The new creation woman is higher than the former.

"When you become a part of the new creation, your weaknesses are transformed into strengths. Most of those who have the great gifts of discernment on the earth are women. Remember, in the new creation all things become new. That is why those with renewed minds do not judge after the flesh, but after the Spirit.

[407]

"The new creation woman is about to be revealed, and all who see her will honor her. Neither my sons nor my daughters can see me as I am unless they begin to look at me together, opening their hearts to what each other sees. My sons and my daughters must prophesy. You must give torches and swords to my daughters as well as my sons, or you, too, will end up as just another statue on this street.

"You are concerned that the daughters are easily deceived. All may be deceived, but the wisdom of women could keep you from much folly, like the folly of cutting down that tree!"

When she said this I shuddered. I knew immediately that something more terrible than I had imagined had happened.

"I just used my sword to cut down a tree which was bearing evil fruit. How could that have been bad? What kind of problems could that have created?" I asked.

"You did not plant a righteous tree in its place. Now it has sprouted again, and the power of evil within it has multiplied. You cannot just dispel the evil, but you must always fill its place with good, or this will happen."

As much as I did not want to leave the presence of this great queen, I turned and began to run back to the place where I had cut down the tree. As I ran, I glanced back for one more look at her great beauty, and I saw her motioning for the eagles to go with me. The deep concern on all of them was so obvious that I stopped.

"Tell me. How bad is it?" I cried out.

The great lady looked at me as if she was measuring the depths of my soul. I knew she was considering whether I could handle the answer. She must have concluded that

I could not handle it because she said nothing. Then one of the eagles spoke up.

"You will understand very soon what has happened. We were not ready, and I don't think you are ready for what is now upon us. Even so, we must go now. The battle for this city and many other cities has begun."

There was a knock at the door, and I woke up with a start. The clock by the bed flashed 5:55. It was hard for me to get oriented. I felt caught between two worlds. I continued looking at the clock and prayed for the grace to make it through what was coming. I knew there was indeed a bridge between the realms of heaven and earth and that what I had seen was very real.

I also thought about how the timing between them was not as it seemed. Sometimes minutes or hours in the heavenly realm turned out to be years on earth. Even so, I knew it was time to wake up. The last battle was really about to begin. Then I realized that there was no one at my bedroom door.

I had to sit for a while. I thought about how the "Jerusalem above" was worth searching for like no other treasure on earth, which is what the church is called to be. There is no question that if she is seen as she really is, the nations will come to her light! Who would not come to her?

How badly I wanted every church and believer to get just a glimpse of her—to hear her words, to feel the majesty of her presence, and to know the dignity of her every move! She was womanhood in all of its glory. She is a bride worthy of the King!

I was consumed with searching for a way to share what I had seen. I wanted desperately to tell all believers what they were called to be a part of, but my words were too inadequate.

"She does not belong in the avenue of monuments. She belongs on the highest hill so that all can see her!" I thought, but my words seemed as dry and dead as the other monuments. I began to long for the words of life.

Then I began to think of the impending battle. A dread came over me like a dark blanket. My strength left me. I was so weary I easily drifted off to sleep.

Then I saw her again. She was no longer a statue on the avenue of monuments—she was a warrior clothed in brilliant armor. She was more regal than human words can describe. Her presence exuded grace and strength, which filled me with awe. She looked me right in the eyes as a most genuine and brilliant smile crossed her lips.

"Do not fear. I, too, was brought to earth for the battle that is now upon us. I must be known as motherhood itself, but I must also be known as a warrior, too. Do not fear. The light that is in us is greater than the darkness. It is time for the light to be seen, and it is time to fight."

CHAPTER VIII

The Tree
and Its Fruit

I was running as fast as I could toward the place where I had cut down the tree with my sword. I knew some-thing terrible had happened, but I could not understand what it was.

Then I began to smell a terrible stench, like rotting fruit, but it was far more pungent than any I had ever smelled. It was then that I saw it—a tree that towered over all others. It reached such a height that it covered a large section of the avenue of monuments. Its leafy boughs were so thick that it was dark beneath it.

As I proceeded toward it, I began to hear crashing noises which became louder as I moved closer. I slowed down as every sense within was telling me that this was more ominous than anything I had ever faced.

I then heard voices. At first there were just a few, but as I got closer it sounded like there were many, maybe hundreds. Then it sounded like thousands. The stench and the air created by this tree wrought a depression that was like a choking fog. I finally had to stop because I just could not bear to go any closer. Then one of the eagles spoke up.

"This is not good!"

"Anyone can tell this is not good!" I retorted. "It would be a little more helpful to know what this is."

"This tree—it is not supposed to be like this," the young eagle said, with an obvious trembling in his voice.

"This is the result of your own impatience, ignorance, and immaturity," the old eagle interjected, who had just landed behind me.

"What happened? How is this the result of my mistake?" I demanded.

"You foolishly cut down one of the trees and did not plant the torch in its place. You know very well that every time you displace the devil, or one of his strongholds, he will try to return, and if he can he will come back many times more powerful."

"I did not think about that. It is still hard to believe that one brief moment of carelessness on my part could have caused all of this!"

"The weapons we have been entrusted with are very powerful, but you must never destroy a work of the devil unless you can replace it with the works of God. If you destroy a planting of the devil, you had better plant that which is of God in its place and be ready to defend it," the old eagle elaborated with obvious chastisement in his tone.

"But the eagle who was with me told me to 'go ahead' when I wanted to cut down the tree," I protested. "We both felt it was the right thing to do."

"The young eagles are here to help you, and they can help you, but they are still young eagles. It does not matter who is with you or who agrees with you; you are always responsible for your own actions.

"Many who are given great knowledge do not have great wisdom. You have walked with Wisdom Himself and He abides in you. It is wisdom to inquire of the Lord before you use the authority and the weapons that He has given to you. Wisdom may still speak to you through one of us, but He will mostly speak to you through your own heart. Your obedience is to Him, not to young eagles or to old ones!"

I felt the old eagle's frustration, but I had to press him for all the understanding I could get. I was overwhelmed by the thought of having caused such a great problem.

"If I had planted the torch in its place, I would not have had it to continue touching the monuments with," I protested.

"First, you should not have cut down the tree without the command of the Lord. Then, if He commands you to do such a thing and you have to plant the torch, you do it even if it means waiting for a time. Every time you plant this torch it will multiply. Everything planted which is the Father's will bear more fruit and multiply.

"It may seem incomprehensible to you to have to wait for that because you are so impatient, but His kingdom grows more through the patient bearing of fruit than through attacking the works of the devil. There is a time for attacking the strongholds of the devil, but that is never the main work of the kingdom.

"Remember this: You will not be judged by how many monuments you awaken, even though it is a part of your calling. Neither will you be judged by how many of these trees planted by the devil that you cut down. You will be judged on how obedient you were. Now, this lesson is over.

"We have a great battle on our hands. It is certainly wisdom that we now press on without delay. This tree is still growing, and the enemy means to have this city, which cannot be allowed."

I started walking forward again. I knew that the old eagle was telling me the truth. I had foolishly used what had been entrusted to me, and now I had brought on a great conflict which had not been necessary and one that we were not ready for.

All of the eagles were walking beside me, including the older one.

"Couldn't you be a little more helpful by flying?" I asked.

"It is hard to fly in this kind of air," one of them answered with the obvious agreement of the rest.

"Hard? Well it's hard for me to walk, but I know I must do it. Can you fight on the ground like this?"

"Not very well," the old eagle confessed. "You are right. We must fly."

With that he lifted slowly into the air, and the others began to follow. They did not go far or very high, and I was glad that they didn't. The farther we walked, the more evil it felt. I did not want to go on. The depression grew into a gripping fear.

Soon I wanted to just abandon the whole city and start again somewhere else. If the eagles had not provided the company and covering above me, there is no way I could have continued. Even so, I was going slower and slower. Shortly, I was gasping because of the great stench.

While still at a distance from the tree, I could see what was making the crashing noise. It was the fruit dropping from the tree. It was so heavy that it crashed through the roofs of buildings and houses. When it hit the street, it splattered with such force that it was like a bomb. When each one hit, a putrid fog would rise from where it fell.

Then I saw where the voices were coming from. There were great crowds of people who had come to eat the fruit. They were devouring it as if it were a delicious delicacy. It was so repulsive that I had to turn away to keep from vomiting. I felt the old eagle standing beside me.

"You had better watch this," he demanded. "You must understand what the fruit is doing to the people. Wave the sword! Hold up the torch!"

I looked down at the sword and torch that I had in my hands. I had almost forgotten them and was just dragging them along. As I began to wave the sword, a gentle, refreshing breeze began to blow around us. It was like getting oxygen again.

I waved it more and more until I could see that the breeze was touching the eagles who were hovering above. With the fresh air, our vision improved quickly. Slowly confidence began to replace our fears.

I then lifted the torch as high as I could. The torch was growing brighter because of the breeze that the sword had released. Hope and resolve began to displace the depression in our group. With the sword and torch we were creating our own atmosphere.

As I looked up I could tell that the eagles all felt the thrill of flying. Great faith began rising in all of us for the coming battle. The weapons which had been given to us were greater than what we were facing. I began praying earnestly for the wisdom to use them the right way this time. I started to move ahead but was arrested by the old eagle who barked:

[415]

"STOP! Do not go one step farther!"

I froze in my tracks. "What's the matter?" I asked, stunned a bit by the force of his command.

"You were all about to be killed. It is good to have courage, but do you not have any wisdom at all?"

"What are you talking about?" I demanded. "How were we about to be killed? What we have is obviously much more powerful than any weapon of the enemy."

"That is true, but the fruit falling from this tree could have wiped you all out at once. As I said before, we need to stand here and watch what the fruit is doing to the people. We must be sure to go only where there is no fruit about to fall."

I knew right away that the old eagle was right. I felt as foolish and immature as a child. I apologized. I could tell the young eagles all felt chastised as well.

I then began to watch the people who were the closest to us and were eating the fruit. I started waving the sword again, which I had stopped doing for just a few moments after the old eagle's rebuke. I was surprised by how foul the air had become in just those few moments.

As I raised the torch again, light came back into our eyes so that we could see better. However, it soon became obvious that the people in the fog could not see us at all. They seemed to be almost totally blind, only able to see for a few feet or so. This caused them to grope like animals for the fruit for which they seemed ravenously hungry.

As the people ate the fruit, they became pale and grew thinner. Some were gorging the fruit down as if they were starving, and the faster they ate, the faster they lost weight as diarrhea was flowing from them. This was a large part of the stench, but these people did not seem to even notice.

As they continued to eat, sores began to grow on them. The pain from the sores was obviously excruciating as they brushed up against one another, causing them to strike at the person they had touched. This drove the people farther and farther from each other.

We watched until those we were observing began to die. Some began to kill others who got close to them. Violence was growing, and so was the paranoia and depression. I could not imagine a scene out of hell itself being any worse.

"The devil does not just like to kill, but he loves to torment," the old eagle remarked. "In everything he does, he tries to reduce human beings to the lowest animal state. He thinks if he can cause such humiliation to men who were made in the image of God, it is a way to mock God Himself."

It was a terrible, grotesque sight, and steadily getting worse. As the depravity grew, it was soon hard to believe that these were humans.

"A pack of dogs has more dignity," I thought.

I then noticed the blood on the ground. It was being sucked into the earth as if by a slow, but powerful, vacuum cleaner. As I watched, I could tell it was being drawn into the roots of the tree. The blood was its food. In the place where there was a terrible battle and much death, I looked up and could see that the branches above it were growing faster and producing more of the deadly fruit.

"We can wait no longer, or the whole city will be lost," one of the eagles cried out. "We must do something."

[417]

I knew he was right, but I also knew if we had proceeded without the knowledge of what we had just observed, we would not have survived our brave charge into the darkness.

I also began to feel that anyone who was working for peace on earth was doing the Lord's work. Any kind of bloodshed was feeding the root of these evil trees, which were producing this evil fruit, and were increasing the evil one's grip on the earth.

"What should we do?" I asked the old eagle.

"That is why you are here," he responded. "I can give you knowledge and sometimes wisdom, but it is not my place to lead in a battle like this."

"But it was my foolishness which led to this, and then I almost got us killed!" I protested. "Certainly I am not the one to lead in a fight like this!"

"Maybe you are now humble and teachable enough to do just that," the old eagle retorted, obviously resolute that he was not going to lead and I was.

I knew there was no time to argue, so I just did what I felt needed to be done until an obvious leader appeared. I called all of the eagles together and organized them into two groups, appointing leaders for each one.

The first group was to fly ahead and find a path where the fruit was not about to fall. They were also to attack any fruit that they could obviously make fall prematurely. This would help clear the path more, and hopefully the premature fruit would be too unripe for the people on the ground to eat.

The second group was to go behind the first. They were to look for any fruit that had been missed or was growing so fast that it became a threat to us. I asked the old eagle to stay close to me, which he agreed to do.

As I began to walk forward, the eagles all flew ahead to do their jobs. I continued waving the sword and raising the torch. As I did this, I felt strength flowing into my arms, and even my feet began to feel lighter. Soon this was purifying the air and giving light for a good distance.

This was crucial because the eagles could go no farther than the light from the torch and air from the sword, or they would choke and start getting sick.

After proceeding slowly for what seemed to be hours, we began to hear a terrible commotion in the distance. There were thousands of raging voices. A chill went through us all. I could even tell that the old eagle was growing tense. Obviously, a great battle was taking place ahead.

Did we dare to continue? Who was fighting? Where was our leader? I looked back to see if anyone was coming to help us. I could not see or hear anyone, but I did notice that fruit was again falling on the path not far behind us. I just could not believe how quickly it was growing.

I also knew that we were trapped. We could not go back, and we could not stay where we were. There was nowhere to go but forward, and I did not need the old eagle to tell me that.

CHAPTER IX

The Warriors

I called a quick conference with the leaders of both groups of eagles. They, too, had already seen our situation—we were now as closed in behind as we were in front, but we were also ready to keep going forward. I asked them to fly as high and as far ahead as they could and report back anything of significance that they saw just as quickly as possible.

As we moved ahead, we grew steadily closer to the clamor of a great battle. It was not long before one of the eagles came to report what they were seeing.

There was a group of about two hundred people with small swords and small lamps. Some of the swords were little more than knives, but they were brave and skilled in using them. They were fighting to hold back what appeared to be a mob, which consisted of thousands.

This little band who was fighting the mob had barely enough light to see, and the air they were breathing was thick with death and depression. They had built barricades and were courageously holding their ground as the mob threw the rotten, poisonous fruit at them. This fruit was so toxic that it would kill or severely wound anyone who was hit by it.

This little band was dodging it skillfully, but it was obvious that they were weary and could not hold out much longer. I was not sure what our little group could do to help against such a horde, but I knew we had to do something.

The old eagle and I approached the scene. Before they saw us, we were able to get very close to the mob because their vision was so poor. When they did see us, they began throwing the fruit at us.

They were too far away to hit us, so some of them started to run toward us. The young eagles swooped down in front of them, and they stopped in their tracks, obviously terrified by the eagles.

I then took just a few steps toward them, hoping the fresh air and light from the sword and torch would awaken them from the darkness. As soon as the light and fresh air touched them, they started fleeing back into the darkness in a great panic.

One of the eagles from above dropped down to tell us the mob was just out of sight and was regrouping. For some reason they were enraged, and it was obvious that they were not going to stop trying to destroy the little band.

I walked over and approached the barricade. A man and a woman who were evidently leaders stepped forward. They seemed glad to see us, but wary at the same time. I told them my name and how impressed we were with their great courage.

"We know who you are," the woman replied. "Your books have helped us."

"If they have helped you, why do you feel so wary of me?" I asked.

[421]

"We are not so wary of you as much as we are of those pigeons who are with you. We're wondering why they would be with you," the man explained, obviously trying to hide his irritation, but not doing it very well.

"Those are not pigeons—they're eagles!" I shot back, trying to control my own irritation.

The man and the woman both looked at me with disbelief. I could tell they were wrestling with not wanting to insult me, but wanting very much to show their scorn for the eagles. The old eagle drew me aside before I could say anything else.

"That they called us pigeons was actually a little gracious. They really wanted to call us vultures. To be honest with you, I can hardly blame them. Young eagles can make a bigger mess of things than pigeons, and even old eagles like me are very hard to be around. I think some of our younger friends here have made problems for these people before. Be patient and gentle."

"I understand," I said. "What will they think when they find out they can blame my foolishness and immaturity for this tree?"

"We have all made a bigger mess of things than most of us will ever realize in this life," the eagle responded. "Even the great saints in Scripture like Abraham, David, and even Paul the Apostle, also released some great problems in the world because of their foolishness or immaturity. We are not better than they, are we?"

"No, of course not," I responded. Realizing how true this was gave me some encouragement.

"The Apostle Paul released an attitude against the church which he himself had to contend with for the rest of his life. It is by the Lord's grace that He also gives us a chance to confront and destroy the evils that we are responsible for releasing," the old eagle continued. "This is your chance with this tree. Our young eagle friends are being given another chance with these people because, like it or not, they will not survive without our help."

"This is true, but for us to get to the place where we can work together could take longer than we have, especially the way the violence is increasing out there and this tree is still growing," I lamented.

"They don't have to call us eagles. I don't even care if they call us pigeons, but we must find a way to work together," the old eagle replied.

As I turned back toward the couple, they seemed a little more at ease. I could tell that the waving of my sword had cleared the air some, and the torch had brightened up the whole area. As I looked at the rest of the people, they were all looking at the eagles who were soaring nearby.

"We did not know that they were real eagles," the man and woman both stated. "I'm afraid that we did much to hurt them and drove them off because we thought they were . . . well . . . I'm very ashamed, but we actually thought that they were vultures."

The old eagle began to speak when one of the younger ones who had landed interjected, "We are eagles, but we know what a mess we made when we were with you. We do not blame you for thinking what you did about us or for driving us away. In fact, you did the right thing. We are the ones who should be apologizing. We're all very sorry for the trouble we caused you and what we did to your congregation."

I just kept waving the sword, holding up the torch and watching. "This is really what it means to clear the air,"

[423]

I thought. It was very touching, but I was still surprised when I turned to the old eagle and saw tears running down his face. When he saw me he was a bit embarrassed but apparently too happy to care very much.

"I have waited to see this for many years. Few things are more beautiful than this," he offered.

"I understand," I said, trying to make both of us feel a little more comfortable. "I suppose if I knew the whole story here I would be as moved as you are."

"If you knew the whole story, you would know that we are witnessing a great miracle. In fact, it is such a miracle that it gives me confidence for this battle that we have gotten ourselves into."

"What do you mean 'we'? I think I am really the one who got us into this."

"If we're going to win, we must stand together and cover each other's mistakes," the old eagle stated. "There was an eagle present with you when you did what you did, so we are all in this together. I, too, knew that it could happen but did not go to warn you. No, we are all responsible."

The atmosphere around the little band and their barricades had obviously changed. I was surprised by how quickly the wariness I felt at first had been changed into trust with just a few apologies and a little humility.

It was obvious that we could not face what was ahead if we were fighting among ourselves, and this reconciliation had to happen. I would have never dreamed it could have happened this fast. If the eagles had been offended by what they were called at first, I knew there was no way we would survive the coming battle. In fact, we could well have been fighting in two directions at once, which was sure to lead to a quick defeat.

Finally, we all turned to look toward the darkness. The falling fruit was now coming down at such a rate that it sounded like distant thunder. It seemed the darkness beyond our little area was getting darker, if that was possible. I looked at the old eagle, and we both knew that we had to get going again soon.

I turned to the couple and said, "As wonderful as it has been to meet you and for you to be reconciled with my friends here, we do not have much time. We must try to destroy the root of this tree soon or the city will be lost."

"Please, you must not leave us!" the woman cried, who was quickly followed by a chorus of many others. "You have brought us such hope and vision again. We need you and the eagles."

I looked at the old eagle and knew we were thinking the same thing. If we left these people, the hoard beyond the light would come sweeping back upon them. They were almost overwhelmed when we came to them, and they would not last long after we left.

"What can we do for them?" I asked the eagle.

"If we do not get to the root of this tree to cut it off soon, these and all of the others in this city who are fighting will be destroyed anyway. We must go on, but we can help them. Gather all of your leaders quickly!" the eagle demanded of the couple.

While the leaders of the group were gathering, the man and woman who I had first addressed drew me aside and began to admonish me.

"You cannot make it to the root of the tree. Just a few years ago we could walk freely anywhere in this city. Even those who hated us treated us with a little respect, but now they are all trying to either make us eat the fruit of the tree or kill us.

"There used to be many other congregations in this city like ours—some had thousands of people. There were whole movements based here with congregations all over the world. Now we are the only ones left.

"If you stay with us, we can hold out; we may even take some ground back and continue to be a light to this city until the Lord returns. If you go, you will perish and so will we, and there will be no witness at all in this city."

"Are you sure that you are the only congregation left in the city?" I asked.

"Quite sure. We were in fact one of the largest and strongest churches in the city. We have been reduced down to this, so I do not think that there could be any others left. If there are any others left, we would have at least heard their battle. We have not heard anything in a long time, and we have not had any more join us from any of the other groups for a long time."

"We must be all who are left in this city," the woman stated. "Other churches used to be an irritation to us, but now we would give anything to know that there were others. Believe me! We just don't think that there are now."

"Let's see what the old eagle has in mind," I replied. "I know eagles quite well now, and they will not do well staying in one place like this, fighting behind a barricade. They would become pigeons, or worse, if they are made to do that kind of thing. If they are not allowed to fly, they will not be any good to you and may be just another problem, which you sure do not need right now."

"Then let them go and attack the root of the tree, and you stay with us," the woman said.

I thought about this. As I looked out into the darkness, it was not very appealing to think about going out into it again. I also knew that the eagles would not be able to get far at all without the light and sword which I was carrying. There did not seem to be a solution.

"I could not let the eagles go alone," I began to explain. "They would not make it. I learned a long time ago that I could not make it far without them, and, in spite of the trouble they sometimes are, I no longer want to be where they are not close. I'm afraid that the eagles and I are a package deal."

"You're right," the man said. "You belong with the eagles."

"I'm sorry for even trying to separate you from them," the woman also offered, very sincerely.

I turned to the old eagle, wondering if he had any kind of solution to our dilemma. When the couple turned to him, obviously wanting to know what he thought, he began to speak.

"There is only one solution," he said. "We must all fight together until we get to the root of the tree and destroy it."

I immediately saw the wisdom in this, but I did not expect the little group to take it well. As expected, some immediately began to protest.

"We've fought for this ground for many years," one man blurted out. "You don't expect us to just leave all of this behind to follow you and the eagles, do you?"

There was silence for a few moments, as everyone seemed to consider this. Then one of the young eagles interjected.

"When we first saw the fight you were in, I had never seen such courage. I can understand how you must feel. You have fought long and hard for this ground and have obviously lost many in its defense. I certainly do not blame you for not wanting to leave.

"However, from what we can see, you would not survive another assault from the evil horde which is now surrounding you, not to mention the continued growth of this tree. There is not much left of your barricades either. I don't think any of us have a choice but to go forward. Our only hope is to put an ax to the root of that tree."

The old eagle then continued, "It is true. You could not have lasted any longer had we not come along, and we could not have gone much farther without some help. It seems that the Lord has brought us together at this time. We need each other, and there seems to be only one possible choice as to what we must do."

"Of course you are right," the leader finally said. "It is going to be the hardest thing we have ever done to leave this place behind. We have paid so dearly for it, but it is obvious that we must now fight for something bigger than our little place. We must fight for the whole city and attack the root of this tree or we will have no chance to survive. We will leave our little place to follow you and the eagles."

CHAPTER X

The
Strategy

Everyone then turned to look at me. Finally the old eagle spoke up.

"What is your plan?"

"Please give me just a few minutes," I said as I withdrew just a little to pray and seek wisdom.

I could not help but to think about the irony of this situation. I have been the major cause of this trouble, yet I am supposed to have the plan for overcoming it.

I also could not help but to think about all of the congregations that had been destroyed in this city, and people lost, because of my immaturity and foolishness with the weapons I had been given. I grew mad at myself but also wanted to lash out at the old eagle. I wanted to ask him why he did not come up with a plan since he was the old, wise, experienced one.

Finally peace came over me. I knew this was not a time for bickering and that a statement like that would only sow doubt in everyone. They did not need any more of that. I breathed a quick prayer for help and then just started talking.

"I need to know your leaders and all of the capabilities they have," I said to the man and woman leading the little band.

"I want them formed into companies according to their weapons and abilities, and I will assign at least one eagle to each who will serve as their eyes. We will march and fight together, but we need to organize. Our unity and organization itself will help to push back this disorganized mob."

I then turned to the old eagle, "Get your best scouts into the air at once and have them find the weakest part of the mob where they think we can break through and then the shortest path from that point to the root of the tree."

"Done," he replied and immediately began sending the scouts out.

"Please report to me the information I need as soon as you get it," I said to both the old eagle and the man and woman.

"We would like to have this mature eagle come and help us determine our weapons and strengths," the woman asked, partly looking at me and partly to the old eagle.

"That is a very good idea," I responded, and the old eagle acknowledged by going with them.

I then went to sit down to think and pray. When I did, the weight of what I had caused settled over me. I could not keep back the grief for all of the great churches which had been destroyed in this city. It had once been renowned for its culture and empire, and now I knew it was known more for the stench of this rotten tree and its fruit.

The mob had thought that the fruit was good food, and they had obviously come from around the world to eat what was in fact killing them. It then occurred to me that if we succeeded in cutting it off at the root, these people would think that we had deprived them of their source of food.

"You give them something to eat," a voice behind me said. When I turned to see who it was, I was astonished

It was the girl from the valley. "What are you doing here?" I asked.

"I have been fighting with these people."

"How did you get here?" I asked, still amazed to see her.

"I don't think you know me," she replied. "I understand that there are many who look like me in other places. You must be mistaking me for one of them."

"Your likeness is remarkable if you are not the same person I was thinking you were. Looking at you more closely, I can tell that there is a little difference, but you must be sisters, if not twins. And how did you know what I was thinking?"

"Some people think louder than others. I can sometimes hear other people's thoughts. I am gifted that way so I can help people."

"I see, but you did not just hear my thoughts—you told me what to do. Where did you get that? How could I give them food to eat?"

"My gift is to know people by the Spirit, not just by appearances. This gift awakened in me when I started spending time with the eagles. That is one of the things they do best—awaken the gifts which are in others."

"How did you do that when everyone here was so offended by them?"

"I had to do it in secret, but I had to do it. Most of the younger ones here have also learned from the eagles. They taught us to hear the voice of the Lord. The Lord was the One who told me to tell you what I just did."

"You seem very sure of that for one so young," I replied. "Can you tell me more?"

"I don't really understand what I did tell you, or how you could feed those people, but I know it was the Lord who told me to tell you. One of the first things the eagles teach is that you do not need to understand to obey, but after you obey you will start to understand," the little girl replied with a disarming attitude of confidence and humility.

"As I have continued to look at you, I know that you are a teacher and a shepherd," she continued. "It is your job to give the sheep their food at the right time. The Lord must have had me tell you what I did because those people must be His sheep too. They just don't know it yet. I think it would help us to look at everyone that way. To win this fight, it won't be by hurting those people, but by helping them."

"You're amazing. What else can you tell me that will help me?" I asked, feeling she was certainly one who spoke for the Lord.

"I can tell you that most of the ones who are very gifted and effective in both fighting, and dodging the evil, are the very young ones. If our leaders would have recognized this, we would not be nearly as small as we are, but we would have many thousands.

"If the congregations that have disappeared would have understood this, they would not have died. I believe

I am here to tell you that if you will choose your leaders according to their anointings and gifts, instead of by their ages or appearances, you will succeed."

I knew right away that this was the word of the Lord.

"Please go, find, and bring to me the man and woman who are your leaders as well as the old eagle," I said.

As soon as they walked up, I could tell that it had not been going too well in identifying the weapons and strengths of the people who were left.

"So, you've had a hard time agreeing," I said, stating the obvious.

"Yes," the man replied. "I appreciate the wisdom and gift of such a mature eagle, but he does not know these people like I do. I have been with them for many years.

Some of the things he says about them I know to be the very opposite of the way they really are. We are having a hard time agreeing on just about everyone."

"What do you say to this?" I asked the old eagle. "It's true. I don't think we've agreed on anyone."

"Sir," I said to the man, "the main reason your congregation has become so small is not because of the battle that you are in, it is because you have not discerned the gifts and callings of the people."

This not only stunned the man, but had obviously offended him. I waited for a minute before continuing.

"There was a time when you could gather great crowds of people. You did it in a number of ways that worked, but the times have changed and you did not. You are a great leader, and you have fought valiantly for the truth with remarkable endurance, but the only ones who can survive and prevail in this battle are those who spend as much time making other leaders as they do leading. This has been your weakness and the others—those you think of as leaders are also weak."

I could tell the man was now even more offended and wanted to argue, but he restrained himself. He had been so humbled by continual defeats and was now so desperate that he was at least to a small degree open to considering that he had been wrong in some things, maybe even very wrong in his approach to both the battle and the leading of his people. As I watched him calm his own spirit down, I continued.

"Sir, please do not think I am implying that you have not done anything right. Your courage and endurance will be the foundation for which any future victory will be built upon. However, I think you must admit something very basic has not been working. Obviously, there must be a change in the way things are done, or the results will just be the same. There is a reason why you need the eagles. We must find the true leaders and raise them up quickly."

"I know you're right," the man finally offered. "I have been a failure in this, and now I can see it is why we lost so many battles . . . and so many people. I just did not see it. I guess that is why I needed the eagles, to see what I could not see for myself. I'll do whatever you say. I know there must be a change, and this is obviously it. I just hope it is not too late."

"Again, I think you are proving to be a true leader," I said. "The eagles can see, but they are not usually very good at leading. You really do need each other. For you to have the humility to acknowledge this will encourage your people, not discourage them.

"I do not think it is too late or we would not be here. I have learned that when something seems impossible, the Lord is about to move. We have definitely provided Him with a good opportunity to move now! We need the right strategy, but more than that we need Him, His grace, and His favor. He gives grace to the humble, and we need to all keep that in mind. You are probably the most genuinely humble one here. Now you must continue to lead your people, but we will help you."

"I really can see how I have missed it by not recognizing other people's gifts and letting them grow by using them," the man responded. "I also have not acknowledged the leadership that others have been given. I confess that I saw them as a threat.

"In the past, it was the gifted ones who caused the problems and the divisions. It was hard to give them more influence by letting them take some leadership. It's obvious, though, I failed even more by not letting them grow."

"Sir, if you only knew how badly I have failed and the kind of trouble my lack of wisdom and immaturity have caused, I think it would make all the trouble that either you or the young eagles have caused seem pretty mild," I replied. "Obviously, we have all failed in some major ways, but I have learned that what often disqualifies us in people's eyes is the very thing which qualifies us for the grace of God.

"We're all that He seems to have here, and He obviously still likes to use the foolish and weak to confound the wise and strong. Our weakness and foolishness is what I think has us here. But I also know that He does not want us to remain weak and foolish, just humble enough to seek His wisdom and His strength."

"Well said, but now we need the plan," the old eagle interjected. "Do you know how we are going to break out and attack the root of the tree? We do not have any more time to look at the past."

"I do have a plan," I responded. "First we must find the true leaders and the effective weapons which we have among us. We must then discern a point where we can break out and proceed to the root of the tree without distraction. Now go back and find the gifts and leaders who are in this group."

Looking at the man, I said, "Trust this old eagle and this young girl," and I directed their attention to the girl. "She has a gift that you need."

Both the man and woman raised their eyebrows as I mentioned the gift in the little girl. They obviously started to protest and then just said, "Okay." With that they all left.

Soon thereafter, the scout eagles began to land and report. As they did, I began to think it had been a very bad idea to send them out without the old eagle. They all came back with seemingly conflicting reports. I quickly decided to just receive them one at a time, in private.

Soon it became clear that they were each seeing just a part of the whole situation, but because they were still so young, they had a tendency to feel that their parts were the whole picture. I felt that all of their reports were probably valuable; they just needed to be put together properly to get the whole picture.

To my dismay, after all of them had reported, I still felt I had a very incomplete picture. There had to be something that we were not seeing since I just could not believe our situation was so entirely hopeless. Not only were we completely surrounded by multitudes, with seemingly no weak points in their lines, but thousands more were joining them from every direction. They were growing in confidence and would soon come pouring in to finish off the little band and us with them.

[436]

I then wondered about some of the conflicting reports that the scouts had brought in. One would see one part of the line as the strongest point, and another would see it as the weakest. As I sat pondering this, I heard my little friend's voice behind me again.

"You don't know what to do, do you?" the little girl half asked and half stated.

"I could sure use a word from the Lord now! Do you have one for me?" I asked.

"Well, I may. I know it does not matter who is out there, but what matters is Who is in us."

"That is certainly true!" I said. "Do you have anything else?"

"I feel this means that we need to discern the gifts and callings that the Lord has given to us and go with the strength He has given to us instead of trying to find a weakness in the enemy."

"Well! I guess that is the whole picture." I replied. "What do you mean?" my little friend asked.

"I'll explain it to you after we are resting on a big pile of firewood from that tree," I said.

CHAPTER XI

The Battle

As I had suspected, it was determined that some of the most powerful gifts were found in the younger people, even some who were very young. Some had already learned to fight very well, using their gifts as weapons. What they lacked in training, they made up for with extraordinary faith.

The young ones did not seem to have any doubt at all about winning the battle or cutting the tree down. I knew the rest of us had very little faith that we would actually be able to do it. We were more or less going out to fight because we no longer had a choice.

I therefore decided to place some of the children and eagles with each group of adults, to fight with them side-by-side. I felt their main leadership at this time would be boldness and courage, which is what we really needed.

The two main words of strategy that I had been given for the battle were to make decisions based on our strengths and not the enemy's. We also could not be distracted from our ultimate purpose—to cut the tree down.

Our greatest strength was the torch and the sword, which I carried, so I knew I had to go first. I did not want to hesitate, so once the people were formed into companies, we prayed, thanking the Lord for all of the great things that He had already done for us, and that He always leads us in His triumph. Then, with a determination to keep thanksgiving and praise in our hearts, we started forward.

I was waving the sword like the rotor of a helicopter over my head. I was also holding the torch as high as I could. I was astounded by the wind that was being generated and knew that my sword could not be generating all of it.

I looked back at the advancing companies, and they had all drawn their swords and were doing the same thing I was. Many of the swords of the adults were chipped and gouged and some were even broken, but they had a brilliance that cast off a great light.

It was now obvious that these swords were living, and they seemed to come more alive from the movement. The more their holders were swinging, the more brilliant they became. The light that was coming from the entire company waving their swords was soon spectacular. As long as we did this, I was sure there was no darkness that it could not penetrate.

The wind that was being created was driving the stench of the rotten fruit away from us. The air became clear and fresh all around us. Just getting out from behind the barricades had done something to release a powerful spiritual momentum, and it was apparent that everyone was feeling it. With each step, the light and wind seemed to increase, as well as our faith. I began to think that I could not have had more confidence had I been leading an army of hundreds of thousands. I knew this little band of a couple of hundred had the power within it to do all that we needed to do.

The eagles had begun soaring above us as soon as we started. As the wind increased, they went higher and higher. After we had advanced a good distance, I was surprised we had not yet encountered the angry mob which had been surrounding the little group.

I was also surprised that none of the evil fruit had fallen on us from the branches of the tree which we were marching under. I knew this fruit was so large and toxic that it would be deadly if it hit any of us directly. However, there was no evidence that any of this fruit had recently fallen anywhere in our path. There were only some piles of what appeared to be a kind of powder lying about here and there, which the wind was blowing away. I motioned for one of the eagles to come down and report what he was seeing.

The eagle said that the evil horde had fled in terror the moment we began to march. I could understand the kind of shock it must have been for them to see this group emerge from the barricades with such light and power. Even so, I could not imagine them not regrouping and attacking us with everything they could. However, they had fled so far that the eagles could not even see them anymore.

I then asked several of them to fly as far as possible in front of us and to the sides, while staying within the fresh air. When they returned, their report was even more astonishing.

The atmosphere that we were creating was killing the branches of the tree and drying up its fruit. This explained why none of it had been falling on us. What was even more amazing was how far this atmosphere we were creating had spread. We would be able to walk without danger all the way to the root of the tree.

Off to the sides, the evil horde had gathered out of reach of the fresh air, but they seemed to just be standing there, dazed and just milling about. They did not even seem to be eating the toxic fruit anymore, and all of them seemed to have the same confused, weak, hungry look.

I gathered the leaders of the little group and explained what was happening. I knew we had to move faster to destroy the root of this tree. They agreed.

We all began to run, and we were able to run like the wind without getting tired. I do not know if I have ever felt such exhilaration. When we reached the root of the tree, the joy was hard to contain for everyone. Even though we had not really engaged the enemy in combat, I wondered if there had ever been a more magnificent charge or a more noble army as I looked at the faces of our little band.

The trunk of the tree was so huge that it took all of us standing at arm's length from one another to surround it. As we did this, we continued to wave our swords. Then, in unity, we all thrust them into the trunk of the tree, and it quickly died.

Its leaves began to fall like snow. The fruit that was in the branches was away from the direction that we had come, and it dried up quickly. The dust of this fruit created a great cloud as it was being blown away by the wind.

Then we all began to hack away at the trunk of the tree until it came crashing to the ground. Some began to cut it up while others went after the roots and the stump. We did not stop until there was only sawdust and firewood left. Where its huge trunk had been was a great crater, but they filled it in, and soon it looked like a freshly plowed garden.

I knew what I had to do. I planted the torch right where this great tree had stood. It took root immediately. It began to blossom right before our eyes. Then fruit appeared. I then gathered all of the people, and the old eagle began to speak to us.

"This victory is worthy of a great celebration," he began. "but we do not have time for that now. Even so, a story must be told so that we will fully understand what happened here." He then looked at me, and I knew what I had to do.

"This terrible thing happened because I used my sword to cut down a small tree but failed to plant a tree of life in its place. The King has shown me mercy by letting me see my great mistake corrected. That has now been done, and fruit of the Tree of Life is already growing where death so recently prevailed. By this we can remember that life is stronger than death.

"The spiritual atmosphere of a good part of this city has been changed now. On the outer edges of it are multitudes of hungry people who are now ready to eat the fruit of this tree. You must take it to them. There will be many great churches here again, all of which will be fortresses of truth and life. You must remember that you are all one."

The old eagle again interjected, "We will have eternity to celebrate our victories here. There will be a great memorial in heaven to this one. You have learned what many before you learned—that one can put a thousand to flight, and two can put ten thousand to flight (see Deuteronomy 32:30). Now you are going to learn that one can gather a thousand, and two of you together can gather ten thousand.

"You are about to gather a great harvest here. Soon multitudes from all over the earth will also be coming to you. They are coming because of the light, the fresh spiritual air that is here, and the fruit of this tree. They are not coming for you or for me. We did nothing today but believe and obey, and for many of us we only did this because there was no other choice. Let us not become arrogant, but humbled by what happened here.

"Even so, every one of you must now lead many. You must lead them here to eat this fruit. You must give them swords and teach them the power of the sword. You will have only led them well when they, too, become leaders. In this way the victory will continue to multiply. Always remember what happens when you begin to build barricades to hide behind. Now go and make disciples of the great multitudes who are now wandering around this city! They will now hear the call."

CHAPTER XII

The
Covering

Again I awoke in my hotel room. Even though I knew it had been a vision, it seemed very real. I wanted to write it all down quickly so that I would not forget it. It was still raining and dreary outside, but I felt energized, as if I was still able to breathe some of the atmosphere of heaven.

Then suddenly I was sitting on a huge white horse. It seemed to be the one that I had found in the valley with the little girl. Even so, it seemed too big for me. I was very high off of the ground to be on a normal-sized horse. Then I noticed the Lord standing next to me.

"Now you have found your seat," He remarked.

When He said this, I looked down at the saddle. It was a western-style saddle, and it felt like leather with a deep purple color which was almost black. It had a golden border around its edge. It seemed to fit me perfectly and was as comfortable as an old chair.

"Lord, the saddle is perfect," I said.

I wondered how I would get on and off the horse because it was so tall. Then, as I looked at the horse's feet, I saw that they were not touching the ground, but we were hovering several feet in the air.

"This is not a normal horse," the Lord continued. *"It can lift you above the earth. When you are on this horse, your journey does not have to follow the contour of the earth, but you can rise above any earthly conditions."*

"Lord, is this the same horse I saw with the little girl in the valley?"

"Yes, it is the same, and it is your mission. It is from the one I will ride when I return, the one that I was given by My Father. They are given to those who are preparing the way for My return.

"Many have ridden them in the past, and many must yet ride them in your time. This is the mission that has been given to you from above. When you have learned to ride this horse, you must then teach others how to ride their horses."

I thought about the little girl in the valley and the one who had just fought with us to kill the evil tree. They were already great warriors and wise far beyond their years. If there are many like them, I knew they would soon be the greatest spiritual force the world has ever known.

I also knew that this horse was capable of wonders I could not yet even imagine. I wondered what an army of children would be like if they all had horses like this.

"You live in the day of great wonders," the Lord said, taking the reins of the horse in His hand and beginning to walk.

"Heaven is a place of continual marvel and awe, and those who I am about to send forth will bring many of those

[445]

wonders to the earth. The children that you are about to meet are for signs and wonders. They will soon go forth to My last mission on the earth before I return."

When we had gone just a few feet, we entered a great hall. There was a long line of people on either side as we passed, and they were all dressed in various clothes from different eras. When we came to the center of the hall, we stopped, and all of the people gathered in front of us.

"These are the ones who helped to prepare you for your purpose. You have received from their teachings or from their stories. They are your witnesses. You are representing them as you are Me, just as those you have a part in preparing will also represent you. We are all one in the great purpose of the Father—the restoration of man and the earth to their purpose."

As I sat on the horse, each one of these people came up to the Lord and bowed and then looked me in the eye and gave me a word, such as *"Be strong," "Be fearless," "Be gentle," "Love your neighbors," "Follow the King...."*

This went on for what must have been several hours, but I would have liked for it to last longer. I felt a special bonding and impartation as I looked at them and they spoke to me. Some I was quite sure I recognized, and others I had no idea what their names were, but I still somehow knew them.

I especially watched them as they approached the Lord. It was obvious they were all His special friends and were great friends with one another. It was a glorious experience to be with them and to be spoken to by them. I had a yearning in my heart to be one of them. There was a nobility and grace upon them which was far beyond mere human elegance.

When the last one in the procession had finished, the Lord turned to me and said, *"You will join them soon enough, but you have work to do first. They are not complete without you. Neither are you complete without them. This is also true of those who are to be called through you and the messengers in your time. Their words will help to keep you on the path that has been chosen for you. You can also give their words to others to keep them on their path. All of those who have life have come from Me."*

Then two of them approached with a large purple cape, which had the same kind of gold border as the saddle. They gave it to the Lord. He examined it and then put it on me, locking the clasp at the front. It was so large that it not only covered me, but covered the horse's entire body.

I looked around at the crowd and then looked back at the cape. I was astonished that it was now a bright red. When I closed my eyes and opened them, it had turned into a blue more glorious than I had ever seen. I closed my eyes again and opened them and it had turned to a pure white. All of these had the same gold border.

"This is your covering," the Lord said. *"It will cover you and your mission. Only here can you see it as you do now. In the realm of earth it looks very different. On earth it is very humble. This is what protects your heart and the heart of your mission. As long as you wear this, you will walk in My grace and authority. Remember this cloak as it really is. It will protect you from the coldness of the evil times that you must walk through."*

Then the Lord motioned for me to step down from the horse, which knelt low for me to do so. I knew that I should also kneel and did so. The Lord handed me the reins as I knelt down beside the horse. Then the Lord poured oil all over my head and began to rub it into my hair like shampoo.

"This is the oil of unity," He said as He continued to rub it in.

As He did this, I felt the oil penetrate deeply within my mind. Peace and clarity took the place of my usual raging thoughts, which often seemed out of my control.

Then I felt the love which I had felt just a few times before. This love caused me to love everything deeply that I looked upon. Of all of the glorious experiences I had received in the heavenly realm, this love was the most wonderful of all. I did not want the Lord to stop until this love had penetrated every cell of my being. I desperately wanted to keep this feeling. Then the Lord stopped, long before I was ready.

"This oil of unity is the anointing," the Lord started as He lifted me to my feet to look me right in the eyes.

"What I have given to you, I give to all of My people. I pour My anointing on each one to cleanse their minds. However, where you must walk on the earth, there is much dust and dirt, which will be thrown at you every day. You must learn to come to Me to be cleansed again whenever your mind has been soiled.

"As you do this often, you will not be able to stand any of the filth in this world in your mind, but you will love the purity and clear vision which comes only by this anointing of the Holy Spirit.

"Holiness is the nature of heaven, and it must be your devotion. True holiness is true love. True love cannot come without true holiness, and true holiness always causes you to love, not condemn. You can come to Me as often as you want for this oil. As you wear it and touch others, they, too, will want to be clean."

Chapter XIII

The Council
is Called

S uddenly I was standing in the valley again. The beautiful little girl was still there, fighting. She was bruised, bleeding, and covered with dirt. Even so, as she looked up at me, I could see her eyes were as filled with fight and resolve as when I had left her.

I looked down at my cloak, now a simple brown, humble fabric. Under it I saw a flash of armor. I had the sword and a flask, which contained the oil. I poured some of this on the edge of my cloak and began washing the little girl's face. She looked deeply into my eyes with a seriousness uncommon for any child.

"They are coming faster now," she started, "they are making more progress than ever before because they are not fighting as much among themselves. I do not know if we can hold this valley long without help."

"Help is coming, but I must first teach you to ride the horse," I answered.

She looked past me to the horse, which was standing just behind me. "Have you learned to ride him?" she asked.

"No, I have only sat upon him. We must learn together," I responded.

The clamor from the evil horde rose to a terrible crescendo. With that I poured the rest of my oil on her head and began to rub it in. I looked down at what should have been an empty flask, but it was full again. I kept pouring it on her until she seemed to be clean. I then lifted her up on the horse and handed her the reins.

"You are going to have to learn to ride this horse in the middle of a battle," I said.

"Then I shall feel quite at home," she responded. "I don't think I have ever known a time in my life without battle."

This touched me deeply. I felt very sorry for this young girl who had already been through so much. I thought that she may truly have never known peace or rest from the struggle in her entire life. A deep desire came over me to take her away to a place where she could just be a little girl, be in a family, play little girl games....

"Don't even think about it!" a sharp, familiar voice behind me said.

It was the old eagle. There was such a fierceness in his eyes, which seemed even greater than when he was in battle.

I also noticed the girl seemed to know him, since she did not seem at all surprised by his presence or that he was speaking.

"Many children are called to a life of battle on this earth. It is their destiny, and you must not rob them of it. Those who fight here like she is doing will have a reward which they can enjoy for eternity, but here she must fight."

"Were my thoughts so far out of line?" I protested. "I was just feeling a little sorry that one so young had to go through so much. I don't think I could endure it if one of my own daughters had to go through so much. What is wrong with my feeling this way about her?"

The attention of all three of us was drawn to the clamor of the evil host which was now very near and obviously advancing. Then the old eagle looked at me with an unrelenting fierceness in his eyes, which I will never forget, as he continued.

"The power that is in her is as great as the power in you. The wisdom and faith to use the power within her has in some ways been greater than yours. You will not last long in the fight without her, and she also needs you.

"I warn you, do not show her pity! Self-pity is one of her greatest enemies. She cannot be defeated by the enemy if she continues to fight, but if she falls to self-pity, she will be disarmed and easily defeated."

The little girl reached out and touched my arm as she said, "He is right. Every time I start to think about myself in that way, I start to lose my faith and my courage. Please do not feel sorry for me. I know I have been given a great honor to even be able to fight in the King's battles. I gave my life to Him, and now I must live only for Him, not myself."

"I know you are both right," I conceded. "Certainly this is not the time or place for the kind of sympathy that I was feeling," I said, even though I was still a bit irritated that such a big deal was being made of my feeling a little pity for a battle-scarred little girl. The eagle did not let up.

[451]

"Self-pity is the deadly enemy of her generation. Do not open the door to that enemy by showing them pity. Give them hope! Give them courage! Teach them endurance! Give them the training and the weapons they need, but I warn you—never, never, never give them pity! That mentality is to fear more than the evil horde out there!"

"I know an age is coming when all children will be able to play," the girl added. "I know they will be able to play with all creatures in peace and safety. Then love, joy, and peace will be the happy abode of all. I have seen this in my dreams, and I have read it in the Scriptures. I am fighting so this day will come. My reward will be to see that day come. That hope is more important to me than children's games. By fighting this fight, I will live a life full of more adventure and glory than any child who dwells in a life of play and fantasy. I should be feeling sorry for them, and I do."

"Of course you are right," I confessed, now feeling very adequately chastised. "I really am going to have to become like this child to enter the kingdom," I thought to myself.

"Now we have important business," the eagle began. "The great council of apostles and elders is about to convene here. This has not happened since the first century. It will mark the beginning of the transition from this age to one which is to come. They will come together here. They are to drink from this stream for which you have been fighting."

I looked around in disbelief. It did not look very likely that anyone would be able to drink from this stream for very long, as the evil horde was already within bow shot of it and getting closer. The look on the eagle's face told me he had discerned my thoughts, but he continued as if he had not.

"When this council meets, we will not be far from the last battle in which those things that must yet be fulfilled will come to pass. Each who is coming represents streams which will water the earth. They are all seasoned warriors who have fought long and with great courage, but few of them have yet seen a victory. Many have lost their own streams, and some will come here badly wounded."

"Are there no better places than this for such a council?" I asked, thinking that this was no place to bring the badly wounded or those who had never seen a victory.

The old eagle looked around carefully before answering, "No. This is the best place. I have already invited them to come, and they are on their way. I expect them to start appearing very soon."

"Sir, I don't want to be talking so much when it seems that we should be fighting, but how are they going to get here? We are surrounded. And what about the badly wounded? Won't they get even more wounded here, not to mention killed?" I asked, still disbelieving that this could be the right place for such a council to be held.

"This is just as good and safe a place as where the first council met in the first century," the eagle stated. "The wounded will begin to be healed in this council. These are all great warriors. After this council they will never again retreat before the enemies of the cross. The fellowship of courage and devotion which they will find here will be their food, and the waters of life which flow through this stream will be their drink. This is the table set for them in the presence of their enemies."

Shrieks from the evil army rose to such a pitch that I could not hear the eagle any more. A great cloud of dust rose and then descended on us so it became hard to breathe or see. I instinctively drew my sword and began to wave it. The dust retreated before it as if it were a giant fan. Soon I could see the horse, the girl, and the eagle.

[453]

We were all looking toward the continuing shrieking and clamor coming from the west. I was astonished as two old gentlemen emerged from the cloud of dust, walking right through the evil host as if on a Sunday stroll. The horde would run at them screaming, screeching, and hurling arrows, which the old men easily deflected with their large and brilliant shields. They seemed completely unperturbed by the attacks. If they just looked in the direction of the evil ones, they retreated in a great panic. I had not seen this kind of authority in men before.

By their walk they created a large swath through the horde which did not seem too close behind them. When they came to the stream they stopped. One bowed to drink while the other stood guard. When they had both finished, they continued walking up to us.

The two older men were probably in their seventies but were extraordinarily fit. They did move a bit slowly because of their old wounds, not because of their age. Even so, their authority and presence was so great, I felt as if an army had reinforced us.

The eagle bowed low as they stopped in front of him, and they did the same. There was an obvious mutual respect and affection between them. They then looked at the horse and girl. She dropped to the ground and also bowed. They did the same with genuine respect for her.

"We have heard much about you," one of them said to her. "No doubt you are well-known not only on earth, but in both heaven and hell as well. We are very pleased to meet you."

I think it was the first time that I had seen this brilliant little girl smile, as she replied, "I never dreamed that I would actually meet you, but having you come here has made all of the battles for this place certainly worth it."

"It is mostly because of you that a great council of warriors, prophets, and wise men are about to gather here," one of the elders replied. "All who have heard of your courage and endurance have wanted to come to this place to help you. The battle will soon rage all over the earth. You have inspired those more than you will ever know to fight with courage and endurance regardless of what they face. Your friend the eagle has made you very famous. I now know just by looking at you that every word he has spoken of you is true."

As I watched the two old gentlemen, I felt almost as if I was in the presence of the King Himself. I thought if there were only a few more like them, and a few more like this little girl, there would not be a battle that we could not win. Obviously hearing my thoughts, the old eagle turned to look at me as he responded:

"You thought you were alone, didn't you? There are many more like these and thousands more like you. There is more evil than you are aware of too. But of this you can be sure—the King will be victorious, and some of us here will still be fighting when He comes into His kingdom. The struggles we have known until now, we will soon consider skirmishes as the great battle unfolds. Blessed are those who have been chosen for the honor of fighting this great fight. Now the great wonders will begin."

"Who is this?" one of the elders said, looking toward me as he asked the eagle.

I, too, waited to hear his reply.

The sound of rain beating against the windows woke me up. I laid there for a few minutes listening. As I did, I could hear in the rain the sound of many feet marching. I knew the veil between the earthly and heavenly realms was getting thinner and the bridge between them was becoming stronger.

"To walk in truth, you must live in both worlds," a voice said.

I desperately wanted to return to my dream. I wanted to see the little girl again, the eagle, and the elders I had just met. Then a great sense of knowing came over me. The dream was real. I already knew or was going to meet everyone who was in my dream. I would fight in the great battle with them. All who follow the King in this time will soon know an adventure greater than any tale, greater than any dream.

CHAPTER XIV

The
Battle Begins

M onths later I sat in a chair listening to the rain beat against the windows. I could hear in it the clamor of the evil horde growing. I was again in the middle of it with my companions, as the evil ones pressed in all around us. Obviously, they would soon overrun the place where we stood. The two elders surveyed the scene, both continuing with a remarkable peace.

"We must make room for the others," one of the elders said as the other nodded his agreement.

"Take these vessels and fill them with water," one of them said while looking straight at the girl and me.

We did as he said, and then he told us to go and give it to those in the evil horde closest to us. The situation was so desperate that we did not have time to question his strange orders but just obeyed, thinking that there really wasn't much to lose.

When we offered our enemies a drink, it stunned them so that they stood still and a great hush came over the place. Not knowing what else to do, they drank what we gave to them. They drank with such a rabid thirst that we were soon rushing back and forth for more of the water. The others around them also seemed to suddenly realize their own thirst and began begging for the water. Everyone who tasted it wanted more. Quickly, we were so overwhelmed that all we could do was to direct them to the stream and invite them to drink.

Expecting them to plunge into the stream, I was astonished at how they treated it with great respect, bowing down and drinking but being careful not to even brush dirt from the banks into it.

As they drank, they changed before our eyes. The hard, tortured, demonic looks softened into human faces. They kept changing until they were like pure children again. After they were transformed, they asked for vessels to take the water to the others in the evil horde. We gave them all that we had, but we only had a few. They then started fashioning containers out of their own clothes. Then some started emptying their quivers and filling them with water to take to others.

This did not entirely end the assault, since many of the divisions were not only resisting the water, but were outraged by what was happening. Even so, I knew that the valley had been saved, and this would be a great victory.

I walked back to the two elders and said, "Well, it does look like this is going to be a good place to hold your council. When do you expect the others?"

"They will be here soon," the one who did most of the talking replied. "They all respond to the sound of battle, and certainly they heard the clamor of this one. I'm afraid if they do not get here soon they will be sorry that they were not at least able to contribute a little to this victory."

"Who could have thought that just offering them a cup of this water would have accomplished so much?" I continued, truly amazed at what was taking place.

"The weapons of our warfare are not natural but are divinely powerful. Their strength is in the life and nature of God. He came to give life, not take it. We overcome evil with good. We overcome by giving the life that has been given to us. Even so, this battle is far from over, and the main business of this council will be how to continue until the victory is complete. We must never again stop a battle until the victory is complete. But the turning has begun. The enemy has gone as far as he can go, and now we will begin to take back that which rightfully belongs to the King."

As I looked I could see individuals making their way through the evil horde that was still fighting. I knew they were the apostles, prophets, and elders who were being called to the council. They all seemed to walk in complete disregard of the threats and clamor of the evil horde surrounding them. Their walk through the midst of such evil was majestic beyond description. They stirred the horde to a frenzy, but I could tell those who had tasted of the living water marveled at this sight. The awe and respect for them was evident on the faces of the newly changed people, which told me that they would be willing to follow these leaders.

"Certainly this is the beginning of a great army who would never again retreat," I thought.

"Certainly it is," a voice beside me said. "This is the beginning of what we have all been waiting for," the old eagle continued. "Just seeing this, the beginning, has made it all worthwhile."

No more words seemed possible as we all stood, knowing we were indeed on the threshold of the greatest adventure of all, but also the greatest struggle. Those who dream dreams and those who see visions would soon see their dreams and visions fulfilled. The last battle had begun. The warriors who had been prepared for this day would all soon be mobilized. They responded to the sound of battle, and the whole earth would soon hear the sound of this one.

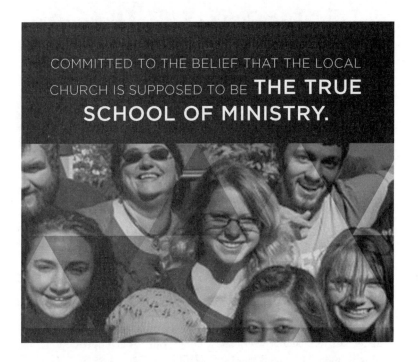

COMMITTED TO THE BELIEF THAT THE LOCAL CHURCH IS SUPPOSED TO BE **THE TRUE SCHOOL OF MINISTRY.**

In recent polls, less than 5% of people in an average congregation know what their gifts or callings are and only about 2% of those are actually equipped and functioning in their calling. **What body could possibly live if only 2% of its members were functioning? MSU exists to fulfill God's purpose for Christ-followers, the local church, and the body of Christ.**

MORNINGSTAR UNIVERSITY

For more information or to apply, visit:
MorningStarUniversity.com

🐦 MorningStar Partners

The most powerful spiritual force since the first century is mobilizing. We are looking at the greatest potential impact for the gospel ever seen. We need Partners to help raise up and send the most high-impact ministries in church history.

Join with us to equip the body of Christ through our schools, missions, conferences, television shows, and publications. Your contributions are used to train and equip all ages in their prophetic gifting. You can become a MorningStar Partner with a regular contribution of any amount, whether it is once a month or once a year.

Partnership Benefits:
- Receive monthly newsletters with rich, timely content from Rick Joyner and others
- Participate in live video webinars featuring key prophetic voices
- Connect with Partners and staff at exclusive Partner events and in our Koinonia Lounge
- Enjoy a complimentary subscription to the MorningStar Journal
- Save money with special discounts on products, hotel rooms, conferences, and more

Become a MorningStar Partner Today:

MStarPartners.org

or call
1-803-547-8495